Art, Moderni

Art, Modernity and Faith

Restoring the Image

Second Edition

George Pattison

SCM PRESS LTD

0 334 02719 5

First published 1991 by Macmillan Academic and
Professional Ltd, Houndsmill, Basingstoke,
Hampshire RG21 2XS and London

Second edition published 1998 by
SCM Press Ltd
9–17 St Albans Place London N1 0NX

Printed in Great Britain by
Biddles Ltd, Guildford and King's Lynn

The first edition of this book was dedicated to Peter Fuller, 1947–1990. This second edition is dedicated to Robert Natkin, whom I first met at Peter's funeral, thereby illustrating one aspect of the motto accompanying the earlier dedication:

'Like Art itself, Death is one of the great interpreters and expanders of life' (P. T. Forsyth)

Contents

Acknowledgements   viii

List of Plates   ix

List of Abbreviations   x

Preface to the Second Edition   xi

1   Art, Modernity and Faith   1

2   The Breaking of the Images:
     Christian Iconoclasm   10

3   The Dream of a Christian Culture   30

4   Christian Theoria   54

5   Pessimism and Progress   78

6   Into the Abyss   100

7   Icons of Glory   118

8   Restoring the Image   134

9   The Theology of Art and the Meeting
     of Faiths   155

10   Seeing is Believing   177

Notes   191

Bibliography   203

Index   205

Acknowledgements

Further to the acknowledgements in the first (1991) edition of this book I should also like to thank Chris Gwillam for setting up the Radio 3 series 'The Power and the Glory' that helped bring into focus several of the works discussed in the new final chapter. Not directly reflected in the book, but important in the development of my own thinking and awareness, have been the friendships of Richard Demarco and Ragni Linnet. I also wish to acknowledge the following sources for permission for use of written and visual materials: the Crossroad Publishing Company for passages from John Dillenberger and Jane Dillenberger (eds.), *From Paul Tillich: On Art and Architecture*, Copyright © 1987; Professor Glynn Williams for the photograph of his work *Pietà*; Bill Viola and Kira Perov for the photograph of *The Messenger*; the Dean and Chapter of Winchester Cathedral and Luis Bestamente for the photograph of Antony Gormley's *Sound II*; the Jerwood Foundation for the inside and cover photograph of Craigie Aichison's *Crucifixion (1994)*.

List of Plates

1. Mark Rothko: *Light Red over Black 1957* (The Tate Gallery)
2. Stanley Spencer: *Resurrection* (The Tate Gallery)
3. Peter Sanraedam: *The Interior of the Buurkerk, Utrecht* (The National Gallery)
4. Tintoretto: *Crucifixion* (The Mansell Collection)
5. Terborch: *The Peace of Munster* (The Mansell Collection)
6. G. F. Watts: *Hope* (The Tate Gallery)
7. Botticelli: *Madonna with the Angels* (The Mansell Collection)
8. W. Holman Hunt: *The Scapegoat* (National Museums and Galleries on Merseyside: Lady Lever Art Gallery, Port Sunlight)
9. Franz Marc: *Tierschicksale* [The Fate of Animals] (Öffentliche Kunstsammlung, Basel, Kunstsmuseum)
10. Andrei Rublev: *The Holy Trinity* (The Tretiakov Gallery, Moscow)
11. Claude Monet: *Waterlilies* (Musée Marmottan, Paris)
12. Hans Baldung (called Grien): *Krönung Mariens* [The Crowning of Mary]
13. L'iang K'ai: *Sakyamuni Descending the Mountain*
14. Glynn Williams: *Pietà*
15. Antony Gormley: *Sound II*
16. Bill Viola: *The Messenger*
17. Craigie Aichison: *Crucifixion 1994*

List of Abbreviations

AA   P. Tillich, *On Art and Architecture*
AS   J. Maritain, *Art and Scholasticism*
CP   P. T. Forsyth, *Christ on Parnassus*
MP   J. Ruskin, *Modern Painters*
RRA P. T. Forsyth, *Religion in Recent Art*
PR   E. Gilson, *Painting and Reality*

For full details see the Bibliography.

Preface to the Second Edition

As far as the United Kingdom was concerned, the first edition of *Art, Modernity and Faith* emerged into a relatively unformed landscape. But although there was at that point little in the way of a coherent and continuing dialogue between art and theology, there were a number of factors working towards the inauguration of such a dialogue.

One important element was the work of the late critic Peter Fuller, whose own avowal of atheism did not preclude a passionate engagement with the question as to whether art could flourish without the support of a shared religious and metaphysical framework. His sudden death cut off one of the hoped-for outcomes of my own book. Apart from the personal loss, it is particularly regrettable that his name is now often taken by those who polemicize against contemporary art on behalf of some supposed substantive ontology, whilst overlooking his own refusal to flinch from the extremely problematic nature of any such ontology, religious or philosophical. Even if it is the case that art needs foundations in belief, the desperate need generated by the evaporation of such belief cannot of itself stand guarantee for the truth of belief. No matter how resounding the tones in which a return to metaphysical ontology are proclaimed, or the re-ascent of theology to the throne of Queen of Sciences trumpeted, wish-fulfilment is by no means the same thing as proof. Whilst not wanting simply to conflate art and theology, I do not see theology as being able to stand outside the crisis of modernity to which modern (and post-modern) art bears such powerful witness. Theology itself is ineluctably gripped by the same crisis, and if it is ever to be able to come to any resolution of it it can only be by purgatively bearing in its own body the sufferings of modernity (see, for example, my article 'Art, Modernity and the death of God' in *The Month*, Second new series, Vol. 30, No. 10, October 1997). Modernity is not simply an ideology or a programme to be refuted on the plane of ideas. It is a destiny to be lived, and only so 'overcome'. Fuller himself was well aware of the uncertainty, the tragedy even, implicit in such a situation – but it is something towards which the more utopistic of the new metaphysicians need to be more attentive.

In other respects there has been an encouraging explosion of interest in this whole field, both amongst artists and in the Churches. The Art and Christianity Enquiry has provided an important forum for bringing together many of those involved in the field, internationally as well as nationally. Conferences and publications (such as the MCU 1995 conference, papers from which are collected in *Modern Believing* Vol. XXXVII, No. 4) have proliferated, as well as the number of artists daring to engage openly in religious issues through their art and being prepared to dialogue with theologians in what politicians call a 'full and frank' manner, i.e., not necessarily reaching agreement but finding the differences interesting, provocative and life-enhancing. This has been happening at many levels and in many contexts. Although artists are by no means invariably the best commentators on their own work, conversations with artists are a vital part of any theological engagement with art. If we cannot listen to what artists think they are doing, our comments on what they have in fact done will be the less interesting. I have been fortunate in being able to listen to many, and although it is always pernicious to single out names, I have been especially stimulated by the words, as well as the work, of Glynn Williams, Antony Gormley and my dear friend Robert Natkin, whose work I have not discussed here simply on account of the self-limiting resolve of my final chapter to deal only with works produced for or sited in Churches that I have myself seen *in situ*. Having been privileged to watch the emergence of what might be called a religious narrative in the work of this primarily abstract painter, I have no doubt that his work in progress on the Stations of the Cross will be a significant focus of discussion on the interface between art and religion (see also my 'Letter from America: Robert Natkin and Friends' in *Arts: The Arts in Theological and Religious Education*, Vol. 6, No. 2, Spring 1994–5).

Of course, the involvement of artists with religion is not quite the same thing as the involvement of theology with art, although the two dialogues constantly and inevitably intersect. It is encouraging that the arts in general and the visual arts in their own right are increasingly reflected in higher level theological study. America has, of course, long led the way here, and British scholars will have a lot to learn from the American experience, as reflected in Doug Adams and Diane Apostolos-Cappadona (eds.), *Art as Religious*

Studies (New York: Crossroad, 1987) or Wilson Yates (ed.), 'Sacred Imagination: The Arts and Theological Education' edition of *Theological Education*, Vol. XXXI, No. 1, Autumn 1994. However, both art and theology are in themselves and in their meetings necessarily local, and British and European discussions will both generate their own agenda and offer stimulation to others.

If the debate has moved on since the first edition of this book, I have not sought to revise it, beyond the addition of a new chapter in which I seek to tie up some of my own loose ends. This is partly because I am still, by and large, committed to the line, if not the detail, of the argument I present here. I still wish to insist on the unsurpassability of seeing itself as a mode of interaction between self, society and world that is distinct from and not entirely translatable into the mode of language. If I am now less inclined to claim ontological status for the 'structural grace in things' revealed to the eye, I value such disclosures of grace no less than I did ten years ago, and am no less – in fact, I hope, still more – ready to trust and treasure them as integral to my own way of being religious. It's just that (as I have already implied) I no longer regard religion as capable of securing its own ontological foundations, neither by reason nor by revelation, neither by theology nor by faith. Neither art nor religion tell us how things 'are': they simply and supremely show us meaning, value and virtue.

The Church, the Studio, the Academy and the Gallery are amongst the various contexts in which the themes of this book will be debated, but it is above all of the essence of the matter that the issues are not merely the province of these institutions. They reflect, articulate and struggle to resolve issues that concern all who are conscious of the fateful, terrible and beautiful possibilities latent in the history of humanity's way of dwelling in its planetary home.

1

Art, Modernity and Faith

Let me begin with a story. I shall call it 'the story of modern art'. I admit that it is not the only story told about modern art but it is widespread and, like all good stories, circulates in several different but clearly related versions. Because it is a 'story' it is stylised and simplified and leaves out many of the obtrusive complexities of real life – which, of course, only adds to its appeal. The story starts with the beginning of modern art. Actually (in 'real life') this is already a problem since no one exactly agrees when 'modern art' began. Was it with the Renaissance? The Enlightenment? Romanticism? Post-Romanticism? And who was the first 'modern artist': Goya? Turner? Manet? – or must we go as far back as Giotto? However, to be diverted by such questions would be to lose the thread of our story before it had properly got under way, so let us say simply that modern art did begin somewhere, sometime, with someone. And whenever that was, it involved the modern artist in a breach with all hitherto prevailing norms, conventions and expectations concerning art. For modern art was from the beginning engaged in the pursuit of artistic autonomy and the critique of established reality. In this aim it resembled other forms of modernism in the fields of science, politics and religion. It was the art of a revolutionary age. Sometimes it set itself, consciously and deliberately to share in the many-faceted creation of a new world order whilst at other times it turned its back on social and political developments for the sake of pure artistic creativity. So, on the one hand we find the Italian Futurists who called on artists to

> breathe in the tangible miracles of contemporary life – the iron network of speedy communication which envelops the earth, the transatlantic liners, the dreadnoughts, those marvellous flights which furrow our skies, the profound courage of our submarine navigators and the spasmodic struggle to conquer the unknown.[1]

In this spirit F. T. Marinetti declared that 'a racing car whose hood is adorned with great pipes, like serpents of explosive breath – a roaring car that seems to ride on grapeshot is more beautiful than the *Victory of Samothrace*'.[2]

At the other extreme we might find Wassily Kandinsky who saw art as a kind of spiritual redemption from the 'nightmare of materialism'.[3] Material and technological progress, so admired by the Futurists, had no place in Kandinsky's spiritual vision: ' . . . that which has no material existence cannot be subjected to material classification. That which belongs to the spirit of the future can only be realised in feeling, and to this feeling the talent of the artist is the only road'.[4]

Either way the style of the modern artist was decisively 'avant-garde' and persistently found itself in conflict with all existing institutions including (perhaps especially) the institutions of art itself, and its history was consequently characterised by a series of secessions, break-away groups and new beginnings. It is therefore no surprise – to continue our story – to find that modern art was constantly fissiparous, ceaselessly splintering into a myriad of movements and counter-movements. Impermanence was all. Faster and faster went the merry-go-round – but where was it all heading? When the established reality had been undermined by repeated attacks and the original substance of art itself drained by the constant war of all against all – wasn't disaster inevitable? In this way the brash enthusiasm which danced so lightly across a chaos of broken forms found itself (inevitably, some said) increasingly haunted by a ghostly emptiness and loneliness. After the fireworks had faded what was left but to continue, chartless, into ever deeper night? The path of modern art, pursued to the bitter end, led to no promised land; there was no rainbow bridge leading from earth to the land of everlasting beauty; there was only the bleak wasteland of aesthetic nihilism. The dynamic exuberance of impressionism, expressionism, futurism, dada and all the rest gave way to the sombre, featureless paintings of Mark Rothko, who called on artists to concern themselves with tragedy and death and whose own dark vision has been described as evoking 'the last silence of Romanticism'.[5] [Plate 1]

The end of our story, then, is the 'death of art', epitomised in the (predictably) short-lived vogue in the 1960s for so-called 'auto-destructive' art. Hadn't all modern art been just that? And what is left? Not much, some say. 'Post-modernism' perhaps? But what does that 'somewhat weasel word now being used to describe the garbled situation of art in the '80s' actually mean?[6] Does it represent a new beginning – or a state of terminal confusion? Jean-François Lyotard, a leading philosopher of post-modernism, has said that it is 'undoubtedly a part of the modern. All that has been received, if only yesterday . . . must be suspected . . . '[7] But here we are again, back with the suspicion, the critique, the negation of established reality! Haven't we heard all that before? And haven't we seen where it all led? Is post-modernism, then, perhaps a final state of self-negation in which criticism consumes itself – just as the technological exploitation of the planet consumes the very basis of human life? What is left but to play meaninglessly with the odds and ends left to us, the detritus, the fall-out, the excrement of that massive act of self-immolation called modernism? And what sort of future is there except a future of waiting (or, more precisely, hanging around) uncertainly for whatever comes next – too used to seeing it all to be bothered even to despair.

It is, you might say, not much of a story, and the ending is appalling. But, the post-modernist might reply – so what? That's just the way it is!

And what of religion, what of the Church in all this? There are those who would point to Christianity itself as the root cause of modernism (and its greatest theologian, Augustine of Hippo, as the first modern man[8]) but, certainly in institutional terms, the Church has been prominent among those aspects of the given reality against which modern art has set its face. Modernism (with good reason, it must be said) has tended to see in ecclesiastical religion everything it loathes: dogma, tradition, authority, establishment, etc . . . We might hazard the suggestion that Van Gogh's decision to give up his frustrated vocation as an evangelical preacher serving the poorest of the poor, and committing himself instead to an equally humble existence as an artist, is a powerful symbol of the relationship between the modern artist and the Church. Art itself became a vehicle for the passions which faith had once inspired. The canals of religious belief ran dry and the life of the spirit, it seemed, moved elsewhere. The paradox of this new situation was well put by Van Gogh himself, who spoke of Sydney Carton in *A Tale of Two Cities* and Kent in *King Lear* as examples of men who had had to hide their goodness under a contrary exterior; and he claimed of himself that he was 'faithful in my unfaithfulness'[9] – faithful, that is, precisely by abandoning the path of an overt Christian faith. Suzi Gablik has argued that *secularism* is one of the leading features of the social context of modern art and, certainly at an external level, the last two centuries have seen a long drawn out separation taking place between artists and the Church. The Church once provided both the subject-matter and the patronage for many of the great works of western art, but that is now less and less the case.

There are, of course, exceptions to this as to every other generalization. The career of the American artist Mark Rothko (which has already been mentioned as an example of terminal modernism) culminated in a commission for a university chapel which some see as one of the great religious works of our time. Don Cupitt (himself very much a theological modernist, it should be said) has, for example, said of Rothko that he 'just invented works of art that are great religion'.[10] In a different situation the rebuilding of Coventry Cathedral brought together an outstanding team of leading contemporary British artists. Individual figures in the Churches have also taken astonishing initiatives in commissioning works of art: Canon Hussey in England and, perhaps most notably, Jean Marie-Alain Couturier in France. Couturier is especially remembered as the guiding spirit behind the Church of Notre-Dame-de-Toute-Grâce at Assy in the French Alps. Couturier secured the services of a formidable team of contemporary French artists for this work: Matisse, Bonnard, Braque, Rouault, Léger, Chagall, Germaine Richier, Jacques Lipchitz and Jean Lurçat. But this is very much a case of the exception which proves the rule, as the whole project was dogged by opposition from the Church authorities. Nor were all the artists themselves believers in any conventional sense. Germaine Richier's 'Crucifix' was the object of special hostility. In it, as described by Jane Dillenberger, a 'strange, weathered, shrunken shell of a creature floats before us'.[11] At one point it had to be removed from the sanctuary because of objections from conservative clergy. This is how John Dillenberger summed up the situation:

> To Couturier's way of thinking great art for the Church comes from great artists, not from their religious stances. In this conviction, he had to stand against the Church of his time . . . He was interested in using the competent artists he knew, quite apart from their religious convictions, as long as they were willing to do the commissions. But for the Vatican in the fifties, modern art, the worker-priest movement, and unbelief formed a single fabric that the Church should reject.[12]

Equally the artists have themselves become reluctant to subordinate the integrity of their work to the sort of constraints which a Church commission is likely to impose.[13]

The problems involved in the relationship between the Church and the modern artist become only too apparent if we actually look at the work of artists who have been regarded as religiously significant. There is certainly no shortage of highly serious works from the modern period which are religiously charged, from Van Gogh through to such diverse contemporaries as Cecil Collins and Anselm Kiefer. The example I am taking, however, is that of Stanley Spencer. Spencer's work is rare among modern artists in the extent to which he calls on imagery from the Christian tradition and, particularly, from the gospel narrative. Nonetheless – quite apart from his intellectual views on religion, and quite apart from the moral and emotional confusion of his personal life – his treatment of biblical themes is quite idiosyncratic. Scenes from the gospels are depicted as occurring in and around his home village of Cookham. One of the most striking of these is the large painting of 'The Resurrection' now in the Tate Gallery. [Plate 2] This shows the resurrection taking place in Cookham churchyard. The graves are opening and figures are seen rising from them. Some are naked, some are in their grave-clothes and others are dressed as if for everyday. In the background a number of those newly-resurrected appear to be going for a boat trip on the River Thames. Many of the figures are recognisable as Spencer's friends and relatives and one represents the artist himself. Now it is quite easy to react to this painting as a genuinely Christian work. But is that so? Compare it with a typical mediaeval painting of the resurrection and striking differences soon emerge. In the mediaeval picture the resurrected bodies would, almost invariably, be shown naked, having left behind all marks of their earthly distinctions. Moreover the whole scene would lead up to the divine judgement throne and show something of the alternative fates awaiting those who have risen. In short it would emphasise the difference between the resurrection state and the present life, and it would point to the finality and inescapability of divine judgement – the separation of the sheep and the goats. In Spencer's painting, however, the difference between this world and the next has collapsed. Cookham in the new creation is pretty much like Cookham in the old creation. The resurrection is not a transcendent state: it is a way of looking at this life, at the people and the places in it, a different way of experiencing the present. Spencer's own comments point in this direction: 'In this life we experience a kind of resurrection when we arrive at a state of awareness, a state of being in love, and at such times we like to do again what we have done many times in the past, because we do it anew in Heaven'.[14] A similar vision is articulated in a later series of resurrection paintings known as 'The Port Glasgow Resurrection Series'. Here the whole event takes on the air of a jolly bank-holiday outing, with people leaning back on their headstones almost as if they were seaside deck-chairs. Now, I am not saying that these works are devoid of religious interest, nor that such a conflation of this world and the next is without precedent in Christian spirituality. The point is simply that this is a unique, distinctive and individual treatment, which we do not approach with the expectation that it will show us what Christianity believes. What we see in it – what we want to see in it – is how Spencer *interpreted* Christianity.[15]

But if this is the case with regard to an artist as passionately (if eccentrically) religious as Spencer, more recent 'religious' works seem to pose even greater problems. The 1983 exhibition 'Prophecy and Vision: Expressions of the Spirit in Contemporary Art' was regarded by several critics as failing in its intention of establishing the existence of a living stream of religious art. After referring to Anthony Green's 'self-portrait as a crucified Christ stretched out over characters from his tiresome little sub-suburban world', Peter Fuller remarks that

> most of the works shown did not even have this sort of contingent relationship to Christian iconography; nor, of course, was there any sense whatever of a Christian style of working. Indeed, taken as a whole, the painting and sculpture section was reflective of that crisis and fragmentation of values which, as we all know, is so typical of Late Modernity.[16]

Suzi Gablik's remarks on the contemporary painter Julian Schnabel's 'Portrait of God' point in an even more disturbing direction. In Schnabel's eyes, she says, God 'is just another image to manipulate',[17] and, she concludes, 'it is difficult to believe in the prophetic consciousness of someone so frankly out to get what he wants – personal success in the New York art world, not metaphysical truths'.[18]

If this, or something like it, is indeed the situation regarding the relationship between art and faith in 'Late Modernity' (or 'Early Post-Modernism') what form might a Christian response take?

It might be tempting, especially for the more conservative-minded, to lean back and say 'I told you so', seeing in the whole business a perfect example of what secularism leads to when it cuts itself off from the resources of a concrete historical faith in a transcendent God. The modernist pursuit of autonomy is no more than that ancient self-love which has dogged human history since the days of Adam and Eve. The most that can be said for modern art on such a view is that at least the violent, disturbing honesty of its images does not attempt to hide the implications of its own logic. As H. R. Rookmaaker said, 'To look at modern art is to look at the fruit of the spirit of the avant-garde: it is they who are ahead in building a view of the world with no God, no norms'.[19] For Rookmaaker Picasso is first and foremost significant as an example of the spirit of nihilism. Picasso, he says, is a 'true nihilist'.[20] Even when he drew on subject-matter from the Christian revelation 'these were curses rather than done in faith'.[21] In Rookmaaker's eyes the crisis of the modern world is 'the question' to which Christianity has 'the answer'.

But such an approach has to be an oversimplification in the present cultural situation. For as Rookmaaker himself is well aware (and who isn't?) Christianity itself has been swept by the winds of modernism. If 'modern theology' does not quite have the ring about it of 'modern art', it is nonetheless the case that considerable theological energy has been expended over the last hundred and fifty years in trying to forge an appropriate theological structure in which to express an authentically 'modern' faith. The fierce resistance to such efforts is itself a testimony both to their significance and, to a certain extent, their success. 'Demythologisation', 'The Theology of the Death of God', 'The Secular Interpretation of the Gospel', 'Man Come of Age' and, more recently, political and feminist revisions of Christianity as well as Don Cupitt's radically 'non-realist' interpretation of religion – all these may only amount to a minority voice in the Churches, but their persistence does indicate that it is increasingly hard for the Churches to declare the simple restatement of 'what has always been believed, everywhere' to be an adequate reflection of Christian truth. Modernism is a question within the Church itself.

Rookmaaker is consistent enough to reject such theological revisionism as energetically as he rejects Picasso and to demand that,

if the Church is to provide 'the answer' to 'the question' posed by
the modern world, then it must speak with one voice. But is this
possible (even if it is desirable)? After all, it is fairly undeniable
that the Churches have not spoken with a united voice for the five
hundred years or so since the Protestant Reformation. Where is this
one voice going to come from?

Peter Fuller is characteristically frank in his answer to the question
'can art be redeemed by taking on board again the social and
spiritual illusions of faith?'

> The evidence of this exhibition [Prophecy and Vision], at least, is
> that they cannot. And the reason seems to me self-evident. Any-
> one who has studied the history of Christianity in Europe over the
> last two centuries will know that it has been confronted by similar
> dilemmas and dilutions to those which have eroded art.[22]

And, he adds, 'most contemporary theologians seem not to have
believed that Jesus was God in any comprehensible sense for many
years now'.[23]

To a certain extent he seems to share (or at the time of that review
to have shared) Rookmaaker's view that only a consistently conservative theology which emphasises the reality of a transcendent
God and the continuity of the faith is at all credible in this situation – although he cannot himself find such a theology believable.

But the modern theological situation is too complex to allow
for any simple skimming off of a supposedly pre- or non-modern
theology from the actual body theologic. If there is a crisis it is
not only a crisis for art and for culture in general. It is also a
crisis within religion. Yet precisely this correlation between the
artistic and the religious situation makes possible the renewal of
a dialogue which has lain dormant for many years. This does not
mean that religion, faced with an internal loss of nerve, is about
to pounce on the resources of art to substitute for its own lack
of faith. There have, of course, been just such Romantic attempts
to make 'aesthetic experience' do the job of religious belief. But
although – as I shall argue – there are paths leading from art to
religion and from religion to art this is not the same as identifying
one with the other, or, more negatively, reducing one to the other.
The dialogue between art and religion is to be just that: a dialogue,
with each partner seeking to appreciate the specific contribution
of the other. Only, we must remember that this is not entirely a

'dialogue' in the strict sense, for art is not a language and does not speak a language. The field of art is that of vision, a point which should not be forgotten in the midst of all the words which are to follow.

The task of this book is not to pass judgement on the present state of this dialogue, still less to make predictions about the course it will (or should) take. It is rather to try to develop an appropriate theological framework by which to extend the dialogue further. To help in this task I shall examine a number of previous theologies of art in the hope that we may learn from both their strengths and weaknesses how best to frame a contemporary theology of the visual arts. In particular I am interested in those theologies of art which contain an explicit response to the impact of modernism. For the relationship between art and religion does not stand outside history and cannot be fixed definitively once and for all. Instead that relationship is constantly acquiring a new shape as each continues on its separate – yet related – way. What sort of theology of art, then, will work best for our time? What will enable theologians to bring to their engagement with the visual arts the great (yet ceaselessly debated) resources of the Christian tradition – but in such a way that the artist is recognised and affirmed in his or her autonomy of working?

In pursuing these questions there is a constant awareness that the double-crisis of religion and of art stands in relation to a still broader crisis of contemporary humanity. Political, cultural and, increasingly, ecological uncertainties encompass us. What style of thinking, acting and making is appropriate in a time when the great ideologies and narratives of metaphysics and of historical progress are being left ever further behind? We do not know; but it may well be a fruitful time for an enterprise such as this, which from the beginning stands outside the lines of demarcation of traditional intellectual disciplines. If there is some new whisper of the spirit in the silence of our present wilderness, we must be both light enough and flexible enough to hear and to follow.

2

The Breaking of Images: Christian Iconoclasm

As we set out on the track of a contemporary theological aesthetic which might help to validate the place of images and of image-making within the life of faith, we can scarcely ignore those theological traditions, so deeply rooted in the Western Church, which declare such a quest to be completely illegitimate. The spirit of Christian iconoclasm is, indeed, pervasive, and if it does not lead to the actual banning of images it creates an almost universal attitude of suspicion and denigration. Many Catholics, for instance, are highly defensive about the use of images in Catholic worship and devotion when challenged on the topic by their Protestant neighbours. Their reply usually goes something like this: 'Ah, but you see we don't actually worship the images themselves. They are only there to help us raise our minds above the mire of everyday worldliness and to prepare us for the consideration of the sacred truth which the image represents. Our images are, if you like, visual aids. We do not dwell on the surface of the image itself but pass through it to what it means. Our contemplation is spiritual and not material, as you suppose'. The Council of Trent, replying to Protestant iconoclasts, insisted that images were only to be venerated, not adored – a distinction by which, as Margaret Aston has said, 'artists were put on notice that the seductions of the world and depictions of the holy belonged to different spheres. And wherever pencil, brush or chisel attempted to outline the invisible, words were to supplement art and compensate for the deficiencies of representation'.[1] But such defensive responses clearly go a long way towards admitting (at least implicitly) the force of their opponents' charge.

It would be hard to imagine that things could have been otherwise if we once pause to consider that both the main sources of Christian theology – Judaism and Hellenism – contain strongly iconoclastic elements. The Jewish objection to images is, of course, summed up in the second commandment itself: 'Thou shalt not make to thyself any graven image, nor the likeness of anything that is in heaven above, or in the earth beneath, or in the water under the earth. Thou shalt not bow down to them, nor worship them' (Exodus 20, v. 4). The repudiation of images enshrined in this commandment was to be one of the most prominent characteristics of Israel's self-defined relation to the religious practices of its neighbours and fellow Palestinians. There is some evidence that things were certainly not as clear cut in the early history of Israel as this suggests. The repeated denunciations of idolatry by the prophets show that the practices which they condemned were both widespread and deeply-rooted. When Josiah set about reforming and purifying Israelite religion (2 Kings 23) idols are taken and burnt not only from previously unsuppressed pagan shrines but also from the temple itself. Nonetheless, by the Hellenistic period the spirit of the second commandment had become a potent tool in ensuring the religious identity of the Jewish community over against Greek (and later Roman) influences. The horror of the desecration of the temple by the Seleucid King Antiochus Epiphanes, who installed a cultic statue in the Holy of Holies (1 Macc. 1. 41 ff.), became an important symbol of what was at stake in the Jewish struggle for national and spiritual self-assertion. The success of the struggle in this respect is evidenced by the special dispensation given to Jewish subjects of the Roman Empire, exempting them from the obligation of making any tribute to the Emperor which might be construed as idolatrous. It was, of course, precisely this issue which became one of the flash-points of conflicts between the Church and the Imperial authorities and the immediate occasion of a number of persecutions and martyrdoms. At the same time recent archaeological discoveries, notably the excavation of the third century a.d. synagogue at Dura-Europos on the Euphrates, show that the visual arts did not totally disappear from Jewish life, although their scope was much less than in some other religious communities.[2]

The Early Church took over the Jewish prohibition of idolatry more or less wholesale and, as already indicated, this became a major part of the Church's practical and theological critique of pagan culture. Here too, however, it would be premature to conclude that the Early Church was entirely aniconic. This was, for a long time, the prevailing assumption in Christian circles. As John Dillenberger writes: 'From the late nineteenth century into our own time, prominent scholars, from Adolf Harnack to Ernst Kitzinger, have assumed that scripture and the early fathers were opposed to the visual arts and that the arts hardly existed until the time of Constantine'. But, he remarks, 'In recent years that outlook has had to be abandoned'. A wealth of material evidence – and again Dura-Europos is an outstanding example – suggests that the attitude and the activity of the Early Church with regard to images was one of variety and diversity.[3] The implications of the Church's iconoclastic inheritance were, however, to break out forcefully in reaction to the spread of images and their veneration in Church life.

Judaism was not the only source from which the Church drew its critique of images. Although the Church found plentiful examples of idolatrous religious practices in pagan culture, that culture itself contained elements which pointed in a similar direction, especially among its philosophers. Plato, for instance, had drawn a strong distinction between the world of Forms, which are eternal, stable, self-sufficient, the sources of all truth and knowledge, and the world of the senses, of material things, changeable and deceptive. The one in the realm of the Idea, of Reality itself, the other the real of 'mere' appearance. Thus, in Book X of *The Republic* the artist is defined as an imitator. Indeed, not just an imitator but (even worse) an imitator of the mere appearance of the object rather than of its real Form. The reality of a bed, for instance, is the same reality from whichever side we see it, but the artist can only paint it from one side or the other as it appears to him. Nor is this the end of the story, for the imitative work of the painter would not be possible without the prior creation of the object by either a divine or a human manufacturer. He is thus 'three removes from nature', nature, that is, in the sense of the ideal nature or essence of the object which he paints.[4] This assertion of a fundamental distance between art and truth recalls the well-known parable of the cave in which Plato / Socrates invites us to imagine a group of men held prisoner in the depths of a cave and chained in such a way that with their backs turned to the mouth of the cave they can only look straight ahead of them. Higher up, between them and the entrance of the cave, is a fire and, between the fire and the prisoners, a road, edged by a wall along which a strange procession of men journeys, carrying 'statues of men and other creatures in stone and wood and other materials'.[5] All the prisoners would ever see would be the eerie shadows cast on the wall of the cave facing them by this queer procession of statues. Naturally, never having known anything else, they would imagine these shadows to be real things. If by any chance one of them were to be released and made his way back up the cave, encountering the fire and the real cause of what he had previously mistaken for reality, and then, later, arriving outside in the clear light of the sun, his journey would clearly involve pain and shock and he could scarcely adjust his eyes to the increasingly bright light of reality. Yet this painful light would be truth and that familiar darkness in which he had previously lived would be falsehood. This parable – like all parables – works on many different levels and is almost infinitely interpretable. It is, in terms of our enquiry, particularly telling with regard to Plato's attitude to art. The statues, the shadows of which are the sole 'reality' of the prisoners, are the most extreme and grotesque distortion of reality and, as such, are identical with the realm of the imitative art of painting, situated at the furthest possible remove from the pure light of truth.

This attitude towards sensuous experience and to visual art as incapable by itself of rising above such experience was widespread in the Greek and Roman worlds, even among philosophical schools which were at many points quite distinct from Platonism. Stoicism, for instance, taught a similar discipline of abstention from the pleasures of sense and the passions which such pleasures arouse. Art was regarded as at best indifferent, and at worst as a link in the chain binding the mind to the changes and chances of this passing world from which it is the duty of the philosopher to extricate himself.

I shall not attempt to offer a full survey of the views of the Early Church on images, but would only refer again to Dillenberger's remarks concerning the complexity of both the material and textual evidence.[6] One thinker who cannot be by-passed, however, is Augustine, whose thought was to have a decisive influence on the whole theological and philosophical development of Western Christianity. Augustine has often been called the first modern man and in this respect his role has a double significance for our enquiry, since it is precisely against the backdrop of the denouement of modernism that we are seeking to formulate a theology of art. In their study of *The Postmodern Scene*, Kroker and Cook interestingly spend considerable time discussing Augustine *qua* proto-modernist as a necessary preliminary to the understanding both of modernism and therefore also of post-modernism in art and culture.[7] My present aim is less ambitious: it is simply to observe how the iconoclastic element in classical thought became fused, in Augustine, to the programme of Christian faith and spirituality.

Augustine was a convert to Christianity and had as a young man been trained in rhetoric, one of the 'liberal arts' of classical education. He had also been strongly attracted by Platonism and always retained a considerable respect for Platonic philosophy, even when he came to hold many of the preoccupations and beliefs of contemporary Platonism in contempt. He deliberately carried over into his own thought what he regarded as the best of pagan thought, appealing to the prototype of the Israelites who took with them in their flight from Egypt the treasures of the Egyptians. So, like the Platonists, he accepted a view of the universe as a hierarchy of ordered levels of being, ranging from inanimate material existence to the intelligent life of human beings. Humanity is distinguished by virtue of intelligence or reason which has the power not only to understand but to co-ordinate and govern the whole range of sensuous experience. This human reason is guided by the 'memory' trace of absolute and eternal Truth which, beyond change and alteration is the transcendent source and measure of all particular judgements and intuitions of truth. The relationship between human intelligence and absolute Truth is ambiguous, for although the human mind is internally and dynamically determined by its fundamental orientation towards Truth it cannot of itself grasp it or contain it. Truth is indeed nothing less than a mode of God's very being and serves as a name by which Augustine addresses God. As such it is virtually interchangeable with another divine name: Beauty. The aim of the Christian life is to come to know this Truth, this Beauty, and to contemplate it in and for itself, apart from and beyond its shadowy reflection in the world of appearances. In relation to this aim the visible world has a double character. On the one hand material things 'offer their forms to the perception of our senses, those forms which give loveliness to the structure of the visible world'.[8] On the other hand this very loveliness can serve to distract the soul from its search for God and tempt it to the sin of the 'gratification of the eye'.[9] In an eloquent passage in which he displays his own literary artistry Augustine exclaims

> I have learnt to love you late, Beauty at once so ancient and so new! . . . You were within me, and I was in the world outside myself. I searched for you outside myself and, disfigured as I was, I fell upon the lovely things of your creation . . . The beautiful things of this world kept me far from you and yet,

if they had not been in you, they would have had no being at all.[10]

Here we can see the ambiguity of his attitude towards material beauty. It is a sign of the divine Beauty – but woe to him who keeps his eyes fixed on the sign and fails to pass on to that which it signifies!

Augustine agrees with other Church Fathers in 'reading' nature allegorically. Nature does not exist for itself but as a reflection of and a witness to its Creator. To help it in this task it has built into it a multiplicity of significations and correspondences which should help even the clouded mind of fallen humanity to glimpse the true significance of the whole: 'For you compensate for the ease with which our mortal senses tire by providing that a single truth may be illustrated and represented to our minds in many ways by bodily means'.[11] The Bible is the key to this system of signs. Thus the Genesis account of creation is ransacked by Augustine for the most subtle allegorical significations, and in such a way that nature itself is transformed via the text into a theological treatise, replete with a truth which yields itself to the truly contemplative eye.

This is how R. O'Connell summarises Augustine's approach to aesthetics:

> . . . he is obstinately convinced, that grasp of intelligible mean-
> ing . . . is the work of the mind alone; sensual imagery can,
> in the last analysis, only distract from that grasp – the true
> appropriation of beauty comes only when sense and imagination
> have resolutely been left behind . . . A grammarian, a rhetorician
> in the twilight of ancient culture . . . armed with the sanction
> of neo-Pythagoreanism: one could hope for equipment better
> designed for the refinement of observation, the sensitivity of
> analysis required in the aesthetic domain, so stubbornly refractory
> to rationalism.[12]

In particular, O'Connell argues, these tools do not serve an aesthetic theory which would be appropriate to a faith which culminates in a relation to a living and personal being. Paradoxically, he also notes in Augustine himself a passionate sensitivity to both natural and artistic beauty and a power of creative imagination which points, in practice, to the subversion of his own rationalistic model. Even so, whatever the extent to which it is possible to rescue

some kind of aesthetic from Augustine there is little here to offer aid
and comfort to a theology of specifically visual art.

Even if we want to attain the vision of the true and lasting Beauty
of God, we must pass through and beyond this world with all its
visual loveliness. In this respect at least Augustine's thought was
to be normative for a millenium and half of Christianity.

Augustine's influence was pervasive through the Middle Ages,
reinforced by the mystical Platonism of Pseudo-Dionysius, but it
also continued on into the Reformation period when his mistrust
of the visual sense was endorsed by a renewed emphasis on the
iconoclastic elements in the Bible. In a reformer such as Jean Calvin
we find once more the familiar themes of Augustinian spirituality.
The way to God is through the interior life of the soul rather than
through knowledge of the external, material world. On the positive
side, the human mind is seen as fundamentally oriented towards
the knowledge of God and has, Calvin says, 'by natural instinct an
awareness of divinity'[13] – even though the idolator may worship a
piece of wood or a stone rather than the true God his action shows
that there is some kind of impression of a divine being in his mind.
Again nature has a positive role as reflecting and setting forth the
divine glory. God, Calvin tells us, 'daily discloses himself in the
whole workmanship of the universe. As a consequence, men cannot
open their eyes without being compelled to see him . . . this skilful
ordering of the universe is for us a sort of mirror in which we can
contemplate God who is otherwise invisible'.[14] But – and it is a big
'but' – none of this can justify the confusion of creature and Creator
typifying the attitude of fallen humanity and finding its supreme
expression in the sin of idolatry, a sin which Calvin, confronting
a Church richly resplendent with costly imagery, saw as a prime
obstacle in the way of restoring true religion:

> . . . since this brute stupidity gripped the whole world – to pant
> after visible figures of God, and thus to form gods of wood, stone,
> gold, silver, or other dead and corruptible matter – we must
> cling to this principle: God's glory is corrupted by an impious
> falsehood whenever any form is attached to him.[15]

Images and pictures of God are, Calvin insists, plainly forbidden
by scripture. But what of the argument that images can be used
for instructing the uneducated? It is no use, for 'whatever men
learn of God from images is futile, indeed false'.[16] If the Church

had been doing its job properly, he adds, there would have been no need for images. From the true preaching of the gospel 'they could have learned more than from a thousand crosses of wood or stone'.[17] Any use of images in religion leads to idolatry. Even where images only purport to represent actual historical individuals or events they are likely to prove damaging. The only images which deserve to be allowed in Churches are 'those lively and symbolical ones which the Lord has consecrated by his Word. I mean Baptism and the Lord's Supper, together with other rites by which our eyes must be too intensely gripped and too sharply affected to seek other images forged by human ingenuity'.[18] Not, Calvin hastens to remind us that 'I am . . . gripped by the superstition of thinking absolutely no images permissible'.[19] It is only images in Churches or images which seek to represent God in physical form against which his polemics are directed. Nonetheless we must remain cautious for even pictures designed for historical instruction have their dangers: ' . . . brothels show harlots clad more virtuously and modestly than the churches show those objects which they wish to be thought images of virgins'.[20] The 'indecency' and 'licentiousness' of the painter's art gives the lie to the supposed religious purpose of his work. As with Augustine it seems that the problem is that any intense desire towards the visible loveliness of the world distracts us from the kind of intellectual and interior contemplation towards which true piety constantly aspires.

In line with Calvin's views iconoclasm was to become a major feature of the Protestant Reformation as the theological critique of images was accompanied by outbursts of iconomachy (the breaking of images) both inside and outside the law. In England legal enactments against images in Churches began in 1536 and for over a century the legitimate scope of images in churches was to be the focus of intense argument. The *Second Book of Homilies*, published in the reign of Elizabeth, added a homily 'Against Peril of Idolatry' to those already written, a move which was significant in several respects. For a start, it runs to twice the length of its nearest rival – 'Against disobedience and Wilful Rebellion' (also an Elizabethan addition) – and is many times as long as the more typical homilies – a statistical index of the importance attached to the topic by the Reformers. The homily is worth examining at some length since it is typical of Protestant iconoclasm and shows that even the Church of England, for all its self-styled moderation, was highly receptive to the iconoclastic spirit of the age.

In many respects the homily recapitulates the sort of argument found in Calvin, but it pursues its case with a heady combination of relentless detail and robust prose which make it quite distinctive. It begins by defining the Church, or House of God, as

> . . . a place appointed by the holy Scriptures, where the lively Word of God ought to be read, taught, and heard, the Lord's holy Name called upon by publick Prayer, hearty thanks given to his Majesty for his infinite and unspeakable benefits bestowed upon us, his holy sacraments duly and reverently ministered.[21]

It follows that there is no need of images in order to fulfil these aims, and, indeed, any false ornaments will only distract the faithful from the proper use of the Church. However,

> contrary to the which most manifest doctrine of the Scriptures, and contrary to the usage of the Primitive Church, which was most pure and uncorrupt, and contrary to the sentences and judgements of the most ancient, learned and godly Doctors of the Church . . . the corruption of these latter days hath brought into the Church infinite multitudes of images, and the same, with other parts of the temple also have decked with gold and silver, painted with colours, set them with stone and pearl, clothed them with silks and precious vestures, fancying untruly that to be the chief decking and adorning of the temple or house of God.

Such corruption, the writer insists, does nothing to help those who are 'wise and of understanding' and can only hurt 'the simple and unwise, occasioning them thereby to commit most horrible idolatry'. He goes on to argue that even apart from the obvious dangers of the sort of excessive veneration of images to be found in late mediaeval piety all use of images in religion is intrinsically dangerous to true godliness. 'Idol' and 'Image', he says, are simply Greek and Latin variants of the one word, being entirely interchangeable, and equally suitable for translating the same Hebrew term. They 'differ only in sound and language, and in meaning be indeed all one, especially in the Scriptures and matters of Religion'. It therefore follows that to allow images to be placed in Churches is virtually by definition to allow idolatry. The Tridentine distinction between veneration and adoration is unsustainable.

The writer continues by appealing to copious testimonies from both Old and New Testaments and from the writings of the Fathers. Despite what he regards as the massive consensus of this testimony the abuse of images crept into Church life.

> First, men used privately stories painted in tables, cloths, walls. Afterwards, gross and embossed images privately in their own Houses. Then afterwards, pictures first, and after them embossed images began to creep into Churches, learned and godly men ever speaking against them. Then by use it was openly maintained that they might be in Churches, but yet forbidden that they should be worshipped . . . But . . . what ruine of Religion, and what mischief ensued afterward to all Christendom, experience hath to our great hurt and sorrow proved.

Indeed, the writer blames such idolatry directly for the collapse of the Eastern Christian Empire, for the rise of Islam and 'the cruel dominion and tyranny of the Saracens and Turks'. In plotting the course of this collapse he lays especial weight on the political and theological crimes of the Empress Irene, whom he sees as a prime mover in 'these Tragedies about images', and, one might add, his writing rises at this point to a truly dramatic pitch in handling this 'tragic' theme.

As well as drawing attention to what he regards as the overwhelming weight of patristic authorities, the homilist points to particular theological problems involved in the case of images of Christ. Christ being both God and man, he regards it as self-evident that, God being beyond all images, no image can conceivably be made of Christ's divinity 'which is the most excellent part'. And, with respect to Christ's humanity, 'no true image can be made of Christ's body, for it is unknown now of what form and countenance he was'. Consequently, 'seeing that Religion ought to be grounded upon truth, Images which cannot be without lies, ought not to be made, or put to any use of Religion, or to be placed in Churches and Temples'. This, he says, confutes the popular argument that images can function as 'Lay-men's Books', for it is now clear 'that they teach no things of God, of our Saviour Christ, and of his Saints, but lies and errors. Wherefore, either they be no books, or if they be, they be false and lying books, the teachers of all error'.

Like Calvin the writer hastens to point out that he is not 'so superstitious or scrupulous, that we do abhor either flowers wrought in

Carpets, Hangings and other Arras, either images of Princes printed
or stamped in their coyns . . . neither do we condemn the Arts, of
painting and image-making, as wicked of themselves'. What must
be insisted on, however, is that neither images nor image-making
have any place in religion. True religion

> stands not in making, setting up, painting, gilding, clothing and
> decking of dumb and dead images (which be but great puppets
> and babies for old fools in dotage, and wicked idolatry to dally
> and play with) nor in kissing of them, setting up of candles,
> hanging up of legs, arms, or whole bodies of wax before them,
> or praying, and asking of them, or of Saints, things belonging only
> to God to give.

Those who indulge in such practices can expect nothing but 'everlasting damnation both of body and soul'.

After all that it is perhaps surprising that seventy years later,
at the time of the Puritan revolution, there was still no shortage
of works for the Puritan iconoclasts to destroy. The best known
of these, William Dowsing, conducted a veritable rampage of
iconomachy throughout East Anglia in 1643 and 1644 in his role
as official parliamentary visitor, enforcing an enactment of August
1643 which required the removal of various images from all churches
by November of that year. Dowsing kept a diary, which, though
perhaps exaggerated in some respects, provides a vivid picture of
the magnitude of the task facing this loyal upholder of the second
commandment. As Margaret Aston put it, 'the tally of proscribed
items seems endless'.[22] Even non-figurative representations of the
Trinity by a triangle or of Christ by the letters IHS along with the
customary symbols of the four evangelists fell under the ban. In some
cases parishioners resisted – occasionally successfully – Dowsing's
incursions, but in other cases local enthusiasts had pre-empted his
arrival. Aston concludes her account of Dowsing's work with the
comment that 'one might well wonder what was left by way of
church decoration, once the iconoclasts of the 1640s had finished
their work'.[23] The process of Reformation iconoclasm in England
was protracted – over a hundred years – but it was thorough. It is
worth reflecting that not a single mediaeval rood now survives in
England.

Even if we are tempted to regard such activities as, in effect, van-
dalism on a grand scale, we may acknowledge that the Reformers

were right in this: that images wield an immense social power. They realised that if they were truly to inaugurate a new era in history they could never do so completely until the visible symbols of the *ancien régime* were removed from the scene. For they recognised that such symbols are potent transmitters of values and ideas. Time, however, has blurred the sharpness of their polemics, and we have become used to seeing even representational stained glass in Protestant churches. Nonetheless the iconoclastic tendency remains a strong feature of Protestantism. Karl Barth firmly restated the traditional Calvinist view that 'Images and symbols have no place at all in a building designed for Protestant worship'.[24] In terms essentially identical with those of the *Book of Homilies* he sums up the aims of Protestant worship as 'prayer, preaching, baptism and the Lord's Supper – and above all the community in action in everyday life. These activities can correspond to the reality of the person and work of Jesus Christ. No image and no symbol can play that role'. In fact such images and symbols 'serve only to dissipate attention and create confusion'. Church buildings must be designed solely 'to be places for the preaching of the Word of God and for the prayer of the assembled community'.

Despite the fierce attack on the place of images in the Church itself the Protestant Reformation was, paradoxically, accompanied by a rapid expansion of secular art, a fact which can, as we shall see, be regarded as a direct outcome of the Protestant spirit itself.[25] Nonetheless a residual suspicion of even such painting as laid no claim to religious significance remained characteristic of much Protestant spirituality. Even if it was not idolatrous art was at best indifferent and at worst a distraction from the path of true piety. These tendencies were, for instance, strengthened by the rise of pietism, with its overriding emphasis on the cultivation of spiritual inwardness and the recognition of emptiness and transiency of the external, visible world – just listen to some of the lyrics of J. S. Bach's sacred music!

A new period in the relationship between religion and art was brought about by the rise of Romanticism at the end of the eighteenth century. In such Romantic writers and thinkers as Schelling and Schlegel it is precisely the aesthetic intuition which is seen as providing humanity with immediate access to knowledge of the divine or the absolute. With such claims art moves to the very centre of human existence. For the artist, art – in the words of the German Romantic writer Wackenroder – 'must take second place only to religion; it must become a religious love or a beloved religion, if I may so express myself'.[26] In his own writings he, like other Romantics, expressed a renascent fascination with the art and culture of the mediaeval world. Raphael's 'Madonnas' were now spoken of with reverence and wonder by Protestants as works of art and precisely as works of art as endowed with religious significance. It must also be said that Wackenroder's placing of art 'second . . . only to religion' was not always clearly sustained, either in his own work or in that of other Romantics. Rather, the tendency was towards the conflation of the two. In this situation the place of 'non-religious' art could no longer be regarded as neutral or indifferent. Romantic claims thus provoked – and still provoke – fresh definitions and counter-definitions of the relationship between art and religion, inside and outside the Church. In a sense this is the general context for many of the theological views examined in later chapters of this book and, indeed, of the book itself.

One outstanding Christian response to the new situation inaugurated by Romanticism is to be found in the work of Sören Kierkegaard, who gave fresh expression to the spirit of Protestant iconoclasm by challenging his readers to choose either 'the aesthetic' or 'the religious'.[27] For Kierkegaard, Romantic claims meant that art was no longer neutral in relation to religion. Instead it was a more or less explicit secular alternative to Christianity which offered a quite distinct – and, to Kierkegaard, unacceptable solution to the riddle of human existence. From his earliest writings he developed a complex but consistent rebuttal of the aesthetic and philosophical premises of Romanticism. He saw the Romantics as the forerunners of the out-and-out 'nihilists' of his own generation, men such as Feuerbach and D. F. Strauss, for whom religion was nothing but an expression of human experiences, ideas and values. By reducing the scope of religion to aesthetic experience, he argued, the Romantics were making it no more than a metaphorical language by which to express purely human concerns. In many respects he subscribed to that 'story of modern art' with which this book began, for he argued that a view of life which founded itself on the principle of human creativity would, since it had thereby cut itself loose from all external moral and religious sources, would lead to despair and, paradoxically, the ultimate impoverishment and withering away of the aesthetic realm itself. In place of the ecstatic utterances of the first generation of Romantics he saw in his own time a turn to themes of darkness, pessimism and death. This, he claimed, was in fact a direct outworking of the premises on which Romantic theory and practice were based.

In his magisterial dissertation *On the Concept of Irony* he argued that Romantics such as Schlegel had effectively replaced God by what they believed to be the infinitely creative human mind. He saw the Romantic doctrine of irony, which maintained the absolute domin- ion of the creative aesthetic consciousness over all predetermining material factors, as no less than the self-assertion of the human will over against the will of God, the sole real ground and guarantor of reality. Refusing to acknowledge their actual dependence on the structure of reality as given and ordered by God, they commit themselves to the pursuit of an illusory creative power, a pursuit which must end with the dissolution of all forms and values as their (literal) non-entity reveals itself ever more clearly behind all the fireworks of artistic virtuosity. Both in theoretical works such as *The Concept of Irony* and in his more literary portrayals of such 'failed' aesthetic personalities as 'Johannes the Seducer' Kierkegaard depicts what he believes to be the emptiness of a life which bases itself on the aesthetic imagination.

He is particularly attentive to two aspects of aesthetic existence which he regards as peculiarly indicative of the failure of art to solve the religious issue, the ultimate challenge of all human existence. The first is the place of suffering and the second the place of time. Let us, briefly, examine his view of these issues.

The aim of Romantic art, at least in its initial phase, had appeared to be the production of images which would correspond to the aes- thetic intuition of the ultimate union of thought and being, ideality and reality, conscious and unconscious, humanity and cosmos. Art is the disclosure of the Idea embodied or reflected in sensuous form, the finite world illuminated or transfigured by the infinite, the coinherence of the many and the one. Each work is, correspondingly, a whole in itself, 'a true microcosm', as Kierkegaard said of Goethe's novel *Wilhelm Meister*.[28] Art thus offers an image of the ultimate rec- onciliation of all life's discords by offering to our view harmonious and pleasing images of the world. It is 'the transfiguration of the finite in the magical mirror of illusion'.[29] Not, of course, that the Romantics themselves would accept the description of their work as 'illusion', but that was how their critical commentator, Kierkegaard, saw it. Even if art deals with tragedy or conflict it must do so by pointing towards an ultimate resolution, a 'happy ending'. Art cuts the corners of life and smooths out its rough edges: 'what the finite life must first attain through toil and trouble is what art portrays as a reality which has already been attained'.[30] This is one of the sources of the power and the uniquely joyous magic of art, but it also reveals something of that gap between ideal and real which the Romantics, in Kierkegaard's view, had overlooked. For the short cut of aesthetic experience can make us think we have arrived when, in fact, we still have far to go. Its images of harmony and joyful reconciliation are illusory – 'I wake up again, and the very same tragic relativity in everything begins worse than ever'.[31] Art 'is *not the true reconciliation* for it does not reconcile me to the reality in which I live'.[32] For Kierkegaard that reality is actually determined by the Christian dialectic of Creation-Fall-Redemption, a dialectic in which suffering is real, the product of human sinfulness, requiring of us a lifetime of constant repentance. Art tries to heal the pain of human life by helping us to forget about it in moments of intense aesthetic experience: but Christianity declares that real healing can only occur when we take upon ourselves the full burden of our contingency and pain, and acknowledge our own nullity 'before God'. This phrase itself contains the essence of Kierkegaard's disquiet over Romanticism, for we are not the creators of our world, we are creatures; responsible for ourselves, yes, but, precisely as such, answerable to One who is greater than we are in every way.

The theme of art and time overlaps at many points with that of art and suffering. Time, like suffering, breaks up the unity of existence. Existence in time is characterised by dispersion, incompleteness, change, decay and death. Art, by revealing a world made whole, 'stops the wheel of time'[33] and lifts us out of the dispersion of temporal existence, breaking the barriers between past, present and future imposed by time. For the Romantics this was particularly significant with regard to the way in which the spirit of art and poetry provided access to the consciousness of past ages. The Romantic philosopher Henrik Steffens wrote that the aesthetic intuition 'wakens the warriors from their graves, gods and goddesses come among us, every sound from long-vanished ages resounds with its unique resonance'.[34] Similarly the pages of early (and later) nineteenth century aesthetics are replete with adjectives such as 'eternal', 'immortal' and 'undying'.

The relation of art to time has a direct bearing on the significance of the visual arts. Kierkegaard himself wrote relatively little about the visual arts, being more concerned with literature, opera and the theatre. Nonetheless it is clear that the visual, image-element in art played a key role in his total concept of aesthetics. Like many of the idealist aesthetic theories which he criticised, he postulated a progression in art from plastic and spatial forms to temporally-determined arts such as music and poetry. The plastic arts, such as painting and sculpture, are defined by their negative relation to time. They exclude time, or, more precisely, can only depict 'one moment in time'. They freeze the image of a passing moment and represent it in motionless timelessness. In effect, such art represents what was known in the moment of experience itself to *be* temporal, a moment of passage from a 'before' to an 'after', as if it were altogether spatial, outside of time. But even if this is pre-eminently true of the plastic arts, it is characteristic in varying degrees of the whole range of aesthetic experience and artistic representation.

This again points to the way in which art resists the full recognition of human frailty, for existence in time means dissolution, above all the final dissolution of death itself. Yet human life is temporal and art, as a human work, cannot finally achieve that denial of time at which it aims. The pathos of this situation pervades Romantic writing. It is, for instance, succinctly summarised by Schiller's lines 'What lives undyingly in song / In life must pass away'.[35] Or, in the words of Kierkegaard's Scandinavian contemporary N. F. S. Gruntvig,

> Enchanting dream
> Of the pearl of eternity in the stream of time,
> You trick the poor wretches who in vain seek
> What the heart desires in images and art
> So that they call 'abiding' what certainly passes away.[36]

The task of the religious person, in Kierkegaard's view, is therefore not to flee from time into the false timelessness of a spatially determined aesthetic 'moment' but to become 'older than the moment'.[37] We are to grow through the full acceptance of time (and with it of our own transiency) to a true relation to eternity.

Kierkegaard's critique of art shows both similarities and dissimilarities to the Augustinian tradition of Christian thinking about art. Like that tradition he draws a sharp contrast between the interior and exterior pursuits of the human subject, and consistently privileges the former at the expense of the latter. On the other hand he is more sceptical of the possibility of the human subject attaining any kind of perception of metaphysical or ideal truth. Certainly he does not seem to hold that whatever access we have to such truth can be objectified in terms of knowledge. Whereas Augustine demoted art in favour of metaphysics, Kierkegaard sees them as bound together, equally incapable of bearing either the tedium or the terror of time, suffering and final dissolution. There is no escape from the cave. All we can do is submit to the divine providence which has placed us there. The faith which enables us to do that can no more be spoken about as knowledge than it can be represented in art.

Looking back at Kierkegaard's work from the twentieth century, it is striking that many modern artists have repudiated precisely those ideals which he regarded as normative for all art. Many have spoken of their artistic goals in terms which Kierkegaard would have held to be religious, and have not evaded the terror of the abyss, as he believed artists must always do, but have confronted and taken into their work themes of tragedy and relativity.[38] Paradoxically therefore Kierkegaard offers an intimation of one area of possible convergence between art and religion in the modern world: the prophetic assault on all consolatory images and premature solutions to the issues of human suffering and death. In particular we can see in him what we might equally see in many artists: the rejection of a bourgeois culture in which 'art' takes on the mantle of religion by assuring us of the meaningfulness and ultimate importance of our lives. Both the iconoclasm of Kierkegaard's theological critique of art and the iconoclasm of much modern art is consequently directed against an aesthetic ideology which hinders society in reflecting on its own contradictions. In this respect Kierkegaard at least would not see 'art' as the sole culprit. In his view the clergy of established religion were on the same level as artists, since they (mostly) assured their flocks that all was well, lulled them with myths – instead of provoking them to a radical reflection on sin, responsibility and Christian freedom.

Kierkegaard's critique of art thus provides a bridge between the long tradition of Christian iconoclasm and key aspects of modern debates about art. In this respect there are interesting parallels between Kierkegaard and the Catholic writer and apologist Léon Bloy. Bloy's work, like Kierkegaard's, expresses a passionate but ambiguous fascination with art. On the one hand he could write

> If art is part of my baggage, so much the worse for me! My only recourse is the expedient of placing at the service of truth *what has*

been given me by the Father of Lies. A precarious and dangerous device, for the business of Art is to fashion Gods![39]

Again, like Kierkegaard, he would nonetheless defend the passion of the genuine artist over against the carping mediocrity of bourgeois society. 'Between a war lord leading his wild animals to their forest pastures and a stock market swindler shoving the crowds to their repasts of acorns, no room is found for a third category of domination'.[40] In terms of this Either/Or artists are at least 'fashioned in the likeness of that Gladiator against nations' rather than in the form of swineherds.[41] Artists have a dream of a greater good beyond the sufferings of the present life which is able to give a certain grandeur to what Bloy calls 'the horrible journey "from the womb to the grave", as it is conventional to call this life laden with wretchedness, mourning, lies, disappointments, betrayals, stenches and catastrophes . . . '[42] 'We are', he states, 'beyond description lacking in everything. We die of home-sickness for Being'.[43] Only art offers a way out, although the true artists will always be few and will almost inevitably suffer rejection and even persecution by the acorn-eating crowd.

Yet for all the heroism of such 'deeply virile' wanderers of the Great Dream,[44] 'art', he asserts 'is foreign to the essence of the Church, useless to her essential life, and those who practise it have not even the right to exist if they are not her *very humble servants*'[45] (my emphasis). Why is this? Because the function of art, even – perhaps especially – the best art is precisely the 'devilish function of wiping out the memory of the Fall'.[46] Thus, even though there may be 'a few rare and aristocratic individuals who are at once artists and Christians . . . there cannot be a *Christian Art*'.[47] If it existed such an art would be a gateway 'open into lost Eden',[48] but no such art exists or can exist. There is no way out from the 'desert of the world', as Bloy calls it. Or, rather, there is only one way: God's redemptive work in Christ, mediated to us by the teaching of the Church.

But what does a Catholic writer like Bloy make of the fact of Church art, of the great religious art of the Middle Ages, for example? Like Calvin and like the *Book of Homilies* he maintains that the Early Church had no art. Only after a thousand years, he says, did the West attempt to adorn its faith artistically. The architecture, music and art of this period convinced Christians that they had at last managed to make Apollo submit to Christ. But this illusion was shattered by the Renaissance when the supposedly subjugated aesthetic forms 'reared up in all-powerful rebellion'.[49] 'Souls were cast, never to emerge, into the burning ovens of form and color'.[50]

John Henry (Cardinal) Newman gives an interesting twist to the metaphor of the artist as 'very humble servant'. 'The Fine Arts', he says, are 'special attendants and handmaids of religion', but this acknowledgement is immediately followed by a caution that 'they are very apt to forget their place, and unless restrained with a firm hand, instead of being servants will aim at becoming principals'.[51] We mustn't let the servants get above themselves! Unless kept in check by the teaching of the Church the natural genius of art could supplant the mysteries of true religion

> by a sort of pagan mythology in the guise of sacred names, by a creation indeed of high genius, of intense, and dazzling and soul-absorbing beauty, in which, however, there was nothing which subserved the cause of religion, nothing on the other hand which did not directly or indirectly minister to corrupt nature and the powers of darkness.[52]

The servant metaphor does not, therefore, imply any kind of recognition of the intrinsic value and dignity of art, but rather expresses in a somewhat different form the same mistrust of art which characterises Protestant iconoclasm. We might, in addition, ask who is the final arbiter of the work of art *qua* servant. The theologian? But isn't theology also a servant task? Who is to regulate the orders of service and determine their respective limits?

Returning to Kierkegaard and Bloy we might sum up their teaching along these lines: the modern bourgeois world is sunk in mediocrity and commercial self-gratification; art offers it the only higher life it can remotely grasp but even art cannot cure its fundamental sickness; therefore we must abandon art and hold out the one thing needful: the recognition of our utter emptiness, our 'homesickness for Being' and our dependence on God's grace to make good what we lack. In an age of confusion no compromise is possible: either art or faith. With this challenge the tradition of Christian iconoclasm acquires the very specific form of a critique of modernity. But does the Christian recognition of the inability of modernism to resolve its own internal contradictions necessarily involve such an iconoclastic approach? Can we not envisage a more positive appraisal of the servant task of art? Might art not prove to be a precious part of a

Christian attempt to rescue the modern world from its self-afflicted sickness? With these questions we come to our next chapter, but, as we do so, let us bear in mind the pervasiveness of iconoclasm in Christian history and let us be careful of dismissing such a powerful tradition too lightly or easily.

3

The Dream
of a Christian Culture

The spirit of Christian iconoclasm, nourished by both biblical and classical sources, has, as we have seen, left its mark on virtually every period of Church history. Yet it is by no means invariably dominant and is matched by an opposite impulse which aims to bring about the integration of artistic production and enjoyment into the life of faith. In the West this impulse has found its supreme monument in the 'Christian culture' of the Middle Ages, which, to its many admirers, represents an unsurpassed – perhaps even an unsurpassable – fusion of art and faith. But it has to be said that our view of mediaeval culture is inevitably shaped by our own modern experience, and the idealisation of the Middle Ages which occurred in the Early Romantic movement, and which has remained a strong feature of many subsequent forms of Romanticism, must to a large extent be interpreted as a response to the impact of the modern scientific, rational world-view. It was almost to be expected that since the intellectual, moral, political and aesthetic programme of the Enlightenment of the seventeenth and eighteenth centuries involved a point by point repudiation of what were perceived as the values and beliefs of the Middle Ages, those who in turn repudiated the Enlightenment should turn back to the Middle Ages as a symbolic focus for the desires and fantasies which the new bourgeois world order was unable to fulfil. It is, at a cultural level, what psycho-analysis has described as 'the return of the repressed', and the repressed ghost of the mediaeval world has never ceased to haunt its bourgeois conquerors. Thus, where modernity is experienced as rootless, superficial, self-satisfied, conformist and unjustifiably optimistic the mediaeval world provided a convenient screen onto which to project longings for rootedness, profundity, reverence, nobility and a sense for the vanity of all 'merely' human enterprises. It was in this respect that Heinrich

Heine described the Early Romantic school as pure mediaevalism, 'nothing but the reawakening of the poesy of the Middle Ages, as that had manifested itself in its songs, images and buildings, in art and in life'.[1] The Romantic movement was not ecclesiastical in its beginnings but it soon forged important alliances with Christian groups opposed to modernity. This combination made for a view of the mediaeval world which was at once religious and aesthetic and which – especially in the period before Vatican II – provided the Roman Catholic Church (and to a certain extent High Church Anglicanism) with a potent apologetic symbol.

The Romantic espousal of what were believed to be the values of the mediaeval world has remained a powerful cultural myth. In a recent study of Gothic art and architecture the critic William Anderson contrasts the attitude of the twentieth century physicist with that of the mediaeval world. The physicists

lacking the support of all the other higher forms of knowledge and of inspiration which they had rejected as superstitious or irrelevant, knowing no moral imperative except the furtherance of their science . . . sold themselves in exchange for government support to the forces of barbarism.[2]

By way of contrast the architectural monuments of Gothic art show us what can be achieved by 'men working together in a common spirit in which their religion, their art, their philosophy, and their science and technology were in harmony'.[3] Most simply the contrast is that between 'an art based on the proper working of conscience' and a 'determinist philosophy' in which 'there is no sanction for the working of conscience'.[4]

Such a view of mediaeval art is, in effect, a mirror image of the story of modern art told in Chapter 1 of this book. Instead of the fragmentation, disintegration and final eclipse of art in the modern world we find in the Gothic achievement a paradigm of unity, harmony and spiritual clarity. Moreover, as Christian apologists of the mediaeval order emphasise, this was made possible because all sections of society, including the artists, accepted the ultimate guidance and authority of faith.

An excellent example of the way in which such a view of the Middle Ages could be pressed into the service of a contemporary Christian apologetic is E. I. Watkin's *Catholic Art and Culture*. Published in 1942 this offered a view of cultural history whose appeal to those living through the age of World Wars, mass unemployment and totalitarian politics is fairly obvious. It was all too easy to contend that such crises and catastrophes were the inevitable result of the triumph of humanism and the rejection of the authority of the Church. Watkin charts the course of this apostasy in the sphere of culture, and his argument is summed up in a striking metaphor which provides the very structure of the book. This metaphor is enshrined in the chapter headings themselves:

THE CLASSICAL AUTUMN, THE CHRISTIAN SPRING.
SUMMER: MEDIEVAL CHRISTENDOM.
LATE SUMMER: THE DISINTEGRATION OF THE MEDIEVAL
    ORDER: THE RENAISSANCE.
AUTUMN: THE AGE OF BAROQUE.
WINTER: THE MODERN WORLD. [5]

He contrasts his own position with with the views of those like H. G. Wells who are 'contemptuous of the culture of the past' and who 'prefer the uncultured civilisation in which we live, where the scientific servant does his work admirably, but there is no master to direct his services to the purposes of an organic religion-culture'.[6] He admits that the modernists are right in pointing out that at the material level the mediaeval world had its share of problems: poverty, ignorance, plague, war and oppression. But, he counters, even summer has its cold and stormy days. In any case, the modern world fares no better in this respect; 'the seamy side of nineteenth-century civilisation' and the twentieth century's 'outbreak of international anarchy' do not exactly gain by comparison with even the worst aspects of the Middle Ages.[7] But, in any case, this is beside the point. The real issue concerns ideals – and at this level the superiority of the mediaeval ideal is plain to see. For although the mediaeval world knew inequality and injustice its ideal rose above such imperfections:

The hovel, metaphorical and actual, below the medieval cathedral does not convince the latter of hypocrisy or make void its beauty . . . the finest art and architecture, since they were devoted to the service of the Church not of private luxury, were accessible to all. The dweller in the hovel worshipped in the cathedral.[8]

It is in fact the Gothic cathedral itself which provides Watkin with the supreme symbol and embodiment of the unitary religion-culture of the Middle Ages, so much so that he can speak also of the 'social cathedral' of a united Christendom, 'the intellectual cathedral of scholasticism' and 'the literary cathedral of Dante's *Commedia*'.[9] But it is the 'literal cathedral of stone' which provides the most accessible point of entry into the mediaeval world-view. Watkin therefore leads us through an extensive exposition of the way in which the cathedral recapitulates the whole outlook of its time. The pointed arch, for example, is not just an engineering device but, by enabling walls to be heightened and transformed into great areas of stained glass, it expresses both the heavenward soaring of the human spirit and its openness to the light of the divine presence. It raises our vision

> to a point from which we can look down on the world, 'terrena despicere', and on the unfinished course of history. But not in contempt . . . In this subordination all these natural and human forms, all these representations of work and study are drawn into this praise of God . . . as in the view of the world which it embodies, everything in the cathedral is directed to God.[10]

The multiple syntheses incorporated into the great edifice of the cathedral – of art and theology, of natural and supernatural, of image and idea, of society, culture and Christian teaching – make of it an all-inclusive ark of salvation, a tangible representation of the key insight of the mediaeval theologian, Thomas Aquinas, that grace is for the perfecting, not the destroying, of nature.

The case for such a correlation between Gothic art and scholastic theology has been made many times. Erwin Panofsky's study *Gothic Architecture and Scholasticism* goes even further than Watkin in making detailed parallels between the histories of Gothic architecture and scholastic thought, and Panofsky analyses the solution of such architectural problems as the siting of the rose window in the west façade, the organisation of the wall beneath the clerestory and the conformation of the nave piers as having been achieved by the methods of scholastic *quaestiones*.[11] But, whatever the 'facts' regarding the 'mediaeval synthesis', our question now is whether the Middle Ages offer us a sound theological basis on which to build an integrative theology of art. Does mediaeval theology itself provide an intellectual basis for the emergence of a unitary 'religion-culture'

such as that described by Watkin? Such questions lead almost
inevitably to Thomas Aquinas who has not only acquired the status
of being the archetypal theologian of mediaeval Europe but whose
theology still exercises a normative role in Catholic theology. Let us
then restate our question, with Thomas specifically in mind: does
the Thomist theology of art itself support the full integration of the
making and the reception of works of art into the life of faith? In
other words, whatever our estimation of the Gothic achievement,
to what extent can the mediaeval world help us in formulating a
contemporary theological aesthetic?

Commentators agree that there was little systematic attention to
questions of art and its relation to religion in scholastic thought.
Nonetheless, it has been argued that it is possible to construct a
coherent Christian theology of art from the scattered discussions
and remarks which we do not find there. A notable example of such
a reconstruction is Jacques Maritain's *Art and Scholasticism*. Like
Watkin, Maritain made no secret of the fact that in his view mediaeval culture was significantly superior to the secular, humanist
civilisation of the modern world – not only in its ideals but even in
the works of art which it actually produced. 'More beautiful things
were then created and there was less self-worship. The blessed
humility in which the artist was situated exalted his strength and
his freedom'.[12] He too emphasised the view that the mediaeval
artist did not pander to the fashions of rich gallery-goers but produced an art that was for the people, an 'art of the tribe', to use
André Malraux's expression. 'Matchless epoch', Maritain exclaims,
'in which an ingenuous folk was educated in beauty without even
noticing it . . . ' (*AS*, p. 22). Like Bloy (through whom he had himself been converted to a lively Catholic faith), he regarded the
Renaissance as a fateful apostasy which would eventually ruin
art itself by giving the artist a false self-consciousness and an
overweening hubris. In this way the artist would come to share
the universal 'frenzy' of modernity, the ultimate end of which 'is to
prevent man from remembering God . . . ' (*AS*, p. 37). But whereas
Bloy insisted that 'Christian art' is a contradiction, Maritain, whilst
acknowledging the difficulties involved in such an art, maintains the
true Thomist faith that 'Nature is not essentially bad . . . However
deeply wounded it may be by sin . . . it can be cured by grace' (*AS*,
p. 212). Applying this principle to art it follows that whatever its
limitations art can be won for Christ. What Maritain expounds, then,
is a natural theology of art, corresponding in general structure to the

broad principles of Thomist theology. On this analysis art can, in its most intimate and essential structure, be shown to be orientated towards and open to the revelation and the working of divine grace. The more true art is to itself, the more it realises what it essentially is, the more appropriate a vehicle it becomes for the reception and the expression of grace. How, then, does Maritain argue his case?

He starts by making a strong distinction between what he calls the speculative and the practical orders. The speculative order comprises those virtues of the mind whose sole end is knowledge, whereas in the practical order knowledge is not regarded as an end in itself but only as a means to an end. In terms of this distinction art clearly belongs to the practical order. 'Its orientation is towards doing, not to the pure inwardness of knowledge' (*AS*, p. 4). The practical order, however, can be further subdivided into the spheres of Action (πρακτόν) and Making (ποιητόν). The sphere of Action is that of morality which, under the guidance of prudence, aims to bring about the overall good of human life. Art, on the other hand, belongs to the sphere of Making, and its aims are (in certain respects) more modest than those of morality. Art is only concerned with the exigencies of the work to be produced, with what serves to make it a good work. Prudential considerations as to the relation of the work to the totality of life and to the final end of personal existence lie outside the scope of art as such. Nonetheless, since art is made by human beings (and, indeed, only by human beings) it is stamped with the rational character of its maker. Thus the formal element of art, 'what constitutes it of its kind and makes it what it is, is its being controlled and directed by the mind' (*AS*, p. 7). This form is therefore 'undeviating reason' itself and, in this respect, art is profoundly intellectual, since it involves the impressing of rational and intellectual form onto a given matter. The mental and intellectual character of art is, of course, of a kind appropriate to its practical nature. Whereas the speculative intellect is concerned above all with knowing its object and gives itself over to the pure contemplation of the divine wisdom, the practical intellect is concerned with directing its object 'according to the rule and the proper disposition of the thing to be done' (*AS*, p. 12). In the case of that act of making which concerns the artist this reminds us that for the artist the work is everything: the artist does not ask about the moral purpose served by the work – he only asks about how it can be well done. The double definition of art as both intellectual and practical therefore involves art in a complex

three-way relationship which Maritain sums up like this: 'The
Man of Learning is an Intellectual demonstrating, the Artist is an
Intellectual operating, the Prudent Man is an intelligent Man of Will
acting well' (*AS*, p. 20). The relationships within this triumvirate
are, however, by no means equally balanced. Art, says Maritain (for
reasons which we shall shortly examine), has a natural affinity with
the contemplative spirit, but 'it is difficult for the Prudent Man and
the Artist to understand one another' (*AS*, p. 85). In confirmation of
this, history reveals recurrent conflicts between Prudence and Art.
Thus, at the Renaissance, Prudence was sacrificed to Art, but in the
bourgeois nineteenth century Art was all too often sacrificed to a
prudential concern for respectability and decorum.

As an intellectual habit art is to be understood primarily as an
intellectual habit and virtue, but for Maritain 'habit' is a technical
term which has little or nothing to do with what he acknowledges
is the prevailing sense of mechanical or unthinking repetition. In
his usage habit means a consistent and stable orientation of the
mind or will towards a good end. Understood in this way habit
is a virtue which raises the intellect 'in respect of a definite object
to a *maximum of perfection, and so of operative efficiency*' (*AS*, p. 11).
'Art', as just such a habit, is in a sense prior to the practice of any
particular art or the making of any particular work of art: it is a
quality of the artist before it is a quality of the work. Those who
have an art, whether it is in logic, music, architecture or whatever,
'are, in a way their work before they create it' (*AS*, p. 12). Moreover,
since a habit is by definition orientated solely towards an end that
is good in itself, it follows that to the extent that art is conformed
to its essential habit it is *infallibly correct* (*AS*, p. 12). This, however,
only applies to its formal and mental aspect, the rationality, that
is, both of its origin (in the human mind) and its ultimate end.
As far as the actual making of works of art goes such infallible
correctness gives no guarantees against the artist's hand faltering,
his eye misleading him or his material proving intractable. At this
level the artist is in 'a strange and pathetic condition, the very image
of man's condition in the world, where he is condemned to wear
himself out among bodies and live with minds' (*AS*, p. 35). Despite
his habitual inclination towards intellectual and speculative truth
he is, in this life, 'condemned to every servile misery of temporal
practice and production' (*AS*, p. 35).

All of this – intellectual truth and servile misery alike – is true
both of the fine arts and of the work of the artisan such as the

blacksmith or carpenter. The lowliest trade is in one respect intellectual and infallibly correct whilst even the highest achievements of poets and artists are limited by their material means. The fine arts are nonetheless distinguished by the fact that they do not aim merely to produce a work, but to produce a work of beauty, an aim which raises the tension between formal and material elements to a still higher pitch.

> The work which involves the labour of the Fine Arts is ordered to beauty; in so far as it is beautiful it is an end, an absolute, self-sufficient; and if, as work to be done, it is material . . . as beautiful it belongs to the realm of the spirit and dives deep into the transcendence and the infinity of being. (*AS*, p. 33)

Where this tension is resolved creatively the fine arts become 'like a horizon where matter comes into contact with spirit' (*AS*, p. 34).

In order to see what this involves we must examine more closely Maritain's conception of beauty (or, we should say, Thomas's conception of beauty as interpreted by Maritain). Beauty belongs to the order of transcendental realities such as unity, truth, goodness and being itself; metaphysical realities which belong to the fundamental structure of everything that is. In two quotations from the *Summa Theologiae* of St. Thomas Maritain tells us that beauty is to be defined as 'what gives pleasure on sight, *id quod visum placet*' (*AS*, p. 23), and as composed, in itself, of integrity, proportion and brightness (or clarity). These two definitions, Maritain says, define beauty according to its effects and according to its essence respectively. With regard to the former definition he says that it indicates a kind of 'intuitive knowledge, and a joy' (*AS*, p. 23). These terms give us an important clue as to what is at stake in this conception of the beautiful and how it relates to other theories which we shall be examining in due course. Following Aristotle and Aquinas, Maritain holds that for an existing human subject there can be no knowledge apart from the conditions of sense-experience. Knowledge, however, is not identical with the data of such experience but depends on a process of abstraction in which the essence or universal aspect of the thing perceived is made present to the mind. For example, when I look at a tree I can only say that I know it to be a tree when in the mass of sensory data I recognise that it can all be subsumed under the concept 'tree'. The medium of sense-experience, which I apprehend intuitively, is the medium and the condition of knowledge, but it is not itself the content of knowledge. Normally, then, there is a clear distinction between intuition and knowledge. But with regard to beauty Maritain tells us that we know it in a kind of intuitive knowledge, that is, a kind of knowledge which bypasses the process of abstraction and 'knows' its object in a simple, direct vision. The perception of beauty thus at one and the same time addresses both mind and senses. Consequently, artistic beauty 'has the savour of the terrestrial paradise, because it restores for a brief moment the simultaneous peace and delight of the mind and the senses' (*AS*, p. 24). Similarly, the enjoyment which the vision of beauty arouses (remember the definition: *id quod visum placet*) is immediately given and, as it were, fused with the actual vision itself. Such joy, we are warned, is not to be confused with emotion or feeling in the normal sense: 'it is a question of a very special feeling, depending simply upon knowledge, and the happy fullness procured to the mind by a sensible intuition' (*AS*, p. 165). In other words it is the element of knowledge which generates the element of pleasure in experiences of the beautiful, and it does so because in such experiences the faculty of knowledge fulfils its own purpose: 'it is the satisfaction of our faculty of Desire reposing in the proper good of the cognitive faculty perfectly and harmoniously exercised by the intuition of the beautiful' (*AS*, p. 165).

Turning to the three elements of integrity, proportion and clarity which characterise beauty, Maritain relates them to the mind's desire for being, unity and light (or intelligibility) respectively. This last element is then brought into connection with another important concept in scholastic metaphysics – form. Form is defined as 'the principle determining the peculiar perfection of everything which is, constituting and completing things in their essence and their qualities . . . above all the peculiar principle of intelligibility, the peculiar clarity of everything' (*AS*, p. 24). Form in this sense is a 'remnant' or a 'ray' of the divine mind itself, impressed on created being in the process of creation. Beauty can now be defined still more closely (in a quotation usually assigned to Albertus Magnus) as 'the *splendour of form shining on the proportioned parts of matter* . . . a lightning of mind on a matter intelligently arranged' (*AS*, p. 25).

Intuitions of beauty are not, of course, confined to the fine arts. Beauty is by definition a transcendental reality and is therefore in some way a quality of everything that is. Indeed the beauty of art is largely dependent on the reality of beauty prior to the activity of artistic production itself. The most supremely beautiful being is, simply, God himself (*AS*, p. 31). God is also the source of beauty in all other beings. However, the transcendental and divine nature of beauty in this pre-eminent sense means that beauty as it is found in all other creatures (eg. sunsets, mountains, mathematical theorems or works of art) is only beautiful by analogy with its divine prototype. To put it another way: by being solely and supremely beautiful in himself God is the measure of all other instances of beauty, which are beautiful precisely to the extent that they are like God. This further underlines the anguish of the artist's situation. Previously we saw how the artist was caught between the demands of intellectual or speculative truth on the one hand and the 'servile misery of temporal practice and production' on the other. Here the same tension emerges in a different and more significant aspect. Compared with the abundant reality of the divine beauty all works of human art are 'rubbish, destined to be burned on the Last Day' (*AS*, p. 36), a distinction, Maritain notes consolingly, which they share with Thomas's own unfinished *Summa*. 'No form of art, however perfect, can encompass beauty in itself as the Virgin contained her Creator' (*AS*, p. 46).

But if the concept of 'intuitive knowledge' bridges the gap between the intellectual and sensuous aspects of beauty, what serves to make the artist a worker in beauty despite the incapacity of his means to embrace the fulness of beauty itself? It is, Maritain says, because the creative artist 'discovers a new type-analogy of the beautiful, a new way in which the brilliance of form can be made to shine upon nature' (*AS*, p. 46). And how does the artist do this? Not by imitation in the crude sense of mimicking or exactly reproducing existing beautiful forms; not, that is, by making copies as Plato thought the artist must always do. For, Maritain tells us, Aristotle at least meant more by imitation than this. Aristotle's conception is formal, such that in addition to '*imitation as a reproduction of things*' there is a metaphysical sense of '*imitation as manifestation of a form*'. What is 'imitated' in this sense is a metaphysical and transcendental form in relation to which the actual representational likeness between the artistic expression of this form and any other created being is purely tangential. The material aspect of the work, its shape, its colour, etc., is not to be regarded as a thing (and, as such, comparable to other things) but is symbolic, pointing beyond itself to the transcendental form which it symbolises (*AS*, pp. 55ff.). In this respect Maritain is prepared to see a positive aspect to Cubism, at least in its intentions: 'Does cubism in our day', he asks, 'despite its tremendous deficiencies, represent the still stumbling, screaming childhood of an art once more pure?' (*AS*, p. 54). Certainly he regards it as an advance upon the ideal of artistic illusion which he believes to have dominated art from the sixteenth to the twentieth centuries. He illustrates the concept of formal as opposed to reproductive imitation by an anecdote concerning his friend, the painter Georges Rouault. As they were returning from a walk through a wintry snow-covered landscape Rouault told him that he had just realised how to paint the white trees of spring. What he had seen in the snow was not the external, sensuous appearance of a wet, cold white matter, but the formal meaning of whiteness itself (*AS*, p. 64). It is in this sense that on the one hand 'artistic creation does not copy God's creation, but continues it' (*AS*, p. 63), whilst on the other 'the artist, whether he knows it or not, is consulting God when he looks at things' (*AS*, p. 64). It is not the external appearance of things that matters but their logical truth: ' . . . every work of art must be logical . . . not in the logic of knowledge and demonstration, but in the working logic of every day, eternally mysterious and disturbing, the logic of the structure of the living thing, and the intimate geometry of nature' (*AS*, p. 52). As examples of such logic he cites Our Lady of Chartres (and mediaeval art generally) together with Virgil, Racine, Poussin, Shakespeare and Baudelaire – a list which does not perhaps entirely clarify what he means!

We might, at this point, ask again: how does the artist gain access to that realm of transcendental beauty if that, by definition, transcends the scope of artistic contrivance? Let us refer back to what was said earlier about the habitual element in art. Maritain's concept of habit meant, as we saw, a fundamental orientation of the mind which directs the intellect towards the sphere of transcendental reality. In this sense he was able to say that those who have an art 'are' their work 'before they create'. The relation to beauty which establishes the possibility of creating beautiful works of art is therefore to be looked for in the mind or the life of the artist. For only when the artist himself is habitually open to the reality of the transcendental order will he be able to produce works of genuine beauty. Although such openness does not by any means guarantee the presence of those skills and techniques which enable good works of art to be produced, it is and remains a necessary and prior condition of such production. Above all, Maritain says, this openness is to be defined as love. In short, 'A Christian work would have the artist, as man, a saint. It would have him possessed by love. Then he may go and do as he likes' (*AS*, p. 71). Quoting Fra Angelico he adds, '*to paint the things of Christ, the artist must live with Christ*'.

This does not mean that he is only willing to commend ecclesiastical art or art with an overtly Christian subject-matter. The artist who lives with Christ 'may go and do as he likes' and paint what he likes. We have already noted Maritain's positive attitude towards cubism, and throughout *Art and Scholasticism* he comments favourably on many works of art (and artists) which might not conventionally be regarded as the works of artists who lived with Christ. Indeed, even outside Christendom, as in the arts of ancient Egypt, China or Greece, 'wherever art . . . has attained a certain degree of grandeur and purity, it is already Christian, Christian in hope . . . ' (*AS*, p. 69). What he supremely deprecates is art for art's sake, an aestheticism which teaches that art is able to constitute a self-sufficient sphere of life, without relation to the other dimensions of existence. Art must, he insists, at all times remain open, above all open to what transcends it ontologically: open to faith, to sanctity, to God.

This means that, whilst rejecting the crude intrusion of narrow bourgeois morality into artistic matters, Maritain ultimately accepts that art is constrained from without and must, so to speak, accept the judgement of a higher court on its works. At a practical level this means that he is prepared to endorse the principle of the censorship of art by the teaching authority of the Church. In the case of a particular work, the 'Stations of the Cross' by the Flemish painter Servaes, Maritain supports the order of March 1921 issued by the Holy Office, banning the work from being exhibited in Church. In acting in this way, he says, the Holy Office acted in 'the sovereign interests of the Faith' (*AS*, p. 144), with 'wisdom' and 'excellent reasons' – and this despite the fact that Servaes is conceded to be 'a painter of very considerable talent, a Christian full of faith' and the work in question 'beautiful and worthy of admiration' (*AS*, p. 145). The work is, however, dogmatically flawed, because it portrays Christ's sufferings as too appallingly human and does not communicate the unique 'sovereign dignity of this soul and body' (*AS*, p. 146). Maritain rejects the argument that the Church is motivated in such cases by a partial or partisan view of truth, since 'Catholicism is not a particular statement of faith any more than it is a religion: it is the religion, confessing the only omnipresent Truth' (*AS*, p. 137). This, however, sounds too much like special pleading, as most contemporary Catholic theologians would acknowledge, and the form of his arguments (whatever the merits or otherwise of the work in question) is horribly reminiscent of the arguments in favour of censorship advanced by those totalitarian regimes of his time which to his credit Maritain robustly opposed. The whole case serves to highlight a problem which is deeply rooted in his overall conception of art, a problem which is, I would suggest, inherent in his account of the analogical nature of material and artistic beauty and the strategy by which he proposes to solve it.

Maritain teaches that beauty is apprehended in an act of intuitive knowledge. Such an act is, as we have seen, complete in itself (and precisely thereby productive of intellectual joy). Yet it does not follow that that transcendental reality which (he claims) is 'known' in this act is known exhaustively. Such knowledge is still, in some sense, deficient, and lacks a fundamental reflection on its own content. Because of its intuitive character it does not itself lay bare the grounds for the truth which is given in it. It must, as we have seen, await the judgement, metaphorical and actual, of a higher court. For alongside such intuitive knowledge there are other levels or degrees of knowledge, for instance, that knowledge which is based on abstraction. But also, and more importantly, we are faced with the question: how can we be sure that the truth which is communicated in beauty is indeed true? Since, in Thomist thought, all knowledge of transcendental reality is analogous (including the knowledge that comes via abstraction) how can we be sure that that which is revealed in the beautiful object is an appropriate symbol of that which it symbolises unless we have some other mode of access to the transcendental order? This is a familiar problem in the context of discussions of religious language, since all analogy is accepted by Thomas as involving both likeness and unlikeness and therefore a degree of equivocation. But if we have no language for speaking of God other than a language permeated by equivocation how do we know whether our God-talk is well-grounded? To speak of our knowledge of beauty as 'intuitive' may, at first sight, seem to offer just such a point of direct access to the transcendental order, but, as we have seen, beauty too, especially artistic beauty, is bound by the limits of all analogy. Now it might be that in such a situation we are driven to accept the revisability of all statements and all forms of knowledge bearing on the transcendental order but Maritain himself seems to accept that there is an ultimate ground for our knowledge, and that that ground is guaranteed by the rule of faith which is authenticated by the magisterium of the Church. The Church is, in effect, the single authoritative ground of truth in this earthly life.

This epistemological problem throws further light on his vision of the harmony between religion and culture in the Middle Ages. The artist functioned in the Middle Ages as a teacher of the untutored poor. In the terms of the Synod of Arras of 1025 visual images were legitimated as 'poor-men's Books'. In other words, images were seen as a means of teaching, of communicating knowledge. As we have seen Maritain is insistent on the element of knowledge in art and in the apprehension of beauty generally. Art, in its sensuous materiality, is (the argument goes) able to communicate directly to the poor a (literal) vision of truth. But the validation of the truth of images rests on the judgements of contemplatives, doctors and pontiffs, who have other perspectives on truth; who, as the guardians of the sacred tradition, are able to pass judgements on the truth in art in a way which those engaged immediately in the production and reception of works of art are unable to emulate. Ecclesially validated faith is thus the measure of art, as of life. All this however strengthens the suspicion that neo-mediaevalism is unable to meet the specific protest by modern art on behalf of artistic autonomy and freedom. One might further suspect that Maritain's personal form of nostalgia for a unitary religion-culture is too narrowly 'Catholic', despite his claim that Catholicism is not 'a' religion but 'the' religion.

Yet despite such suspicions it must be acknowledged that Maritain's vision had a significant appeal to many artists, especially those who found themselves recoiling from the incipient nihilism of contemporary art or who were wearied by the trite vacuity of 'art for art's sake'. The myth of the mediaeval religion-culture was, as I have already suggested, an attractive focus for those who were discontented with the negative aspects of modernism. Maritain's writings on art were, for instance, taken up by Eric Gill, the British artist and craftsman whose conversion to Catholicism had a powerful impact on his generation. Gill argued that all human life is ultimately governed by what it conceives of as reality, 'the discovery and grasping of the real'.[13] It follows that some kind of religion or philosophy is presupposed in all human activity, a fact which is as true of Russian Communism and of bourgeois democracy as it is of mediaeval Catholicism. Moreover, all religion and philosophy is, at bottom, concerned

with God, even if it refuses to name him as such. From this Gill
concludes that

> ... what we call the 'great periods' of 'art' always coincide
> with the great periods of religion, and that what we call the
> 'great period' of religion is one in which there is a 'unanimous
> society'. A unanimous society is one in which there is one mind,
> one attitude towards life, one pervading sense of its meaning,
> a universal acceptance of a certainly defined finality, and that
> finality, that final cause, God, a final cause outside material life
> but pervading, directing and ruling it.[14]

In this respect that art of mediaeval Christendom is closer to the art
of Hinduism than it is to the art of the modern world which has lost
such unanimity. Both Hindu and mediaeval art

> are made according to hieratic canon, both are devoid of idiosyn-
> crasy. Both are negligent of anatomical verisimilitude. Both are of
> public rather than private significance. Both are concerned with
> the expression of conceptions of general importance and wide-
> spread belief, and not with personal and particular likings.[15]

It was in the light of this recognition, he tells us, that tired of
the vacuous and 'merely idiosyncratic' cult of self-expression, he
'decided to abolish art, art as an end in itself, a thing desirable for its
own sake. Such was the choice, such was the necessary decision'.[16]
In practical terms this meant not only his conversion to Roman
Catholicism but his involvement in a series of communal living
projects through which he hoped to overcome the self-consuming
individualism which threatened the modern artist.

At the same time he remained sufficiently modernist to resent
the sort of control of art by the Church authorities which Maritain
defended. Maritain had himself pointed out the problematic relationship between art and prudence, and the dangers of a narrowly
conceived bourgeois morality intruding into the proper sphere of
art, but Gill's approach was still more confrontational. In an extraordinary essay 'Art and Prudence', which for some reason takes
the form of a didactic poem (elsewhere, in, for example, the essay
Id Quod Visum Placet he adopts a thoroughly pretentious pseudo-
scholastic style, setting his argument out in the questions, objections and responses typical of a mediaeval treatise) he speaks with

scarcely concealed contempt of those who would make prudence the rule of art.

> With good art prudence should have no quarrel . . .
> But many prudent men quarrel with art, however
> good, because many prudent men are prudes.
> The prude is afraid of the pleasure of the senses.
> And many prudent men quarrel with art, however good,
> because many prudent men are proud.[17]

Since in the same essay (or poem?) he asserts that the Church as 'the guardian of faith and morals' is 'Prudent Man',[18] the stage seems set for a situation of conflict and recrimination which ill suits the concept of a 'unanimous society'.

Gill is painfully aware of the scandal of what he calls 'repository art', the bad religious art – religious kitsch we might call it – which is characteristic of much popular Catholic devotion.[19] Although he is willing for himself 'to continue our present practice of hiding our best works when the parish priest comes to tea',[20] he frankly accuses the clergy of having become 'the most abject patrons of the loose and undisciplined and sentimental'.[21] The conflict which Gill is highlighting here is reminiscent of the controversy over Couturier's 'modernist' Church at Assy. Do we look to the theologian or the artist to solve these disputes? If Maritain, as a theologian (albeit a lay theologian) looked in the last resort to the teaching authority of the Church, Gill, as an artist (and, in many respects, a modern artist despite himself) protested vociferously against the ecclesiastically sanctioned degradation of Church art. These different responses to a common problem once more raise the question as to how far the ideal of a unitary religion-culture is a viable ideal in our own situation, especially in the form associated with the dream of the Middle Ages as the great and unsurpassable age of Christian art. Don't the interests of artists and theologians, however close, ultimately point in different directions?

So far I have considered Maritain's view of art in its own terms as a valid exposition of the Thomist conception of art and beauty. But is this so? Umberto Eco's study, *The Aesthetics of Thomas Aquinas* (recently translated into English) throws considerable doubt on this. Eco attacks Maritain's notion of 'intuitive knowledge' as essentially a modern and romantic idea, which is not only untrue to Thomas's own thought but is actually incomprehensible in terms of Thomist epistemology. 'Intuitive knowledge', as we have seen, appears to offer a way of approach to transcendental beauty which bypasses the process of abstraction (although, as we also saw, it does not elude the fundamental limits of analogy). Eco however engages in an extensive analysis of Thomas's understanding of the aesthetic *visio* and concludes that this cannot possibly be a kind of intuition. According to Thomas, he argues, intuition can only occur in the sphere of sensibility. As such intuition cannot be the basis for any kind of knowledge, since this requires the further activity of the intellect. But 'the act of abstraction, the *simplex apprehensio* through which the intellect formulates concepts, the act of knowledge prior to which the aesthetic intuition is supposed to occur, is in fact the epistemological *primum*'.[22] 'It is', he says, 'absolutely impossible to posit an intuition of form in the concrete, before the abstraction'.[23] Maritain's notion of 'a lightning of the mind on a matter intelligently arranged' would, Eco asserts, involve the denial both of sensible intuition and of abstractive knowledge as Thomas understood them. Far from aesthetic pleasure preceding the act of abstraction (as Maritain contends) Eco concludes that such pleasure is dependent on the completion of a process of abstraction through which the mind comes to a thorough knowledge of its object. 'It signifies, not an absence, but a cessation, of effort. It is a sense of joy and triumph, of pleasure in a form which has been discerned, admired, and loved with a disinterested love, the love which is possible for a formal structure'.[24] Eco's interpretation of Aquinas is, then avowedly intellectualist:

> Beauty, in Aquinas's aesthetics, is not the fruit of psychological empathy, nor of the imaginative transfiguration or creation of an object. Instead, it sinks its roots deep into a complex knowledge of being. And so, intellectual travail is a necessary pathway to the knowledge of beauty.[25]

These epistemological considerations have important cultural implications. For a start they render the notion of a non-intellectual teaching of divine things by means of images redundant. Beauty, in its intellectual truth, cannot be attained by those who are unwilling or unable to enter on the paths of 'intellectual travail'. As an example of what this might involve we could, perhaps, consider Eco's fictional detective-monk William of Baskerville, who solves the riddle of a series of grim monastic murders by journeying along a complex and tortuous path of signs interpreting signs interpreting signs . . . [26] There is no place here for images as 'poor men's books': truth cannot be had cheaply. Eco's interpretation, if correct, also sets up an ultimately unmanageable strain within the conception of a unitary religion-culture. Although Eco accepts Panofsky's careful correlation of theological and architectural patterns he rejects the view that either architecture or scholasticism provided an adequate reflection of the economic, social and even artistic realities of the time. The 'optimum convergence' between the multiple elements of the system could not be maintained, and certainly cannot be guaranteed outside the process of intellectual exploration and interpretation itself. This also indicates that it is no longer possible – or at least extremely difficult – for religious authority to claim the kind of finality in questions of beauty which Maritain's Neo-Thomism allowed it to have. (Again the novel *The Name of the Rose* provides an interesting commentary on the theoretical situation.) By making intellectual factors paramount, Eco is in fact sowing the seeds of dissolution at the very heart of the mediaeval synthesis and inviting the move into a more individualistic social and aesthetic culture. Naturally Eco's own semiological preoccupations may colour his interpretation of Aquinas, just as Maritain's neo-mediaevalism affects his interpretation – but his criticism nonetheless exposes a complex of presuppositions in Maritain's work for which Maritain himself does not appear to have a sufficient explanation.

It would, however, be unfair to Neo-Thomism to suggest that its aesthetics are indissolubly linked to the myth of a mediaeval religion-culture and it is quite possible to conceive of an application of Thomist principles which would give a much greater value to the development of a modern, secular artistic culture. This is, in fact, the thrust of Etienne Gilson's 1955 Mellon Lectures *Painting and Reality*.

In some respects Gilson's interpretation of Aquinas is virtually the opposite of Eco's intellectualising account. Gilson minimises the intellectual element in art and concentrates instead on the physical reality of the work. As the title suggests he is particularly concerned with painting and he takes pains to draw attention to the very physical nature of painting. Painting, as opposed to poetry or music, has, he says, the quality expressed by the German word *Dasein*: it is *there*.[27] A painting 'is a solid, material thing, enduring in a certain place and enjoying a continuous mode of existence so long as it lasts' (*PR*, p. 11). Although there is a sense in which, as an aesthetic object, it is discontinuous (according as to whether it is actually being looked at in an appropriately aesthetic manner), even when it is being regarded aesthetically, as a work of art, its physical mode of presence makes itself felt as such in the aesthetic experience. 'This solid physical presence is part and parcel of the aesthetic existence of paintings' (*PR*, p. 20). This physical quality is a recurrent theme in many of the aspects of painting towards which Gilson draws our attention. He insists, for instance, on the 'manual' as opposed to the 'white-collar' nature of the painter's art: paintings, he says, 'are not only man-made . . . they also are hand-made' (*PR*, p. 29). In this respect he rejects the distinction between liberal and servile arts made by Aquinas, for the specific dignity of painting is to be found in its manual character and nowhere else. The 'mentalism' which such a distinction betrays is not in his view authentically Aristotelian. Those whose viewpoint is grounded in the Bible should also remember that even Yahweh is said to work with his hands! The physical presence of painting is again illustrated by way of contrast with the dramatist or composer whose work is taken up by others – but 'the painter is to himself his own executor' (*PR*, p. 37). The work which he produces is forever what it is, an individual and unrepeatable creation. It follows also that if we really recognise the irreducibly material and singular character of painting then ' . . . strictly speaking, no picture can be duplicated' (*PR*, p. 64). The reproduction of a picture in a book or a magazine is never the picture itself, nor could it ever be so, no matter what advances occur in the field of printing technology. The uniqueness and irreproducibility of the actual physical painting belongs to its essential character. For similar reasons Gilson deprecates some of the attempts to restore 'old masters'. A restored picture is not the picture it was. We must accept that perishability and mutability belong to the material nature of painting and that if this were not the case then paintings would not be what they are (*PR*, pp. 91ff.).

The materiality of painting invites comment on the form/matter distinction. Whereas Maritain invited us to rise above the work of art regarded simply as a thing and to see it, by virtue of its formal element, as a symbol, Gilson wants us to remain close to the thingly, material character of the work. In fact, he says, this whole form/matter distinction arises only for philosophical reflection – it is not a distinction which has any relevance for human experience. 'In human experience', he says, 'the two notions of being and of form cannot possibly be separated' (*PR*, pp. 122f.). Instead of seeing 'form' as something transcending the actual physically existing object it is, he argues, form which makes a thing the individualised thing it is. Equally, matter is not some kind of indifferent stuff onto which each and every form can be imposed. Matter itself can be said to desire form, to aspire to form (*PR*, p. 109), so that the task of the artist is to work with the matter she has at her disposal and to give it that form which the matter itself requires.

In looking at a painting, then, we are not looking for some formal quality which will raise our minds above the level of mere sensory perception. What we must look at is simply the painting itself in its unique matter/form singularity. The meaning of the picture is to be found nowhere except in the picture itself, although we must be careful even of speaking about a meaning 'in' the picture, since a picture 'does not teach; it does not explain; it does not talk; it just is one more thing among things' (*PR*, p. 128). But what value can looking at such things have? Much, says Gilson. What painting offers us is an entrance into the presence of being, 'the simplest and most primitive of all acts' (*PR*, p. 28). Usually this act of being, simple and universal as it is, is not manifest as such, it lies 'hidden and unrevealed, behind what the thing signifies, says, does or makes' (*PR*, p. 128). In painting, in a manner quite different from that of philosophical reflection, being is brought out from its customary concealment and made present. This is supremely the case with those paintings which do not attempt to portray what lies outside the actual reality of painting itself – as in action scenes when 'whirls of apparently frantic motions stay frozen solid in an everlasting immobility' (*PR*, p. 21) – but remain within the boundaries of painting's peculiar capabilities, thus, with a minimum of action and a maximum of composition. It is in the light of this requirement that Gilson particularly commends still-life: 'now, precisely, this is what painting is best equipped to depict' (*PR*, p. 25). But these remarks apply also to a quality of stillness which is larger than that of 'still-life' painting in the narrow sense. It is, for instance, a quality of the interior of houses or Churches in many Dutch works of the seventeenth century. [Plate 3] In such works we can sense a 'quiet presence and motionless existentiality' (*PR*, p. 27). Similar possibilities are to be found in abstraction. Whatever the style or school to which a painting is assigned however, 'the true work of art is "the one which *is*"' (*PR*, p. 131), that is, the one by which we find ourselves placed in the presence of being. Commenting once again on the role of still-life

Gilson writes that 'there is a sort of metaphysical equity in the fact that this humblest genre is also the more revealing of all concerning the essence of art and painting' (*PR*, p. 28).

Having emphasised the unity of matter and form in the art-work, and the importance of the actual physical *dasein* of visual art, Gilson rejects any attempt to assess the value of such art in terms of knowledge. Citing Gauguin he says that we must learn 'to see without understanding' (*PR*, p. 145). Art is not unrelated to knowledge and cognition but these are not at stake as such in aesthetic intuition. Such intuition is prior to all reflection. The contrast with both Maritain and Eco is striking. We may say that Gilson here dissolves Maritain's concept of 'intuitive knowledge' in a direction opposite to that taken by Eco. Knowledge is simply a distraction in relation to that presencing of being which occurs in painting. Our enjoyment of painting and of beauty in general is 'by sense and in sense' (*PR*, p. 178). To want to know – as when we allow our eye to gravitate towards the title of the picture or the name of the painter before we look – is precisely to miss what we really need to see.

Gilson speculates that it is probable that the pleasure of seeing arises out of some kind of biologically given accommodation of the senses to their objects.[28] But, because it is a human being who has such experiences, a human being oriented towards cognition and the perception of intelligible relations, 'the pleasure at stake finds its source in the very intelligibility of being' (*PR*, p. 184). The perception of beauty is therefore cognitive and intelligible but, he emphasises, not intellectual. The possibility of such perception is rooted in the fact that matter and form are indissolubly linked in human experience in such a way that experience is never uninformed even if it does not yield intellectual knowledge.

What sort of relationship between art and nature does Gilson envisage? Maritain had the artist in search of the logical and intellectual aspect of nature. This is clearly not the case here. Gilson prefers to see nature working in or through the artist. 'Nature produces no works of art, nature produces artists who, in turn, produce works of art' (*PR*, p. 204). In this way painting participates in the biological fecundity of the natural world. Instead of simply 'imitating' nature the artist works from within nature and, in accordance with the desire of nature itself, aims 'to make "something" appear where, heretofore, there was "no thing"' (*PR*, p. 115). The artist thus makes a new thing, a thing which in one sense has no place among the things of nature, a new being, which adds to the plenitude of being (already engaged in a process of bringing forth new particularisations of itself). A painting simply fulfils its function by coming to be. It is not a second or third hand type of knowledge as Plato taught. It is a modest but irreplaceable contribution to the perfection of being. Gilson therefore wants to affirm both the freedom and the creativity of art in respect of the making of new forms of art. Modern art in particular has, he says, been concerned to explore and to reveal 'this universe of visible qualities' (*PR*, p. 275) which is 'one particular instance of what was, to its Creator, the inexhaustible realm of possible reality. There still remains more to reality, either real for us to discover or possible for art to actualize' (*PR*, p. 257). By creating new forms and structures art shares in the ongoing work of creation. Painting is thus truly 'Christian' when it is conceived as a kind of co-operation with God 'by increasing, to the extent that man can do so, the sum total of being and beauty in the world' (*PR*, p. 295). This participation in the process of natural creation is seen by Gilson as justifying 'the long pilgrimage of painting on the road to total abstraction' (*PR*, p. 257). What painting learns in the course of this pilgrimage is that it is not dependent on nature in an external sense but participates in those processes of being through which nature too is actualised. After the advent of the most extreme abstraction (which he believes to have occurred in the work of Mondrian) we have now arrived at a new situation in which we are aware that actually painting never was imitative in the popular sense. We now know that there is a real sense in which a Van Eyck can also be called supremely abstract, since, like all genuine painting, it has 'its own rule, its own justification in itself' (*PR*, p. 265), it is a unique instantiation of being. In our new situation, consequently, 'no particular type of art enjoys any privilege' (*PR*, p. 259). Art is at last free to be itself.

In rejecting the reduction of art to knowledge or to cognitive processes of any kind Gilson is also attentive to the difference between painting and language. In the case of painting, 'whatever one can say about it will really be about something else' (*PR*, p. 210), for speech is always oblique, and the best works of art, as language itself testifies, strike us speechless. It is clear, however, that many pictures do have a literary or allegorical meaning which cannot simply be seen but which invites reflection, discussion and explanation. Gilson therefore distinguishes between what he calls 'pictures' or 'images' on the one hand and painting proper on the other. The production of images in this sense 'is a branch of literature' (*PR*, p. 266). Of course a great deal is written and spoken about art (including books on the theology of art!), but in the face of this Gilson reminds us that we must remember the basics. Amidst the flood of commentaries, interpretations and reproductions, the boom in art publishing and art journals, we must learn to resist 'the dangerous pedagogical inflation' which betrays 'the growing aggressiveness of the disciplines of language' (*PR*, p. 231). We must recall the simple fact that 'the pleasure of art itself can be found only where art itself is – . . . in paintings' (*PR*, p. 237). Gilson's whole book is thus in one respect – as he himself states in the preface – an attempt to draw attention to painting, an invitation to look and, whilst asking what philosophy has to learn from painting, not to allow such questioning to falsify what takes place uniquely in the event of looking itself. It is in that looking, made possible exclusively by the material quality of painting, that art reveals itself to be a powerful discloser of reality and a resource against the growing hegemony of knowledge and language in human affairs.

This then is a very different kind of development of Thomist principles from what we found in Maritain, and it shows that Thomism is not as such limited by nostalgia for a lost mediaeval religion-culture. It would, of course, be unfair to Maritain to imply that he looks exclusively backwards in the direction of such a mediaeval golden age, since he responds sensitively, perceptively and positively to many twentieth century artists and was very much at home in contemporary art-circles in Paris. Nonetheless, although his tone is different from that of his mentor Bloy, for Maritain too it is, at the end of the day, true that the role of the artist is that of a 'very humble servant'. He is reluctant to take contemporary art in its own terms and, more or less explicitly, sees it as needing to be tested against a given rule of faith. Gilson shows no such reluctance. His way of applying the principle that grace perfects nature is to seek to find in art itself a unique mode of reality which provides the sole avenue by which we can assess the religious significance of art. His programme is indeed at many points close to that of this present enquiry, though, as I shall argue, it is probably necessary to go further than he does in rethinking the philosophical basis of a Christian aesthetic. Nor does *Painting and Reality* itself finally clarify the relationship between art and knowledge. Gilson is. I believe, right in seeking to distance art from knowledge, but if, as he maintains, the philosopher is able to have knowledge of being, what is the relationship between such knowledge and what takes place in aesthetic experience? Is there an order of priority between them? And what is the role of faith in determining that order? Where does the knowledge to which the philosopher has access meet the intelligibility which art expresses and embodies? What is it for something to be intelligible and yet not an object of knowledge? From another angle we might ask whether it might be possible (with Gilson) to affirm the proper integrity of artistic practices and yet to couch that affirmation in terms which relate more directly to the specific shape of Christian theology? And can we do that without slipping back into the kind of heteronomy of faith over art which we encountered in Maritain? To achieve this we shall, I believe, need a theological vocabulary and framework which the natural theology of Neo-Thomism has been unable to supply, and we shall need to explore further dimensions of the encounter between art and faith in the modern world.

4

Christian Theoria

John Ruskin's *Modern Painters* began life as a defence of J. M. W. Turner against his critics, but over the seventeen years which separated the publication of its first and last volumes it grew into a thorough-going philosophy of art. For not only does it comprise innumerable analyses of works by Turner and other artists, it also lays the metaphysical and epistemological foundations which Ruskin regarded as essential for a true understanding of art. But it was not merely a philosophy of art, it was a theology of art, since, Ruskin maintained, the ultimate task of the artist was to reflect and recapitulate in his work the beauty given by God to created things as a perpetual witness to his eternal glory. When this task is accomplished successfully it can be said of the artist, as Ruskin said of Turner, that

> He stands upon an eminence, from which he looks back over the universe of God, and forward over the generations of men. Let every work of his hand be a history of the one, and a lesson to the other. Let each exertion of his mighty mind be both hymn and prophecy, – adoration to the Deity, – revelation to mankind.[1]

Of his own aim in *Modern Painters* Ruskin declared 'there is no variation, from its first syllable to its last. It declares the perfectness and eternal beauty of the work of God; and tests all work of man by concurrence with, or subjection to that' (*MP*, V, p. xviii).

The overall structure of Ruskin's argument resembles the familiar pattern of natural theology, for its prevailing assumption is that the works of God in creation provide a timeless and universally accessible testimony to their divine origin. The artist is gifted with the ability to see and to represent in his work a truthful image of that testimony and so to be able to direct the less perceptive to see it for themselves. The term 'nature' is, however, somewhat ambiguous in theological parlance. On the one hand it can be taken in a physical

54

sense as referring to the non-human environment: plants, animals, rocks, trees, rivers, the weather, and so on. On the other hand it can be used in a metaphysical sense, in which case it refers to those structures which characterise created being as such. The natural theology of Thomas Aquinas takes nature in this latter sense, and we have seen how, in relation to art, this means seeing the human perception of beauty and human creativity in relation to transcendental realities – being, truth, unity, beauty itself – that are held to have have a kind of metaphysical ultimacy. In Thomist terms the power of mediaeval art does not lie in either the faithfulness or the delightfulness with which the artist captures the forms of physical nature in his work but in its formal, metaphysical quality. Later forms of natural theology, however, do not share this metaphysical horizon. The arguments from design which postdate the scientific revolution of the seventeenth and eighteenth centuries are significantly different. For these later Protestant forms of natural theology are very much shaped by the expansion of empirical knowledge of the world. It is not the metaphysical dependence of the world which engages such natural theologians as William Paley but the intricate good order of its design – a design which we discover in and through the complex detail of scientific observation. It is in this later sense that Ruskin's argument in *Modern Painters* may be said to constitute a natural theology of art. Nature in the physical sense of the tangible, visible environment of human life stands in the foreground of his view of art and of the relation to God on which good art depends. Although he deprecates the reduction of the sense of beauty to mere sensory stimulation, his notion of the seeing that is integral both to art and to faith stands much closer to the realm of empirical investigation than it does to any metaphysical investigation of being as such.

Whether metaphysical or empirical, however, the programme of natural theology is, notoriously, open to fundamental objections philosophically and theologically. Hume's incisive criticism of arguments from design was already familiar in Ruskin's time and would be as relevant to Ruskin's project as it was to those arguments which it consciously addressed. The more recent theological assault on natural theology, associated with Karl Barth and the dialectical theology of the twenties and thirties of this century, is also significant in relation to the case put forward by *Modern Painters*, a point which has been highlighted in Peter Fuller's recent study of Ruskin, *Theoria*, which we shall be examining later in this chapter. At the same time the method of natural theology has powerful attractions for a theology of art, indeed it would be hard to see how an argument which started, as Barth required, 'from above', ie. with divine revelation, could incorporate the rich and complex concern for what is disclosed in physical vision into such a theology. But if theology of art is driven to place itself on the side of a theology which works 'from below', ie. from the facticity of human experience, to what risks does it allow itself to be exposed? Before returning to this question, however, let us firstly examine Ruskin's argument in *Modern Painters* in greater detail.

Ruskin distinguishes five basic 'Ideas' which, he says, are constitutive of 'all sources of pleasure, or any other good, to be derived from works of art' (*MP*, I, p. 12). These are:

I.   Ideas of Power;
II. Ideas of Imitation;
III. Ideas of Truth;
IV. Ideas of Beauty, and
V.   Ideas of Relation.

These, he quickly tells us, are not all of equal value. Ideas of power and imitation as 'the perception or conception of the mental or bodily powers by which the work has been produced' and 'the perception that the thing produced resembles something else' are soon dealt with and assigned to the lowest place in the hierarchy of ideas. Conversely, whilst ideas of relation are described by Ruskin as 'the most important part of our subject' (*MP*, V, p. 149) his treatment of such Ideas (in the late-appearing Volume Five) adds little of systematic significance to what he has already said concerning 'Ideas of Beauty'. I shall therefore concentrate in this account on his exposition of what is meant by 'Ideas of Truth' and 'Ideas of Beauty', since this contains the essence of his natural theology of art.

The discussion of Ideas of Truth involves Ruskin in a detailed discussion of works by Turner and his 'rivals' and in an extensive exposition of the significance of the forms and structures of the natural world. As has already been noted he has little time for conventional concepts of imitation and his concept of truth in art is far removed from that of photographic verisimilitude. A pencil outline of a bough of a tree on a piece of white paper may convey truth, he says, although it does not look 'like' the bough any more than the white paper looks 'like' air. Truth can also be related to moral, intellectual and symbolic levels of reality where imitation in any normal sense is clearly out of place. But with regard to material things truth does include 'the representation of facts', as in the line drawing of a bough, but it does not stop there. There is also a 'higher' truth involved which art is suited to convey: the truth of thought, the vision of the artist himself. Landscape painting, for instance, aims to represent both facts and thoughts. However, whilst the representation of thoughts is said to be 'the real and only important end of all art' he regards 'the representation of facts' as 'the first end' for 'it is necessary to the other and must be attained before it. It is the foundation of all art; like real foundations it may be little thought of when a brilliant fabric is raised on it; but it must be there' (*MP*, I, p. 43). This foundation itself depends both on painterly technique and on a keen-sighted and accurate observation of the forms and structures of the natural world. Thus the discussion of Ideas of truth embraces both the truths of tone, colour, chiaroscuro and space on the one hand and the truths of skies, clouds, earth, water and vegetation on the other.

The discussion of the truth of tone provides a good illustration of how Ruskin differentiates between truth and imitation. Look at nature, he says, not only does she (*sic*) surpass us 'in power of obtaining light as much as the sun surpasses white paper, but she infinitely surpasses us on her power of shade' (*MP*, I, p. 132). She can therefore indulge in a far greater gradation of tonality than any painter can ever manage within the frame of a picture. 'It cannot but be evident at a glance', Ruskin assures us, 'that if to any one of the steps from one distance to another we give the same quantity of difference in pitch of shade which nature does, we must pay for this expenditure of our means by totally missing half a dozen distances not a whit less important or marked' (*MP*, I, p. 133). And this, he adds, is precisely what the so-called 'old masters' (whom he generally compares unfavourably with Turner) did: for the sake of one piece of 'exquisite accuracy of imitation' they sacrificed the truth of the whole. Turner, however,

> makes every degree of shade indicative of a separate degree of distance, giving each step of approach, not the exact difference of pitch it would have in nature, but a difference bearing the same proportion to that which his sum of possible shade bears to the sum of nature's shade. (*MP*, I, p. 134)

In other words the work of art is not a copy but an analogy of what we find in nature. Although it depends on a faithful knowledge of the visual facts of nature its truth consists in the representation of those facts in a manner consistent with the limitations and means of art.

The requirement that the artist have both an extensive and an intensive knowledge of the facts of nature is brought out by Ruskin in his long discussions of the various 'truths' of aspects of the natural world: skies, earth, water and vegetation. It is here too that the theological implications of his work begin to be apparent. For these aspects of the natural world have all been designed to move our minds to wonder at and delight in God's wisdom and power in creation. Take, for example, his opening remarks about the truth of skies.

> It is a strange thing how little people know in general about the sky. It is the part of creation in which nature has done more for the sake of pleasing man, more, for the sole and evident purpose of talking to him and teaching him, than in any other of her works, and it is just the part in which we least attend to her. (*MP*, I, p. 194)

For, Ruskin adds, the practical function of the sky could perfectly well be accomplished 'if, once in three days, or thereabouts, a great ugly black rain cloud were brought up over the blue, and everything well watered, and so all left blue again till next time, with perhaps a film of morning and evening mist for dew' (*MP*, I, p. 194). But what we actually experience is quite different.

> There is not a moment of any day of our lives, when nature is not producing scene after scene, picture after picture, glory after glory, and working still upon such exquisite and constant principles of the most perfect beauty, that it is quite certain it is all done for us, and intended for our perpetual pleasure. (*MP*, I, p. 194)

But although this conviction that it is all 'done for us' seems to betray an extraordinarily naive view of the ecological functions of sky and weather it is certainly not Ruskin's intention to ignore a proper scientific investigation of the laws of the natural world. He had himself a life-long fascination for geology and was intimately involved in contemporary debates about the origin of geological formations. These, of course, were occurring in a time when the Genesis accounts of creation and the flood still had to be reckoned with by those advancing a scientific interpretation of the world, with the result that virtually all the models proposed by participants in such debates seem irrelevant today. The important point, however, is that for Ruskin the aesthetic attraction of the natural world is not ultimately separable from the knowability of the world, just as art depends both on facts and on thoughts. Indeed, in promoting the unity of facts and values, Ruskin and such contemporary scientists as Sedgwick were arguably saying something which, if flawed in its particular formulation, has been recently readmitted to the forum of scientific discussion and the philosophy of science.[2] As we shall see, however, the way in which Ruskin himself formulated this unity turned out to be only too vulnerable to the attacks of positivism and the emergence of an aggressively de-sacralised scientific world-view.

Ruskin's account of the various truths with which landscape painting needs to be concerned includes many painstakingly thorough descriptions of the phenomena concerned. These descriptions combine both the detailed accuracy of controlled observation and the rhapsodic fervour and exuberance of a great prose poet. On the one hand stands 'the absolute necessity of scientific and entire acquaintance with nature' (*MP*, I, p. 241), and on the other the awareness that all this exists for the sake of 'bearing witness to the unwearied, exhaustless operation of the Infinite Mind' (*MP*, I, p. 224). These descriptions fill page after page of *Modern Painters* and are worth reading in their own right, though too extensive to quote here.[3] Whilst not 'scientific' in the modern sense they do evoke Ruskin's prevailing concern to see art rooted in a faithful attention to empirical reality. It is for the lack of such concern that he constantly castigates the 'old masters' such as Claude, Poussin and Cuyp. Their approach to nature, however accurate in the imitation of parts, is essentially untrue to nature. Their concern for artistic effect vitiates their attention to truth. With regard to the representation of clouds, for instance

the old masters attempted the representation of only one among the thousands of their systems of scenery, and were altogether false in the little they attempted; while we can find records in modern art of every form or phenomenon of the heavens, from the highest film that glorifies the aether to the wildest vapour that darkens the dust, and, in all these records, we find the most clear language and close thought, firm words, the true message, unstinted fulness and unfailing faith. (*MP*, I, pp. 250f)

Concluding the discussion of the truth of clouds he pictures the scene of a sunrise in the Alps. Watch, he says, 'and then, when you can look no more for gladness, and when you are bowed down with fear and love of the Maker and Doer of this, tell me who has best delivered this His message unto men!' (*MP*, I, p. 253). (Turner, of course!).

The pinnacle of Ruskin's 'system' is to be found in his discussion of Ideas of Beauty, in particular his account of what he calls the theoretic faculty, the faculty, that is, by which we see beauty. This account makes no secret of its theological motives, as Ruskin proceeds in almost catechetical style to argue for its pre-eminence over all other aspects of human existence and experience.

That is to everything created, pre-eminently useful, which enables it rightly and fully to perform the functions appointed to it by its Creator . . . Man's use and function . . . is, to be the witness of the glory of God, and to advance that glory by his reasonable obedience and resultant happiness. Whatever enables us to fulfil this function, is in the pure and first sense of the word useful to us. Predominantly therefore whatever sets the glory of God more brightly before use. (*MP*, II, pp. 159f.)

This concept of usefulness is expressly aimed at the contemporary philosophy of utilitarianism, which Ruskin associates with the industrialisation and commercialisation of life. The simple teaching that 'to live is nothing, unless to live be to know him by whom we live' (*MP*, II, p. 164), is, he believes, especially needed in an age when

the iron roads are tearing up the surface of Europe, as grapeshot do the sea, when their great sagene is drawing and twitching the ancient frame and strength of England together, contracting all its various life, its rocky arms and rural heart, into a narrow, finite, calculating metropolis of manufactures, when there is not a monument throughout the cities of Europe, that speaks of old years and mighty people, but is being swept away to build Cafés and gaming-houses . . . (*MP*, II, pp. 161f.)

In this torrent of destruction we are, he claims, in danger of losing not only our architectural and artistic heritage but also, and perhaps more terrifyingly, our awareness of the loveliness of the natural creation.

In this spirit Ruskin goes on to distinguish between that which is the object of life and that which is subservient to it, a distinction which corresponds to that between the theoretic and practical aspects of life. Thus the work of the geologist or architect, concerned as it is with knowledge, is theoretic, whereas the work of the miner or bricklayer is subservient. (Although Ruskin is well aware the ideas of the architect could scarcely be realised without the labour of the bricklayer.) But in contemporary life he sees the virtual eclipse of theoretic activity in favour of practical, material and, broadly speaking, utilitarian activities. In a better-ordered world 'those pursuits which are altogether theoretic, whose results are desirable or admirable in themselves and for their own sake . . . ought to rank above all pursuits which have any taint in them of subserviency to life . . . ' (*MP*, II, p. 165).

There are, it seems, two faculties concerned with such theoretic activity, the theoretic faculty itself and the imaginative faculty. The former is 'concerned with the moral perception and appreciation of ideas of beauty' (*MP*, II, p. 166), and the latter is exercised by the mind 'in a certain mode of regarding or combining the ideas it has received from external nature, and the operations of which become in their turn objects of the theoretic faculty to other minds' (*MP*, II p. 166).

There are two initial points to make about the activity of the theoretic faculty as that by which we perceive beauty whether in nature or in art. Firstly, as has already been mentioned, there is a substantial area of overlap between the vision of the artist and the study of the scientist. Ruskin's bitter attack on the technocratic and exploitative spirit of the nineteenth century was not intended to denigrate the proper achievements of a disinterested scientific study of the material world, nor, within limits, the application of the results of such study. Secondly, however, the theoretic faculty is characterised first and foremost as concerned with the moral perceptions of ideas of beauty. This emphasis involves Ruskin in making a firm distinction between theoria and aesthesis, as a result

of which he distances himself from the term 'aesthetic', which he
regards as having connotations of a purely sensory response to
pleasing stimuli. Aesthesis, he says, is 'the mere animal consciousness of the pleasantness', whilst theoria is 'the exulting, reverent
and grateful perception of it' (*MP*, II, p. 171). Although sensuous
pleasure is a perfectly legitimate accompaniment of the theoretic
contemplation of beauty it cannot explain such contemplation. This
'higher' theoretic activity is, moreover, not just a matter of being
sharp-eyed or sharp-minded but, as Ruskin repeatedly emphasises,
depends on a proper moral disposition. The moral self, Ruskin
says, is motivated by a desire towards 'whatever is an object of
life, . . . whatever may be infinitely and for itself desired' (*MP*,
II, p. 170). In any such object, he adds, 'we may be sure there is
something of divine, for God will not make anything an object
of life to his creatures which does not point to, or partake of
Himself' (*MP*, II, p. 170). The moral factor in our perception of
beauty thus requires what might be called an aptitude for disinterested desire, desire that is, which does not consume or annihilate
its object but which affirms it and, in doing so, heightens the
sensual pleasure which accompanies its fulfilment: 'first . . . joy,
then . . . love of the object, then . . . the perception of kindness in
a superior intelligence, finally, with thankfulness and veneration
towards that intelligence itself . . . ' (*MP*, II, p. 172). And if men's
minds are unable to attain the theoretic appreciation of beauty it
is almost certainly on account of the hardness of their hearts, which
makes such beauty as they do see 'a mere minister to their desires,
and accompaniment and seasoning of lower sensual pleasures' (*MP*,
II, p. 172). The sense for beauty ultimately requires nothing less
than the cultivation of the full Christian character, since those
dispositions which enable the perception of beauty to take place
correspond precisely to the disposition appropriate to Christian
discipleship.

> The temper, therefore, by which right taste is formed, is first,
> patient. It dwells upon what is submitted to it, it does not trample
> upon it lest it should be pearls, even though it looks like husks, it
> is a good ground, soft, penetrable, retentive, it does not send up
> thorns of unkind thoughts, to choke the weak seed, it is hungry
> and thirsty too, and drinks all the dew that falls on it, it is an
> honest and good heart, that shows no too ready springing before
> the sun be up, but fails not afterwards; it is distrustful of itself, so

as to be ready to believe and to try all things, and yet so trustful of itself, that it will neither quit what it has tried, nor take anything without trying. (*MP*, II, p. 170)

The constant allusions to the language of the Bible and, especially, the parables, is not accidental, for, as Ruskin states quite categorically, the operation of this disposition 'is in analogy to, and in harmony with, the whole spirit of the Christian moral system' (*MP*, II, p. 180). Theoria is described quite specifically as 'Christian theoria' (*MP*, II, p. 173).

That which is the object of the theoretic faculty both 'points to' and 'partakes of' the divine life itself as evidenced in the visible forms of the natural world. Our sense for such objects is, Ruskin says, 'instinctive' (*MP*, II, p. 200) and inscribed in our own nature. This 'instinctive' kinship with the things of God is, in turn, stressed by Ruskin in his description of what he calls the 'typical' forms of beauty, forms by which we are naturally attracted yet which also reveal to us different aspects of the life and being of God. These forms of typical beauty are infinity, unity, repose, symmetry, purity and moderation. They reveal, respectively, the divine incomprehensibility, the divine comprehensiveness, the divine permanence, the divine justice, the divine energy and the divine government by law.

I do not intend to enter into a detailed exposition of all these forms of beauty, but, in order to show the general thrust of Ruskin's argument, I shall highlight some of the points he makes with regard to infinity and unity. He invites us first of all to put ourselves back into the receptive state of mind of a child in its instinctive and not yet rationalised encounters with the world. He is confident that we will remember 'the emotion . . . caused by all open ground, or lines of any spacious kind against the sky, behind which there might be conceived the sea' (*MP*, II, p. 193). This childhood response is modified by time and experience into a general love 'common to all' (an assertion which Ruskin claims to have tested empirically) 'of a light distance appearing over a comparatively dark horizon' (*MP*, II, p. 194). What such an effect suggests (instinctively and unconsciously) is 'Infinity. It is of all visible things the least material, the least finite, the farthest withdrawn from the earth prison house, the most typical of the nature of God, the most suggestive of the glory of His dwelling-place' (*MP*, II, p. 195). This yields a fundamental rule of priority as regards the pictorial arrangement of light and darkness. It is the 'one grand division' which separates the sheep from the goats in painting. Any painter of any intellect at all, Ruskin says, will show a feeling of 'the most intense pleasure in the luminous space of his backgrounds' whereas 'I know not that the habitual use of dark backgrounds can be shown as having ever been co-existent with pure or high feeling and . . . with any high power of intellect' (*MP*, II, p. 196). This instinctive pleasure offers escape, hope and infinity: the promise of a greater and better life.

It is not the only manifestation of the human taste for the infinite with regard either to the contemplation of nature or the beholding of works of art. Another quite different feature which nonetheless evokes the same principle is, Ruskin tells us, curvature. Here again he proceeds with supreme confidence: 'That all forms of acknowledged beauty are composed exclusively of curves will, I believe, be at once allowed' (*MP*, II, p. 200). Again too he seeks to root this truth in our instinctive response to nature. A similar pattern emerges in relation to the gradation of shades of colour which, he says is 'their infinity' and is to colour 'what curvature is to lines' (*MP*, II, p. 201). These laws of light and shade, of curvature and the gradation of colour are not just rules of artistic practice, not just means of evoking sensuous pleasure. They are to be seen as vestiges of the Creator in his creation. We respond to them with theoretic delight precisely because our relation to the cosmos is ordered in such a way that it brings us to the knowledge of God.

A similar structure characterises what Ruskin writes about the type of unity, the 'type of divine comprehensiveness'. He understands 'the unity of God' to be 'That Unity which consists not in his own singleness or separation, but in the necessity of his inherence in all things that be, without which no creature of any kind could hold existence for a moment' (*MP*, II, p. 203). The pattern of such comprehensive unity is found throughout creation since ' . . . there is not any matter, nor any spirit, nor any creature, but it is capable of a unity of some kind with other creatures, and in that unity is its perfection and theirs, and a pleasure also for the beholding of all other creatures that can behold' (*MP*, II, p. 204). 'Some species of unity', he adds, 'is in the most determined sense of the word essential' for the 'perfection of beauty in lines, or colours, or forms, or masses, or multitudes' (*MP*, II, p. 204). So, whilst the curvature of line evokes the infinity of God and leads the mind towards the divine incomprehensibility, the divine unity simultaneously asserts itself in the proper proportion of curvature.

In *The Seven Lamps of Architecture* Ruskin had argued that mediaeval architecture expressed precisely those proportions of curvature and division which are to be found in the most beautiful forms of the natural world.[4] The truly beautiful curve, whose archetypes are to be found on all sides in nature, is not that which resolves itself into circularity but that which is structured in such a way as to maintain its curvedness infinitely (as we, at least, might imagine). Ruskin's examples range from the eroding effects of mountain streams to the simplest shell spirals. Again there is a convergence between beauty in nature and in art, and both are seen as disclosing what is essentially a divine truth.

In addition to 'typical beauty' Ruskin discusses what he calls 'vital beauty', 'the appearance of felicitous fulfilment of function in living things, more especially of the joyful and right exertion of perfect life in man' (*MP*, II, p. 183). Whereas typical beauty is, for instance, to be found 'in the lines and gradation of unsullied snow', vital beauty is displayed by the 'slender, pensive, fragile flower' *Soldanella alpina* which pierces its way through the edges of the ice sheet in early May. When we see this 'we shall, or we ought to be, moved by a totally different impression of loveliness from that which we receive among the dead ice and the idle clouds. There is now uttered to us a call for sympathy, now offered to us an image of moral purpose and achievement' (*MP*, II, p. 240). This image is no less valid because the creature which evokes it is unconscious of the significance of what it is doing. The living world (or the 'organic creation' as Ruskin calls it) 'is in its nature, its desires, its modes of nourishment, habitation and death, illustrative or expressive of certain moral dispositions or principles' (*MP*, II, p. 240). It follows that it is no accident that we equate certain animals with moral qualities or attitudes since they are all put into the world as objects of instruction, 'whether it be of warning or example, of those that wallow or those that soar, of the fiend hunted swine by the Gennesaret lake, or of the dove returning to its ark of rest . . . ' (*MP*, II, p. 241). The purposes of creation are readable in the creature. We may, perhaps, be reminded of that didactic pedantry so wilfully parodied in the illogical world of Alice's Wonderland, but we should note that Ruskin insists that this lesson can only be learned by those whose minds are ready to learn. Like is known by like, and the moral reality of the universe can only be disclosed to those whose own moral nature is already activated. For example, the activity of the theoretic faculty in relation to vital beauty involves the ability to delight in the happiness and self-fulfilment ('the felicitous fulfilment of function') of that which is being observed. But to delight in the happiness of another creature is, precisely, to practise the theological virtue of charity, 'of which', Ruskin remarks, 'the entire essence is in God only' (*MP*, II, p. 241). Thus it follows that for the proper exercise of this faculty in relation to vital beauty 'there is necessary the entire perfection of the Christian character, for he who loves not God, nor his human brother, cannot love the grass beneath his feet and the creatures that fill those spaces in the universe which he needs not, and which live not for his uses' (*MP*, II, p. 241). Equally, 'none can love God, nor his human brother, without loving all things which his Father loves' (*MP*, II, p. 241). There is thus a triple correlation between the divine, the human and the cosmic dimensions of love. All things work together well for the eye which is guided by love, by the desire to affirm the happiness of the other. The possibility of such an affirmative desire, already adumbrated in earlier remarks about the theoretic faculty in general, is an important element in the theology of art which I shall attempt to outline in a later chapter.[5] Whether this necessarily requires us to affirm without qualification the objective good order of the cosmos as a whole, as it 'really' is, 'in itself', quite apart from the eye which beholds it, is, of course, another question. It is however fairly clear that at this stage Ruskin wished to affirm the harmony of objective and subjective elements, and that the human love of beauty was in a real sense in touch with 'the love which moves the sun and other stars'.

Ruskin's discussion of vital beauty concludes by looking at such beauty in human beings, both in life and in art. He subscribes to the view that the inner life leaves its mark on external appearance. But things are not as simple as in the Greek view of a perfect harmony or balance between the two. The situation is more complicated than that. The external appearance of a human being may be 'seamed by sickness, dimmed by sensuality, convulsed by passion, pinched by poverty, shadowed by sorrow, branded with remorse', and many other ills (*MP*, II, p. 261). On the other hand the activities of intellect, moral feeling and what Ruskin calls 'soul culture' may bring about the ennobling of human features. This may 'interfere with some of the characters of typical beauty belonging to the bodily frame' since the soul aims to achieve 'an ideal glory of perhaps a purer and higher range than that of the more perfect material form' (*MP*, II, p. 265). As an example of this he offers a contrast between St.

Paul and the prophet Daniel: 'We conceive, I think, more nobly of the weak presence of Paul than of the fair and ruddy countenance of Daniel' (*MP*, II, p. 265). He is also attentive to the differences which characterise human beings: there is no one model of noble demeanour, since it is precisely in the field of our differences from one another that the exercise of charity and other moral virtues lies. Since

> the Love of the human race is increased by their individual differences, and the Unity of the creature, as before we saw of all unity, made perfect by each having something to bestow and to receive, bound to the rest by a thousand various necessities and various gratitudes, humility in each rejoicing to admire in his fellow that which he finds not in himself, and each being in some respect the complement of his race. Therefore, in investigating the signs of the ideal of perfect type of humanity, we must not presume on the singleness of that type . . . (*MP*, II, p. 266)

Indeed not even those aspects of humanity which can be seen as results of the fall are necessarily excluded from the ideal of vital beauty in human beings, since even in the redeemed state towards which we are journeying in Christ we shall bear the marks and mementoes of that fall. The final state at which we hope to arrive is nonetheless greater and more beautiful than that of paradise. It follows that 'we have not to banish from the ideal countenance the evidences of sorrow, nor of past suffering, nor even of past and conquered sin, but only the immediate operation of any evil . . . ' (*MP*, II, p. 268).

Once more it is essential to note that the perception of vital beauty in human beings is itself determined by our own moral disposition – 'nothing but love can read the letters . . .' (*MP*, II, p. 271). All this adds up to the conclusion that there is no rule book, no definitive guidelines, by which to judge what is acceptable in human portraiture. Although Ruskin warns us that the depiction of pride, sensuality, ferocity and fear always tends to degrade the ideal type of vital beauty, everything depends in the last resort on the moral insight both of the painter and of those who see his work. Everything comes down to context, point of view, the eye which looks and the heart which directs the eye. Thus there is no fixed rule regarding the appropriateness of the nude. The 'daring frankness' of those Ruskin calls the 'old men' is quite a different thing in this respect from the 'mean, carpeted, gauze-veiled, mincing sensuality of curls and crisping-pins' of contemporary nude painting (*MP*, II, p. 276).

But what of that which Ruskin calls 'the superhuman ideal', the life of 'beings supernatural'? How can such being(s) be represented in the forms of the visible, phenomenal world? Here we are not just looking for the operation or the effects of the divine energy in creation but for the actual presence of the divine itself in creation, in creaturely form.

Ruskin lists four ways in which supernatural beings have conventionally been represented in art. The first of these is by 'external types, signs, or influences' (*MP*, II, p. 360). An example of this would be the appearance of God to Moses in the form of the burning bush. The second is 'by the assuming of a form not properly belonging to them' (*MP*, II, p. 360), as when the Holy Spirit is shown in the form of a dove or the second person of the Trinity by a lamb. In both of these cases we are very much in the field of allegorical or symbolic art. The third category is described (somewhat obscurely) as being 'by the manifestation of a form properly belonging to them, but not necessarily seen; as of the Risen Christ to his disciples when the doors were shut' (*MP*, II, p. 360). The four and last mode is 'by their operation in the human form which they influence or inspire, as in the shining face of Moses' (*MP*, II, p. 360). All four categories have this in common: that they reflect what is little less than an artistic paradox. For 'wherever there is form at all, it is the form of some creature to be known. It is no new form peculiar to spirit, nor can it be. We can conceive of none' (*MP*, II, p. 360). It is therefore necessary for the artist who seeks to resolve this paradox in some way to modify the creaturely form which is all he can represent. This may be done by distorting the creaturely form in some way, but Ruskin is more interested in another stratagem: to retain the 'actual form in its full and material presence' and yet to portray it in such a way that 'cannot but assert and stamp it for superhuman' (*MP*, II, p. 361).

In this respect he finds the Christian conception infinitely superior to the Greek. Despite all the words lavished on the achievements of classical sculpture 'The Greek could not conceive a spirit; he could do nothing without limbs; his God is a finite God, talking, pursuing, going journeys' (*MP*, II, p. 370). It is only the advent of Christianity which enables spiritual life to be truly represented in art.

But how? We can find some clues in an earlier discussion when Ruskin enquired into the visual and imaginative means by which a painter might portray ideal truth. Rejecting both the direct depiction of such truth and the merely extrinsic approach of allegorical art he asks whether there do not exist purely painterly means by which such truth can be manifested. And, he believes, there are. His prime example of an outstanding achievement in this direction is Tintoretto, whom he contrasts favourably with 'the morbid and vulgar Sentimentalism of Correggio' (*MP*, II, p. 323), and the 'intolerable, inconceivable brutality of Salvator' (*MP*, II, p. 325). Tintoretto, he says, combines both 'the absolute truth or statement of the central fact as it was or must have been' with 'the elevation into dignity and meaning of the smallest accessory circumstances (*MP*, II, p. 328). As an example of this (all his examples being drawn from the evangelical narrative) he takes Tintoretto's 'Crucifixion'. [Plate 4] Here the artist 'despising all outward and bodily appearances of pain' has not sought to show 'the rack of nerve or sinew, but the fainting of the deserted Son of God before his Eloi cry' (*MP*, II, p. 327). He has therefore avoided the depiction of a face contorted by physical pain and, in fact, put the face into shade.

> But the agony is told by this, and by this only; that though there yet remains a chasm of light on the mountain horizon where the earthquake darkness closes upon the day, the broad and sunlike glory about the Head of the Redeemer has become wan, and of the colour of ashes. (*MP*, II, p. 327).

Yet this is not all. To bring out the full pathos of the passion story the artist has included a telling detail.

> In the shadow behind the cross, a man, riding on an Ass colt, looks back to the multitude, while he points with a rod to the Christ crucified. The Ass is feeding on the *remants of withered Palm-leaves.*

This use of 'the smallest accessory circumstances' is seen by Ruskin as a 'master-stroke'. Whatever the extent to which we agree with his interpretation what is interesting, from a theological point of view, is the possibility which the discussion raises of depicting supernatural realities through physical, material forms yet in such a way that these forms are not falsified but become the indirect disclosers of divine truth. Just because there can be no direct revelation of God in a beautiful human form (as in the Greek ideal) does not mean that the human body cannot become – albeit under certain not readily objectifiable circumstances – a vehicle for some kind of indirect revelation.

Ten years later, when the third volume of *Modern Painters* was published, Ruskin himself seems, however, to have become more cautious about the representability of the divine. In dealing with what he calls the 'false ideal' of religious art he argues that the increase in artistic power associated with the Renaissance in general and Raphael in particular has led to the diminution of the religious interest of painting, even when it deals with specifically religious themes. He acknowledges the sincerity of feeling but deprecates the lack of truth in such early Renaissance painters as Francia and Perugino, for whom

> the word 'Virgin' or 'Madonna', instead of calling up the vision of a simple Jewish girl, bearing the calamities of poverty, and the dishonours of inferior station, summoned instantly the idea of a graceful princess, crowned with gems, and surrounded by obsequious ministry of kings and saints. (*MP*, III, p. 47)

The result of such a development was that

> all true grounds of faith were gradually undermined, and the beholder was either enticed into mere luxury of fanciful enjoyment, believing nothing: or left, in his confusion of mind, the prey of vain tales and traditions. (*MP*, III, pp. 47f)

But the further transformation of the 'Queen-Virgin of Perugino' into the 'simple Italian mother' of Raphael's 'Madonna of the Chair' was to be no less disastrous. In a passage marked by fiercely Anti-Romanist rhetoric he claims that this new realism was simply a result of the fact that 'the painter had no longer any religious passion to express' (*MP*, III, p. 49). The Madonna was no longer an object of veneration but 'an available subject for the display of transparent shadows, skilful tints, and scientific foreshortenings'. (*MP*, III, p. 50). What this is, in fact, is simply 'the opera and drama of the monk' (*MP*, III, p. 54). Protestantism has not, however, fared much better, with Evangelicals rendering their religion 'an offence to men of the world by associating it only with the most vulgar forms of art' (*MP*, III, p. 57). But, he says, to paint Christ's miracles 'discreditably' is no better than to sing his praises 'discordantly'. The conclusion seems ineluctable. 'Has there, then (the reader asks emphatically), been no true religious ideal? Has religious art never been of any service to mankind? I fear on the whole not' (*MP*, III, p. 55). Art and Christianity have largely gone their separate ways, although he remains hopeful that 'those bright Turnerian imageries . . . and those calm Pre-Raphaelite studies' point the way to a better future, and lay a new foundation, indeed 'the first foundation that has ever been laid for true sacred art' (*MP*, III, p. 57). This foundation, of course, hinges on that loyalty to facts which is the proper foundation, as we have seen, of all art, and on the ability to add to that loyalty the thought which the facts serve to represent. The maximum of visual sensibility is to keep one's eyes fully on the visible world and in that world to see the expression of the divine life in its many aspects. Yet this maximum also requires the activation of the moral vision, an openness and charity, which gives to a one-sided scientific knowledge of the world human – and religious – value. In this way, Ruskin's natural theology of art draws both on the structure of what were in his own time well-established arguments from design, and also on an awareness of a moral or subjective element which serves to establish important connections with other approaches to religion with which Ruskin himself was not in sympathy.

But were Ruskin's hopes for a 'first foundation' for sacred art themselves well-founded? Does the basis which he believes to have been laid stand up to the theological requirement which he places on it?

In a recent study of Ruskin's thought and its influence on subsequent developments both in art itself and in art criticism, Peter Fuller has been particularly concerned to draw attention to the theological aspect of Ruskin's thought and to what, in his view, is its failure. He notes that at some point between 1858 and 1874 (that is sometime after the Third Volume of *Modern Painters* appeared) 'Ruskin abandoned conventional Christianity'.[6] Still attempting to hold on to the 'laws and facts of nature' he seems to have found little joy even here. 'Those laws of beauty and of help which Ruskin derived from the study of nature seemed as deeply threatened as precepts derived from the Bible itself'.[7] Fuller links this less optimistic view of nature with the rapid expansion and impact of industrialism and mercantilism in this period. 'Nature', in an industrial society, no longer comes naturally; exploited, alienated, it becomes an object of indifference and even dread. In Ruskin's case his initial 'unconversion', which was associated with an almost Nietzschean delight in physical power and vitality, seems to have given way to a state of 'fear and literal trembling'. Paranoid observations about an ominously lowering storm-cloud become frequent in his writing, and the storm-cloud itself becomes a symbol of the nineteenth century, as in the title of two lectures he delivered in 1884 entitled, simply, 'The Storm-Cloud of the Nineteenth Century'. He seems to have believed that the weather itself had degenerated. 'The plague wind now constant', he noted, 'and the sun virtually extinguished'.[8] As in Shakespearean drama or biblical prophecy the external world came to reflect only too plainly the moral failure of humanity. Here the correlation between 'facts' and 'thoughts' and moral sentiments takes on a quite different tone from that which it had in *Modern Painters*[9]. Nature is now seen to be as futile and as cruel as the human beings who exploit it. Now Ruskin speaks of 'the cruelty and ghastliness of the nature I used to think so divine'.[10]

All this is not merely of psychological interest but, as Fuller argues, conceptually interesting as well. The links between humanity and nature and between nature and God are broken or eclipsed, and even Ruskin's eventual return to a friendlier view of nature is, Fuller believes, significantly altered by what he had experienced in the meanwhile. His later writings, Fuller claims, are an attempt 'to elaborate an aesthetic and spiritual response to a world in which a conventional God seems to play an ever diminishing role'.[11] Ruskin, in his own thoroughly un-German way, had passed through the 'Death of God' prophesied by Nietzsche and dominating so much of twentieth century theology. Fuller sees Barth's attacks on natural theology as a highly significant episode in this development. Barth's decisive 'No!' to natural theology and his insistence on the 'wholly other' character of God seem to strip the world of all theophanous possibilities, whether in relation to the forms and structures of nature (in either a physical or a metaphysical sense) or with regard to the moral arrivings of the pious 'soul culture'. Neither the direct nor even the indirect testimony of the creature to the Creator can be taken for granted. Barth's iconoclasm is, Fuller maintains, only a short step away from the proclamation by a later theological generation of the Death of God, since a God who has no intrinsic or reliable connection to any of his creatures is, in effect, a redundant

God, a God whose existence makes no difference to the way things are, and who might just as well not exist at all.

Fuller sees Ruskin's own journey from *Modern Painters* to the period of the 'storm cloud' as anticipating this theological development, but he also finds in Ruskin a further move, namely, the move to a naturalism which has lost all Christological emphases yet which retains a kind of spiritual orientation, a spirituality without God. The values of this spirituality are those of a humanity which is ecologically aware and sensitive to its place within the complex fabric of its environment. This, it turns out, is precisely the position which Fuller himself wishes to commend. His most succinct statement of it can be found in exhibition notes on recent work by the landscape artist Michael Williams, where he writes

> Even if God has disappeared, can we not, perhaps, root a spiritual, though secular aesthetic in a careful and loving attention to every detail of the visible world? Can a modern ecological sensibility replace the old Christian sense of wonder and awe in the face of God's creation? Williams's paintings suggest that the answer to these questions may be yes.[12]

Clearly Fuller himself also hopes that the answer will be yes. 'It is', he has written elsewhere, 'a moot point whether art can ever thrive outside that sort of living, symbolic order with deep tendrils in communal life, which, it seems, a flourishing religion alone can provide'.[13] His own hopes however seem to look more in the direction of biology and ecology than religion. He argues that the intuitive response to certain natural forms which Ruskin observed is not to be explained – as the early Ruskin thought – in terms of the intricate fine-tuning of creature to creature by the divine artificer, but, more simply, by the fact that we, as fully biological beings, participate in the laws of the natural world. He cites the Harvard mathematician Benoit B. Mandelbrot in support of his thesis that we are indeed instinctively responsive to an immense range of complex shapes. Not just the spheres, cones, cylinders, cubes and circles beloved of early cubists and abstractionists but 'waves and "wiggles"' should be added to our fund of inbuilt shape-responses.[14] He applauds the biologist E. O. Wilson's concept of 'biophilia', defined as an innate urge on the part of living beings 'to affiliate with other forms of life'.[15] Aesthetic responses are said to play an especially important part in this process. According to Wilson '"Beauty in some fashion can be said to lie in the genes of the beholder".'[16] Is this biologistic interpretation all that can be rescued for a contemporary aesthetic from *Modern Painters*?

Fuller's interpretation of Ruskin and his proposals concerning a post-modern biologistic Ruskinian aesthetic raises interesting theological questions. His account of the failure of Ruskin's natural theology of art exposes the vulnerability of that theology on many fronts: the falsifiability of its scientific component, the insecurity of its emotional investments and its susceptibility to the sort of theological critique offered by Karl Barth. But is there nothing left for theology to salvage from the wreck?

Firstly, we might venture a comment as to the character of natural theology in general. If natural theology is seen as a kind of foundation on which to build the edifice of faith then it would indeed be disastrous if that foundation were to be shaken or even overthrown. But is that the case? Aquinas, for instance, did not seem to see natural theology as foundational in that way. For him it was more a matter of corroborating and making sense of a faith which was assured on other grounds. We have in this study, for instance, seen how Maritain's 'natural theology' of art in fact presupposed the final authority of faith all along. But certainly, in the context of Enlightenment and Post-Enlightenment controversies, natural theology came increasingly to be regarded as a kind of foundation for faith or a stepping-stone from unbelief to faith. But if arguments are required to perform tasks or to sustain burdens which they were never designed for then it is no surprise when they fail. The study of nature, whether that is conceived physically or metaphysically, never can lead us to God. But this does not make natural theology redundant if the task of such a theology is conceived in terms of exploring the ramifications of belief in God in relation to the natural world – including, of course, the world of art. Can we then attempt to see Ruskin's 'natural' theology of art as an explanation of what nature and the artistic relation to nature might mean from the standpoint of faith? Such a natural theology, although presupposing the standpoint of faith, aims to show how faith makes sense in the context of a potentially unlimited range of human concerns and activities. This certainly does not mean that it is immune from the sort of attacks associated with Barth and his followers, but it does mean that it should not be accused of putting faith and theology in thrall to scientific, psychological or aesthetic prejudices. Instead its task is to give faith a recognisable human content. Unless or until such a task is ventured it is hard to speak of faith as meaning anything at all.

This way of construing the task of natural theology is especially pertinent if we turn to that aspect of Ruskin's account of theoria which Fuller conspicuously neglects: its moral or subjective element. Again it would be futile to try to set up subjectivity as providing some kind of epistemological stepping-stone from creature to Creator. Ruskin's German contemporary, Ludwig Feuerbach was already propagating a hermeneutics of suspicion and arguing that God was nothing but a projection of psychological needs, a line of argument which Nietzsche and Freud were to exploit with great panache. Subjectivity provides no refuge from the storm clouds of the modernist critique of religion, but attention to the subjective element in Ruskin's thought does help us to find a way past the dilemma implied by Fuller in his reinterpretation of theoria, a dilemma which he poses more explicitly elsewhere. The dilemma is (roughly) this: either Christianity identifies itself in terms of objective doctrinal truth or it abandons all claims to a coherent and distinctive identity. Thus he argues that because Ruskin's account of theoria has no distinctive doctrinal content it is not distinctively Christian. But the moral character which Ruskin sees as essential for theoria is *very specifically* related to the requirements of Christian conversion and discipleship. In this way the concept of theoria can be seen as an exposition of the implications of a very specific tradition of faith for art. The passions of the Christian soul which Ruskin sees as essential to theoretic activity – passions such as patience, courage, wisdom and love – are not just the names of 'natural' emotional states, but correspond to or grow out of existential commitments of a highly specific kind.

But we have still not touched on what is really important about the subjective dimension. We may approach this by way of contrast with Fuller's biological reduction of theoria to biophilia, an evolutionary, genetically-determined affinity between living forms. A theological understanding of art does not, of course, preclude a biological element – we have, for instance, already noted Gilson's willingness to relate beauty to the biological structure of human life in a way which in some respects anticipates Fuller's own argument. But what such an explanation gives us is only the 'outside'. Granting the validity of the biophilia-hypothesis in its own terms we may still go on to ask about what it does not explain, about the 'inside' of the experience of beauty, how it feels to us within the horizons of our subjective experience. Assuming Ruskin and Fuller to be correct in asserting the 'leading role' of nature in shaping our sense of beauty, we might put it like this: alongside the view of nature which a rigorous scientific approach has to offer is the view of nature as we experience it, as we feel it speaking to us, luring us, mocking us, delighting us, humbling us and revealing to us the deep things of God. This is precisely the view of nature which art is eminently suited to give us. Indeed, Fuller's study *Theoria* can to a large extent be read as an essay on the changing image of nature (in this subjective sense) in Ruskin's own development and in the subsequent history of art. So far, I would suggest, there is little difference between Fuller's approach and my own: the fact of such a dimension of experience is not in question. Differences emerge, however, with regard to the relative value placed on the scientific and the subjective approaches. My impression is that Fuller holds a scientific approach to be ontologically well-founded in a way in which a subjective view is not. The implication of Fuller's case is that to claim otherwise would be to fall back onto the pathetic fallacy which our western culture abandoned two centuries ago. It is at the end of the day 'only' a metaphorical way of speaking to say that nature speaks, feels or acts with any kind of intentionality towards us. I shall, on the contrary, argue that an approach which allows subjective experience to be treated as ontologically significant, as a path on which we may be graced by unsurpassable disclosures of being, is not in any way inferior to the objectivities of science.

Ruskin was highly suspicious, not to say scathing, about contemporary German philosophy, but that philosophy, rooted as it was in the dynamics of subjectivity, was preparing the way for theoretical developments which provide a framework for appropriating Ruskin's own emphasis on the place of 'thoughts' and 'moral' commitments in theoretic activity. This is particularly so with regard to the phenomenological methods of Husserl, Heidegger and subsequent thinkers such as Maurice Merleau-Ponty. We shall examine some of these at length later,[17] and for the present I should just like to make one cautionary remark. To appeal to subjectivity is not to appeal to private or interior experiences. Subjectivity is not the same thing as either individualism or solipsism, nor is it an open invitation to all manner of arbitrary or capricious whims and fancies. It is precisely the guiding assumption of phenomenology that what we call subjective consciousness is not in fact locked up in its own 'subjective' self-preoccupation but is, in its most fundamental structures, open to or concerned with an encompassing reality apart from which it would be 'without form, and void'. In Ruskin's own account of theoria, for instance, our subjective outlook is inextricably intertwined with our responsiveness to a world which is experienced as radiant with beauty and as ontologically prior to and independent of ourselves. To 'turn to the subject' in this sense is not, therefore, necessarily to turn away from nature or from reality. Nonetheless it must be conceded that the German philosophy which Ruskin so distrusted tended in several of its representatives to forget or to disparage the natural matrix of human thought, feeling and action, a point to which we shall recur as we turn to examine the theology of art of a British theologian, Peter Taylor Forsyth, who was influenced both by Ruskin and by the great tradition of German idealism.

5

Pessimism and Progress

In the early years of the twentieth century the Congregationalist theologian Peter Taylor Forsyth produced two major books on theology and art, both based on public lectures: *Religion in Recent Art* and *Christ on Parnassus*. The former consists of a series of studies of works by leading Pre-Raphaelite artists – Rossetti, Burne-Jones, Holman Hunt, G. F. Watts – and Wagner. The second book presents more of an overview of the historical and systematic relationship between Christianity and the arts, with considerable space being given to the visual arts. In both sets of lectures, Forsyth is very much concerned to forge a distinctively Protestant aesthetic which is at the same time prepared to meet art, especially contemporary art, on its own ground. Like Ruskin he sees nature as a key element in the relationship between art and religion, but his philosophical basis is very different from Ruskin's. For Forsyth wrote under the influence of that German idealism which Ruskin eschewed. This influence, however, takes different forms in the two books.

An underlying theme of *Religion in Recent Art* is the theme of the significance of pessimism for religion and art alike, a theme which is most explicit in Forsyth's discussion of Wagner and Schopenhauer. Here he argues that whilst Christianity is not itself ultimately pessimistic (as Schopenhauer believed), it must be ready to sympathise with the spiritual travail expressed in pessimism. 'Pessimism', he says, 'when it is in moral and mental earnest, may be foreign to our crowning Christian instincts and our final Christian faith, but it is not all alien to the secret or the method of Christ'.[1] It is, he believes, far more religiously significant than either positivism or agnosticism because although it is unable to embrace the reality of either resurrection or revelation:

It is one side of Christianity, nevertheless, because it is not pure Naturalism, because it is a creed of sorrow, because it distrusts the easy optimism of the merely happy creeds, because it has a heart for the world-pain, something like a sense of sin, and a horizon as large as human fate. (*RRA*, p. 221)

In short, 'It is Christian in the force with which it insists upon a historic degeneration, a moral Fall, as the obverse of Redemption' (*RRA*, p. 221). Although pessimism is therefore untrue in its final conclusions it does contain and express a certain truth as a dialectical moment in the unfolding of the full reality of the human situation. On this basis Forsyth is able, quite courageously, to see a Christian significance in what many of his contemporaries regarded as the morbidity, not only of Wagner but of, for example, Rossetti and Watts. With regard to Rossetti's 'The Blessed Damozel' he warns us that 'If we dismiss the whole thing as morbid, we should remember that there is such a thing as being 'morbidly robust' . . . ' (*RRA*, p. 17).

However, a willingness to affirm the relative truth of pessimism is only one side of the coin. If Schopenhauer is the secret debating partner of *Religion in Recent Art* it is Hegel who stands very much in the foreground of *Christ on Parnassus*, where, in Forsyth's own words, he is 'preaching Hegel'.[2] In particular he acknowledges a heavy dependence – especially as far as aesthetic theory is concerned – on Hegel's *Aesthetics*. There are, I shall argue, significant points of difference between Forsyth and Hegel, points of which Forsyth himself does not seem fully aware. These relate both to the religious tenor of their respective works and to the fundamental manner in which the relationship between humanity and nature and religion and art is construed. Indeed, in certain respects Forsyth is closer to Kierkegaard, an arch opponent of Hegelianism, than to Hegel himself. Having said this, however, the similarity between Forsyth and Hegel both in general conception and in method is quite apparent. They approach art in a double perspective which might be described as both historical and structural. This means that art is understood historically – and for both of them the decline of the classical world, the rise of Christianity and the Protestant Reformation are of paramount importance – and also structurally, in terms of the interrelationship between the various arts. Painting is thus understood both in terms of the historical conditions of its emergence into a place of pre-eminence among the arts and in terms of its specific two-dimensional visual character over against, for example, both sculpture and music. The overall thrust of their thought is conducive to what might be called a 'liberal' assessment of the relationship between Christianity and culture, with so-called 'secular' culture itself providing a field for the expression and exploration of religious meaning. Equally, neither of them regard art as capable of finally exhausting the content of Christian truth, even when it is most markedly 'Christian'. Finally they are both attentive – from opposite ends of the century – to what Ruskin called the 'storm-cloud of the nineteenth century', the whole problematic of humanity's alienation from nature and the fragmentation of culture. In one respect it is a basic characteristic of their respective programmes that they are seeking to formulate a credible Protestant response to that very situation which, for Ruskin, seemed to mean the eclipse of faith.

In this Chapter our procedure will be to outline the broad conception of art set out in *Christ on Parnassus*, before turning to follow Forsyth in his wrestling with works of 'recent' art. We shall then turn to Hegel and bring out those points where there are the most significant divergences between them, especially, of course, with regard to the theology of art.

Forsyth's view of Christianity is (here at least) governed by the familiar Hegelian dialectic of thesis-antithesis-synthesis, with Ancient Greek and Ancient Hebrew culture playing the respective roles of thesis and antithesis to which Christianity was to provide the synthesis. This same pattern holds good for his view of the history of art. Following a well-worn path – a path which Nietzsche was to close forever – Forsyth describes Ancient Greece in glowing terms:

> We have there the gay adolescence of a mind and body perfectly balanced and sane, the sunny gladness of a time and a clime where Nature and man met each other half-way, and matter and spirit kissed without stooping. This religion was the apotheosis of natural joy. What wonder that its worshippers became artists in spite of themselves, and, without knowing, touched a completeness of perfection which the world, now larger, sees no more, nor ever again perhaps shall see. (*CP*, p. 13)

The Greeks in this way brought to perfection the Indo-European conception of humanity which 'began with Nature' (*CP*, p. 49). This conception had not always produced fruits of blithe and genial harmony, however. The Greek view of things is contrasted with the earlier Indo-European civilisations of India and Egypt. Indian art began, like that of Greece, with Nature. But in this case nature dominated the human spirit, crushing it with its vastness. The artistic representation of nature therefore laid enormous emphasis on the colossal, the abnormal, on whatever surpassed man in size and force. 'It is the worship of the vast. It is the dominion of bigness. Spirit . . . is the victim of a despotism of sheer mass and force' (*CP*, p. 8). Following (with Hegel) the track of the world spirit on its journey westwards Forsyth arrives in Egypt where he finds a new element. There is still an emphasis on what is vast or colossal but there is also science, geometry, exactness and a dawning faith in immortality. 'You have, that is, the laws of the reason, and the separateness and persistence of the spirit, asserted over against the vastitude of Nature' (*CP*, p. 9). This new relationship between spirit and nature finds its supreme expression in the sphinx, 'the specific Egyptian symbol', where human form is revealed in the very process of struggling free from its animal embodiment; or, as Forsyth put it, with his customary eloquence, we see a creature which is 'half beast half woman, half Nature half Spirit, half mystery half mastery' (*CP*, p. 10). But, as Hegel had said, the Greek world solved the riddle of the sphinx and emancipated humanity from its residual entrapment in nature. In Forsyth's words: 'In Greece man found his own eternal law as imprinted, reflected on nature, and by a pre-established harmony she became his friend, his ally, his equal, his consort' (*CP*, p. 11). We have already heard his admiration for the cultural achievement which followed. Yet there was that in which this 'gay adolescence' fell short – it, and its art, was without grief. He concludes his discussion of Greek art and religion by referring his listeners to a painting by the Greek artist Timanthes, known to us only by reports and a sketched copy on a wall in Pompeii. It is a picture of the sacrifice of Iphigenia, the daughter of the Greek commander Agammemnon, a sacrifice required by the gods as a necessary condition of the Greek fleet sailing for Troy. 'The spectators stand round the victim with various degrees of grief and pity depicted in their faces. Chief among them is her father Agammemnon. But the painter has covered his face with his hand in his robe' (*CP*, p. 40). Why is this? Forsyth does not believe it to be on account of any lack of ability on the part of the painter, as if, that is, he was technically incapable of portraying such powerful emotion. It is rather, he says

an evidence of the artist's truly Greek strength and self-control, his true Greek sense of the proper limitations of Art . . . Art could represent it, but it would be with such a contortion of feature and strain of agony that the horror of it would destroy the dominant beauty, and reduce the work below the level of worthy Art. (*CP*, p. 41)

Greek art, like Greek consciousness generally, was in fact constrained by its own ideal of a natural harmony. Such harmony, however, lies *below* the level of Christian reconciliation which embraces and takes into itself 'holy, saving sorrow' (*CP*, p. 42). Holiness, sorrow and the love that brings about a new and more abiding reconciliation between God and humanity are themes which lie outside the range of Hellenism. Yet, he finishes, 'the new beauty was impossible without the old' and we should not forget that 'Greece was one of the schoolmasters that bring us to Christ' (*CP*, p. 42).

The other great schoolmaster was the religion of Israel. Here we find a quite distinct set of presuppositions which distinguish the Hebrew spirit not only from that of Greece but from that of the Indo-European world in general. If the Indo-European mind began with nature, the Semites 'began from within. They began with Mind or Soul. Nature was but the product of Spirit, its creation, its tool' (*CP*, p. 49). This demotion of nature leads, consistently, to the demotion of art. The second commandment 'killed plastic imagination . . . Neither painter, sculptor, nor dramatist could live under the shadow of this stern law, or in the midst of this grimly earnest people' (*CP*, p. 43). Forsyth notes parallels to this development in Islam and, more recently, in Scotland, although, he claims, English Puritanism has a quite different temper. Consequently, 'a lecture on Hebrew art is like the chapter on lions in Norway. There is no Hebrew Art' (*CP*, p. 45). In recompense for this loss the intensely theocentric character of Jewish spirituality gave the world something of even greater value than art, 'that new creative life of the soul which makes art possible. They produced that which produced Art . . . (He) who by new creation gives us an eternal faith, also opens infinite possibilities to the creation in Art' (*CP*, p. 72). Whereas the downfall of Hellenism occurred when the blithe harmony of its great creative period was crushed by an inexorable fate from which it found itself unable to struggle free, the Hebrew subordination of nature (and, with nature, art) to the interests of religion gave humanity a newly confident basis on which to approach nature.

In Christianity therefore there is a synthesis of Hellenism and Hebraism in which the Hebrew confidence in spiritual reality is allowed to express itself freely 'in the beauty of Nature and Art' (*CP*, p. 74). Or, to reduce Forsyth's argument to the briefest theological shorthand: if Hellenism represents the principle of divine immanence and Hebraism the principle of divine transcendence, then Christianity 'is not transcendence, and it is not immanence. It is the immanence of the transcendent' (*CP*, p. 82). For the Christian spirit nature can, in art, become once more a vehicle for the life of the soul, although in a manner quite different from that manifested in the Greek world.

This difference shows itself in many ways, for instance in the rise of painting itself. Still keeping close to Hegel, Forsyth contrasts the culmination of the Greek ideal of beauty in the great works of classical sculpture with the efflorescence of painting in mediaeval Europe. This is no mere historical accident but is a direct result of the Christ event itself. For sculpture represents the God as *there*, standing over against the community as an object of worship. But painting, as Hegel had said, 'converts the external shape entirely into an expression of the inner life . . . '3 In Christ the community acquires a new imagination of its God; the gospel narratives portray this God in an individual and actual subjective life; and, in the New Testament itself and in subsequent Christian literature, the life of the Spirit of this God is seen extending itself through the actions and sufferings of the living community. Thus from Christ himself the subject-matter of Christian art spreads out to embrace the Holy Family, apostles, martyrs and saints, indeed any and every situation where human feeling is enlivened and excited. The God who appears as subject makes all manifestations of subjective life religiously significant. This sets the stage for the emergence of what Hegel calls romantic art with its three categories of painting, music and poetry. The Christ event both gives to art a new theme and requires of it a new mode and manner. In this sense the rise of painting, as an art which enables us to participate in the subjectivity of that which is represented, is a distinctively Christian event.

The new painting, like all romantic arts, has, according to Forsyth, three distinctive tendencies, which he defines as the fantastic, the grotesque and the picturesque. He lists a further five distinctive features of painting which enable it 'to reflect, though not adequately to express, the Christian soul' (*CP*, p. 111). These are, firstly, the attenuation of the material element itself; in place of the three dimensions, the solidity and the mass of sculpture painting offers only a flat surface, and, Forsyth reminds us, 'whatever . . . decreases the material extension of the work of art brings it so far nearer as an expression of the spirit' (*CP*, p. 111). Moreover, in place of marble the painter works in light, shade and colour. Light, as the ultimate medium of painting

> . . . is ideal, pervasive, piercing, and bathing all things. Its affinity is with the inward light, the reason, the spirit; and it is the outward semblance of that uncreated word which pierceth to the dividing asunder of the joints and marrow, and is a discerner of the thoughts and intents of the heart. (*CP*, p. 112)

Or, as Hegel had put it, in sculpture the light shines on the work from *outside*, in paintings, from *within*.

Secondly, Forsyth points to the 'variety', 'individuality' and 'power of expressing particular character, and shades of character' which painting possesses in contrast to sculpture. This in turn corresponds to 'the stress and value which that faith [Christianity] lays upon the individual soul and its history' (*CP*, p. 113). He connects this with the realism of recent art, a realism which he regards as distinctively Christian in so far as the 'egoist passion' of the high ideal of perfect beauty (ie. Greece) gives way to the 'pity and love' which find the divine in the actual concretion of life – 'a definite faith at close quarters with the reality of human life, in its pathos, tragedy, and sin, personal need met by personal salvation through a personal Redeemer in His personal crisis of the Cross' (*CP*, p. 115). But the consequent 'sympathetic particularization' of Christian art extends not only to the human subject, but also sets in motion the rise of landscape painting, which, Forsyth says, is 'in a special way . . . the product of the Christian Revelation' (*CP*, p. 117). Whereas Greek art idealised nature and made it divine, Christian art pursues the way of particularisation, the giving of divine value to individuals, 'God running down into all Nature' (*CP*, p. 118). And it is this process, he believes, which has occasioned the rise of landscape art.

Thirdly – and here, I think, Forsyth speaks for himself rather than for Hegel – painting is characterised by a unity which demands sacrifice. If on the one hand Christianity opens up a virtually infinite multiplicity of situations and feelings for the new art of painting to explore 'with the new freedom there must enter a new law . . . the law of subordination, sacrifice, perspective, to quell atomic self-assertion' (*CP*, pp. 118f). He illustrates this point by referring to such undefined figures as appear in Turner's great landscape paintings, arguing that because of their relation to the total effect of the work 'the figures must limit and sacrifice their self-assertion' on the principle that 'greatness involves self-erasure' (*CP*, p. 119). Consequently 'It is not only, nor chiefly, in great altar-pieces of the Crucifixion that Art bears witness to the power of the Cross, just as it is not in the heroic moments and scenes of our own life that for the most part we have to show forth the Lord's death' (*CP*, p. 120).

Fourthly, the picture requires a very different attitude on the part of the spectator from that required by sculpture. Whereas the statue is independent and self-sufficient the painting draws the spectator into the field of its own occurrence and engages us in the subjective illusion 'that the lines are really vistas, the angles really corners, and the curves really spherical' (*CP*, p. 123). In other words, the subjective interest which we bring to the picture is a part of its reality.

Fifthly, the *colour* of painting provides 'a fit vehicle of the intensity and passion of love in Christianity – love holiest and most human too' (*CP*, p. 123). If the Christian world cannot be said to be sunnier or brighter than the Greek it is nonetheless 'richer and more wondrous' (*CP*, p. 123). That is, it is more colourful. In his earlier discussion of the picturesque element in Christian art, Forsyth laid particular emphasis on colour, quoting Ruskin to the effect that 'colour is the spiritual power of art'. 'Colour', Forsyth adds, 'is the religion and form the theology of art' (*CP*, p. 95). 'It is', he says, 'the melting shades of colour, and the melting contours of landscape, whether in poetry or painting, that best suit with those suggestions of the Infinite which abhor the sharpness of definition and transcend the limitation of form' (*CP*, p. 96).

With these 'structural' elements of painting in place Forsyth proceeds in his next lecture with a survey of the history of painting from Byzantine, through Italian, Flemish, German and English art. In each of these he sees painting as entering more fully into its inheritance. He regards Byzantine art as ultimately limited by the Greek tendency towards typical, rather than individualised, forms. The result of this is that 'saints in pictures become more and more like mummies . . . there was no melting, no chiaroscuro, no perspective' (*CP*, p. 135f). The West, by way of contrast, in what he sees as a single grand development from the tenth and eleventh centuries through to Raphael, was to allow individualisation – and

with it the true spirit of painting – to run its course. From Cimabue
and Giotto onwards the way was prepared for the five great masters:
Michael Angelo, Leonardo, Correggio, Titian and Raphael, of whom
he singles out Raphael as the one in whom 'the qualities which
singly, perhaps, were as strong in others, co-exist in him in a fusion
and harmony so entire, in such admirable proportion and exquisite
balance, that he becomes the apex and epitome both of his age and
of his art' (*CP*, p. 149). In Raphael's Madonnas (compare this with
Ruskin!) 'we have the triumph of the weak things of the world over
the things which are mighty' (*CP*, p. 150). Here he remains close to
Hegel's view that in respect of beauty these Madonnas represent
the supreme expression of that love which is the central theme of
all Christian art. As Hegel had said

> the supreme and unique form of this love is Mary's love for
> the Christ-child, the love of the one mother who has borne the
> Saviour of the world and carries him in her arms. This is the most
> beautiful subject to which Christian art in general, and especially
> painting in its religious sphere, has risen.[4]

He does, however, agree with Ruskin that Raphael 'is the summit
which unites the upward slope and the downward' (*CP*, pp. 150f).
From here on 'the future of painting lay . . . with another school, the
product of another race . . . the succession passed from the South to
the North . . . ' (*CP*, p. 151). Italian art was now to be eclipsed by the
rise of Teutonic art in its Flemish, German and English variants.

In the realism of this new art, in its secularity and worldliness,
Forsyth sees a reflection of the political freedom inspired by the
Protestant faith of Northern Europe. Still in the company of Hegel,
he affirms both the Reformation critique of the mediaeval confusion of religion and art and the secularisation which accompanied
the Reformation. Both these elements contributed to a fresh 'leap
forward' in art, for both religion and art had to find 'a type of
faith more concrete with life and to the complete reconciliation
in beauty of the soul and the world' (*CP*, p. 149). Thus the fresh
subject-matter of Dutch art – the everyday life of the bourgeois
world – is itself a reflex of a political emancipation which was also,
at bottom, religious. [Plate 5]

> Not saints alone, even those canonized from near the artist's own
> time, were now represented. A new class came to the front and to

freedom about this time – the citizen or burgher class – the man who does not give his whole life and soul to religion . . . yet is ready to serve the cause of religion with all his energy and resources when the call arrives . . . an alliance is struck between piety on the one side, and, on the other, industry, freedom, commerce, peace, patriotism, courage of a stubborn if not brilliant sort, and the well-to-do-ness of municipal life. (*CP*, p. 148)

It is an effective summary of the world of Frans Hals, Vermeer, Peter de Hooch and the other great (and lesser) names of Dutch art.

This is more or less the point at which he takes up the tale in *Religion in Recent Art*, the point, that is, of a cleavage between the institutions of religion and a newly secular art. He compares this situation with the breakdown of the religion-culture of the classical world and at once sees a notable difference. 'In Greece it was Art that destroyed Religion; in Europe it was Religion that destroyed Art' (*RRA*, p. 2). The strife which followed the break-up of the mediaeval order 'was a healthy strife, it was the ferment of life, it was the break up of the old historic sward by a resurrection . . . It was the Spirit of God in man taking fresh flight into a new heaven . . . ' (*RRA*, p. 2). For whilst 'Art cannot revive Religion; Religion can revive and regenerate Art' (*RRA*, p. 3). He – like Ruskin – regards the time as now ripe for a renewal of religious art, an art which would take up into itself all the lessons of modern secular art. Such an art would remain true to the world and, in Forsyth's sense, realistic but would show nature on a newly upward curve, rising towards union with the divine. He does not therefore see what some regard as morbid pessimism as a sign of the terminal decadence of art without faith, but as the furthest parameter of the great dialectical movement which is to bring all things into union with God.

It is particularly to the Pre-Raphaelites that he looks, not only as the prophets of a new order of art but also of a new age for humanity; although, he warns us, 'Pre-Raphaelitism is but the overture to an artistic performance which our children only will see at its highest' (*RRA*, p. 4). Observant of the 'dark' side of the Pre-Raphaelites he declares that whilst 'they are caught by the riddle of the painful earth' this does not mar their teaching, since 'their sorrow is not the sorrow of this man or that, but of mankind, and of the heart' (*RRA*, p. 8). Through Rossetti, Burne-Jones, G. F. Watts and Holman Hunt he discerns a progressive potentiation and intensification of religious truth and feeling which approximates ever more closely to the fulness of Christianity itself. He describes the stages of this development as 'The Religion of Natural Passion', 'The Religion of Praeternatural Imagination', 'The Religion of Supernatural Hope' and 'The Religion of Spiritual Faith' respectively. Instead of the historical and systematic treatment of the subject to be found in *Christ on Parnassus* he engages in a detailed examination of a series of works by the artists concerned. One of these expositions, that of Holman Hunt's 'The Scapegoat', has been described by Peter Fuller as 'a *tour de force* of twentieth century art criticism'[5], and we might add that these lectures – at least as far as their form is concerned – arguably provide an excellent model for a working theology of art.

Forsyth is well aware of the sort of criticism which the work of Dante Gabriel Rossetti is likely to draw from a conventionally-minded English Protestant spectator. 'There is', he acknowledges, 'a sultry, tropical feeling around, the heavy opulence of lands not ours, and passions to which our common lives are strange' (*RRA*, p. 9). This world is romantic, passionate, melancholy but for all this it is not morbid or bitter. Rossetti's sense for 'the riddle of the painful earth' may have broken his heart but it did not rob him of hope. Even if he is described as morbid there is, Forsyth tells us, 'such a thing as being "morbidly robust"' (*RRA*, p. 17). Yes, perhaps there is in Rossetti 'a morbid wealth of broken-heartedness' (*RRA*, p. 28) but 'still he felt that we should be better were we able to feel more' (*RRA*, p. 34).

He is certainly not trying to claim that Rossetti's work is directly Christian. His view of life as overshadowed by the constant presence of death falls short of that. 'He was familiar with the Angel of Death, but he did not see the Angel of the Resurrection ever close behind' (*RRA*, pp. 29f). This does not, however, lead him to adopt the attitude we might imagine a Christian philistine taking. Whereas such a one might see in Rossetti only a decadent aestheticism, exacerbated by an equally decadent Mediterranean religiosity, Forsyth sees here a point of contact with genuine and serious religious issues. We have already indicated that one of his underlying aims in these lectures is to embrace the relative truth of the kind of pessimism he associated with Schopenhauer and to acknowledge its authentic passion. This is the core of his response to Rossetti.

In an interesting series of asides in the lectures he draws special attention to the role of women in the work of the various artists with whom he deals. Of Rossetti's women he says, they 'interest us' (*RRA*, p. 21), in contrast to Raphael's Madonnas 'they have other interests than sweet maternity' (*RRA*, p. 21). Rossetti's concern with women is, moreover, prophetic, since, Forsyth asserts, 'there are signs that the great battle of society will be fought round the position of women, and their relation to men. And as Art will be more and more in touch with the social condition, Art must feel this and utter it in its own way' (*RRA*, pp. 23f).

He calls the work of Burne-Jones 'The Religion of Praeternatural Imagination'. What this means is that 'while his beauty is unearthly in its exquisite excess, it is still not pure heavenly in its spiritual strength' (*RRA*, p. 49). Burne-Jones 'is not supernatural' (*RRA*, p. 55). For what he paints is 'the astral body of Nature'. Even if, as in his depiction of the resurrection, this treatment of the subject is highly mythical, it does nonetheless recapture a dimension which is lost in too many ecclesiastical presentations of it. What Burne-Jones gives us is 'the unaffected and exquisite solemnity of the hour' (*RRA*, p. 80). In such works Burne-Jones teaches us that art must learn to discard 'the common conventional grandeurs' (*RRA*, p. 80).

As in the case of Rossetti, so here Forsyth is attentive to the role of women in Burne-Jones's art. His relation to the feminine is, he says, peculiarly distinct. For he has 'access to regions which are closed to the foot of man, and where feminine sensibility alone may tread. Nature has her virginal hours and her conventual solitudes . . . And Burne-Jones is their confessor' (*RRA*, p. 55).

If, like Rossetti, Burne-Jones fails to express a fully supernatural faith in his art we may concede that 'the soul in search of a praeternatural beauty will not be repelled from the source of true spiritual beauty'. for whilst 'the path of beauty is not the way, . . . it is a way to God' (*RRA*, p. 80).

Rossetti, Burne-Jones and Holman Hunt (to whom we shall come shortly) remain well-known and their works are still widely reproduced. But the painter to whom Forsyth turns next, George Frederick Watts, is one whose reputation has suffered an almost total eclipse in the course of the twentieth century. It is almost true to say that outside the art world itself Watts is unknown today. It is therefore hard to realise the very high esteem in which he was held by his contemporaries. He was, for instance, the first artist in Britain to be offered a knighthood (which he declined) and in his work as a portrait-painter he created a veritable gallery of the best-known faces of Victorian England. At the close of the nineteenth century an exhibition of his work in New York attracted half a million visitors, a number which would by no means be contemptible even today. 'He is our Michael Angelo' (*RRA*, p. 97), wrote Forsyth, an epithet first applied to Watts by Lord Leighton and later taken as the title of a study by Wilfrid Blunt.[6] But even in 1904, the year of Watts' death, G. K. Chesterton, in a highly appreciative study, wrote that Watts was first and foremost a man of the Victorian age and of Victorian idealism, and in many respects altogether out of tune with the dawning spirit of the twentieth century. The atmosphere in which Watts lived and worked was 'an atmosphere completely vanished from the world of art in which we now live'.[7] In this respect Chesterton's judgement was surer than Forsyth's (whose *Religion in Recent Art* was published in the following year). Chesterton, however, did not hesitate to offer his own eulogy on Watts' greatness:

> Standing before a dark canvas upon some quiet evening, he has made lines and something has happened, In such an hour the strange and splendid phrase of the Psalm he has literally fulfilled. He has gone on because of the word of meekness and truth and of righteousness. And his right hand has taught him terrible things.[8]

Forsyth agrees. Watts 'is an artist, a thinker and a prophet at once' (*RRA*, p. 102).

Towards the latter part of his career Watts produced a series of highly allegorical paintings which at one point he wanted to incorporate into a kind of modern temple of art, the 'House of Life', which might be for England what Bayreuth was for Germany. The project was not realised, but it was with these allegorical paintings, rather than his portraiture, that Forsyth was chiefly concerned. We see in them, he said, not the interpretation of old myths but the creation of a new mythology. Or rather it is allegorical in the sense that whilst 'the mythic painter takes a story and interprets it, the allegoric makes a thing for us to interpret' (*RRA*, p. 100). These allegories of Watts are, in effect, 'painted parables'. What then is the compass of this new mythology or allegory?

Compared with Burne-Jones's 'religion of praeternatural imagination' Watts' standpoint is that of a genuinely 'supernatural hope', and his work expresses the conviction that 'Beyond life there is a

destiny, above Nature there is a power' (*RRA*, p. 98). His work is
both more intellectual and more 'masculine' than that of Burne-
Jones. For Watts 'Art . . . is a branch of sacred hermeneutics' (*RRA*,
p. 88). 'Let natural beauty be what it may, artistic beauty is higher.
And why? because it is spiritual. Because you have in Art the
finished product of which Nature is but the initial stage' (*RRA*,
p. 89). Art is nature 'born again' and 'is to Nature what salvation
is to the soul' (*RRA*, p. 90). It is this spiritualisation of nature which
Forsyth sees as coming to the fore in Watts' work. Like Rossetti
and Burne-Jones he has experienced the Victorian 'soul-weariness'
'but he has risen above its frailty' (*RRA*, p. 99). His fascination
with death is not to be condemned as morbid since 'Like Art
itself, Death is one of the great interpreters and expanders of life'
(*RRA*, p. 98). Indeed 'Mr. Watts is our only artist who is capable of
wrestling with death and therefore the only one who understands
life' (*RRA*, p. 130). For beyond death Watts has seen the power of
love triumphant and has recognised in death itself 'the arm of the
Lord and the shadow of His wing' (*RRA*, p. 115). Thus his paintings
can be described as expressive of a truly 'supernatural hope'.

Forsyth pursues his interpretation of Watts through a series of
vigorous commentaries on these 'painted parables': 'Psyche', 'Hope',
'Mount Ararat', Love and Death', 'Love and Life', 'Sic Transit', and
'Woman'. Let us take as an example his interpretation of 'Hope',
today perhaps the best-known of Watts' pictures. [Plate 6] The
picture shows a female figure sitting on a sphere which we take
to be the world. The figure is blindfolded and curved over a lyre
of which every string but one is broken. In the sky above a single
star shines. The whole picture is painted in tones of blue and grey.
At first we might take it to be a representation of 'despair', but a
second look, Forsyth believes, should prove otherwise. Who is this
figure? Not hope itself, but one who hopes. She – like the nineteenth
century – has conquered the world, and yet her face is turned away
from 'heaven's light' 'and now, with earth searched and heaven
to explore, her gaze is not up but down, her heaven-searching
power of faith is quenched' (*RRA*, p. 108). Nonetheless, this is not
despair, for

> . . . the thirst to believe is still there. Look how the darkened soul
> stoops and strains for the one string's note, for the one voice to
> tell her a gospel that all her achievement has not yet attained,
> and all the round and mastered world cannot promise. The soul

has in its own self and nature a note that Nature has not. But is that note of nature only in the soul? Is it a subjective dream of its own? Is there any promise in the 'not-ourselves'? . . . Yes, there is one star, though the poor soul sees it not. The painter sees it, and we see it. A star is there and a dim dawn. (*RRA*, p. 108)

This is a paradigm of the way in which the painter can assume a prophetic role. In holding up a mirror to the age the artist enables us to see that which the age itself does not recognise – in this case the recognition that death and the *fin-de-siècle* 'soul-weariness' are not the last word.

In connection with the painting 'Woman', which, Forsyth tells us, portrays woman 'in her vast ideal allegorical significance', we learn that 'humanity . . . is the real link between heaven and earth' (*RRA*, p. 139) and that it is through woman that humanity will attain the consciousness of its highest vocation. Forsyth firmly believes, and finds an endorsement of his belief in the painting, that it is precisely in our time that this consciousness is taking shape.

These lectures on the Pre-Raphaelites conclude with an extensive study of Holman Hunt, whose religious attitude marks an even higher stage than that of G. F. Watts. It is 'the Religion of Spiritual Faith'. Hunt's religious art 'is not only Christian in the complexion . . . but specifically Christian in character . . . doctrinally, spiritually, experimentally' (*RRA*, pp. 153f). Even more boldly Forsyth declares that 'what Bach did for music, that Hunt has done for painting' (*RRA*, p. 150).

Hunt's Protestant painting is rooted both in a deeply studied appreciation of the natural world and in faithfulness to biblical revelation. The Christian God is, according to Forsyth, not merely transcendent but transcendent-within-immanence: 'He is a God of whom Nature is a constant Incarnation and living Revelation' (*RRA*, p. 143). As in his comments on Watts' 'Woman' the link between nature and God is clear and well-defined: 'The key to Nature is human nature' (*RRA*, p. 145). Moreover 'the key to the human spirit is the Spirit of Christ . . . and the Nature of Christ is intelligible only by the Nature of God' (*RRA*, p. 145). This law of progression, Forsyth believes, can be clearly recognised in Hunt's work, which 'shows us that Nature, in her wonderful veracity, her fixity of law, her fluidity of process, her swell of evolution, is rising with Christ . . . ' (*RRA*, p. 158). The passion for natural veracity which Forsyth sees in Hunt is, he says, typically Protestant – although in this sense

Dante and Giotto are also said to be Protestant! Here the foundation for a renewal of sacred art, for which Ruskin had hoped in Volume Three of *Modern Painters*, is seen as having been laid, and, in its power, Ruskin's 'storm-cloud' is dissipated, as nature is seen to be 'rising' towards Christ.

The Bible is the other great source of Protestant spirituality and here too Forsyth sees Hunt as being paradigmatically Protestant. For Hunt the Bible is not merely 'a record of life, but a source of life' (*RRA*, p. 153). Hunt's journey to Palestine is seen by Forsyth – and he quotes Hunt himself to this effect – as an affirmation of the artist's commitment to the veracity of the scriptures. In this respect the journey was a kind of symbolic prophetic act which repudiated the rise of what was widely seen as the relativising and sceptical methods of historical biblical criticism. Renan and D. F. Strauss, who wrote two of the great revisionist 'lives of Jesus' of the nineteenth century, are named by Hunt as representatives of this tendency, a tendency against which he saw his path as being resolutely set.

Forsyth concentrates on three of Hunt's works, 'The Triumph of the Innocents' – described as 'Browning translated into pencil' (*RRA*, p. 175) – 'The Shadow of Death' and 'The Scapegoat'. Of these let us focus on 'The Scapegoat', a work which brings to a head many of Forsyth's arguments about the three-way relationship between nature, art and religion. [Plate 8] It is Forsyth's commentary on this which Peter Fuller has, as already mentioned, described as 'a *tour de force* of twentieth century art criticism'.

'The Scapegoat' could easily make the impression of being a very dreary painting, and a closer examination of its theme does not readily dispel such a view. It shows the scapegoat of the biblical scapegoat ceremony wandering in the wilderness, carrying with it the sins laid on it by the High Priest, and stumbling along the barren edges of the Dead Sea, with skeletal remains and other debris scattered all around. Hunt, Forsyth says, has found in this scapegoat a fitting image for the agony and travail of nature. He has 'made the groaning of the innocent creature a solemn symbol, nay more an organic part of the great and guiltless sorrow which bears and removes the curse of the world' (*RRA*, pp. 181f). 'The creature groans, the saint groans, the Christ groans; and it is all the groaning and the travail . . . of the one redeeming Spirit' (*RRA*, p. 182). The painting, which Forsyth acknowledges is for him 'fragrant with the holy mood' (*RRA*, p. 183), centres on the disparity 'between the dumb distress of the creature and the divine agony which submits to be hinted thus' (*RRA*, p. 183). Yet even in this dismal scene there are suggestions of an ultimate resolution of the world-pain which it expresses. In the background the sun upon the hills points us to the beauty of nature, whilst a rainbow symbolises the redemption of nature from the curse under which it has been laid.

It is, perhaps, difficult for us to entirely empathise with Forsyth's treatment of Hunt. Both religious and aesthetic sensibilities have changed so dramatically since the turn of the century that our initial reaction is probably closer to that of H. R. Rookmaaker, who sees in the religious tenor of Hunt's work nothing but 'sheer sentimentality' and in his quest for historical accuracy a surrender of art to photography.[9] Of 'The Scapegoat' he says, 'Does the painting change at all if we tell each other that the scapegoat was a sacrifice, sent away into the desert yearly bearing the sins of the people of Israel?' Clearly he does not think so! Peter Fuller, however, is more appreciative, although he picks up on a small but important fault in Forsyth's exegesis. Forsyth lays great emphasis on the presence in the picture of a rainbow. 'It is the symbol of the Encircling Father, the triumph of inclusive bliss, beautiful above all the curse . . . and full of promise for a new heaven and a new earth, wherein dwelleth righteousness and there is curse no more' (*RRA*, p. 182f). Yet, Fuller points out, the rainbow was omitted in the final version of the painting, and, he asks, 'Without the promise of the rainbow what was left except the naked shingles of the world?'[10] Without the rainbow we are back in the shadow of the dark 'storm-cloud', we have lost the exegetical key which makes of nature a text expressive of the divine life pointing towards and partaking of God and rising towards Christ. But, if there is no natural language in which the things of God can be expressed how can art, whose materials are drawn entirely from the natural order, be truly 'religious'? This is, of course, bad news for a natural theology of art which wants to start with nature and work its way towards God! But, we may say, what difference does the presence or absence of a rainbow in a single picture make? Does it really affect our assessment of the religious significance of Hunt's work that much?

The point is this: where do we derive our understanding of the religious significance of a painting from? From the picture itself? Or from a knowledge which is based on other grounds and which we, as it were 'apply' to our 'reading' of the picture? The issue raised by 'The Scapegoat' – an issue which feeds back into our whole assessment of Forsyth's approach to art – is whether the pictorial element is allowed to work in its own right or whether it is in fact reduced to a cipher, a code, a language illustrative of a different order of non-pictorial truth. Does the discussion about the rainbow take place inside or outside the space of the picture itself? Is nature really being taken in its own terms or is it simply being used by the artist as a 'means' to a strictly non-natural 'end'? Forsyth claims that this is not the case. The artist, he says, 'does not impose himself on Nature . . . It is Nature's idea uttered, and completed, and coming to itself through the artist' (*CP*, p. 260). But does the expression of nature in art have a religious significance in its own right or is it only an image of a religious truth which comes from elsewhere, perhaps from revelation, in which case art is no longer being treated in its own proper autonomy of existence. Forsyth claims to be committing himself to the first alternative – but is he really consistent in this commitment?

At this point we might usefully turn to his relation to Hegel. Forsyth, as we have seen, regards nature as ultimately intelligible only in relation to human nature, and ultimately only in relation to the divine nature revealed in Christ. At the same time he insists that nature, and with nature art, is 'rising' of its own accord towards such a revelation of its own meaning and purpose. Hegel, however, seems to take a less appreciative view of nature. Humanity is the source of all spiritual significance: 'Even a useless notion that enters a man's head is higher than any product of nature'.[11] Man exists as spirit

> by altering external things whereon he impresses the seal of his inner being, and in which he now finds again his own characteristics. Man does this in order, as a free subject, to strip the external world of its inflexible foreignness and to enjoy in the shape of things only an external realization of himself.[12]

As an example of this Hegel adduces the spontaneous impulse of a child sitting by a smooth surface of water to disturb it by throwing in a stone and watching the ripples spread out. What the child enjoys is the fact that he himself has created this new pattern, this new order, which does not derive from the natural 'given' arrangement of things themselves. What Hegel sees in this is the essential *nisus* of spirit to negate the given. In sharp contrast to Ruskin, for whom nature was a ready made treasury of divinely ordained meanings which human beings had only to discover, Hegel sees the creation of meaning as a specifically human task – if necessary in opposition to nature. Spirit, for Hegel, is essentially subjective in the sense that there is no objective reality 'out there' which determines or constrains the meaning of human life in history. The meaning of life is not inscribed within any already existing state of affairs but is to be attained through human action, reflection and interpretation. The motivation of spirit is self-knowledge and in order to achieve this it must subordinate and transcend the given natural order of things.

Now although Forsyth does not believe that nature has any kind of absolute value or meaning apart from its relation to spirit, his emphasis is quite different from that of Hegel. But there is more to it.

For Ruskin both man and nature stand within a divinely appointed order which is greater than either of them and it is by virtue of their relation to this order that the one becomes meaningful to the other. For Hegel, however, there seems to be no mode of divine action relevant to our purposes other than that which occurs in and through human subjectivity. On this issue at least Forsyth is closer to Ruskin. Forsyth's 'spirit' is by no means primarily or exclusively human. It is first and foremost transcendent. Forsyth, in other words, finds himself closer to the Hebrew element in the Christian synthesis than Hegel was able to be. For in addition to the line of historical evolution Forsyth affirms the reality of an axis of divine-human relationship which is indicated by such words as *revelation, redemption* and *faith*.

> We have marked in the history and nature of Art the action of certain processes of reconciliation, redemption, spiritualisation and so on. How do we know that these will converge and close in a reconciliation and glorification of all things? Have we any access already in history to an act which is the final reconciliation and manifestation of the whole creation revealed in advance? (*CP*, p. 261)

In a sense this was (or is) perhaps *the* question which has haunted European theology since Hegel. Are we adrift in a sea of relativity or do we have some sure and certain ground on which to stand? At this point the preacher parts company with the philosopher. For Forsyth the only 'answer' is that of revelation, and faith in the redemption won by Christ. To the rhetorical question 'The Christ who is so mighty in history, has He the throne in eternity?' (*CP*, p. 261) his answer is, in faith, 'yes'. For Hegel on the other hand the once-for-all element in such a confession cannot be sustained, but is dissolved into a process of appropriation and interpretation. Forsyth's insistence on the transcendent nature of God and the finality of the Christian revelation has direct implications for his theology of art. For, he says

> it should be clear that the Christ merely historic and humane is not equal to the perennial control of an interest so great and unusual as Art's treatment of nature's text . . . Nothing less than a dogmatic Christ is adequate to the spiritual control of the greatest aspects and interests of mankind in every age. (*CP*, p. 288)

This difference has implications for the way in which each thinker sets out the ultimate limitations of art. Hegel sees the process of spiritualisation as leading to a state of consciousness which art itself cannot encompass. Art, in his view, represents a middle stage between the sheer exteriority of nature and the interiority of spirit (for which language is the most appropriate vehicle). The image must yield to the word, and the word is comprehended in the laws of logic. Historically, Hegel sees the Reformation as a key point in the discovery of this truth. But for Hegel there can be no return to art as a vehicle of spiritual truth, no renewal of sacred art, once this point has been passed. 'No matter how excellent we find the statues of the Greek gods, no matter how we see God the Father, the Christ and Mary so estimably and perfectly portrayed: it is no help; we bow the knee no longer'.[13] The time of art is over: 'art, considered in its highest vocation, is and remains for us a thing of the past . . . '[14] and 'the peculiar nature of artistic production and of works of art no longer fills our highest need . . . thought and reflection have spread their wings above fine art'.[15] Art *represents* reality in forms and materials drawn from the external world of nature. Our task now is to *understand* the inner spiritual meaning in a spiritually appropriate way, *conceptually*, in *language*, by means of *logic*.

But if for Hegel there can be no interest in the whole issue of a new religion-culture Forsyth clearly believes in the possibility of a new era of religiously important art. It is precisely this which he sees anticipated in the works of those painters to whom *Religion in Recent Art* is largely devoted. He too sees art as ultimately limited, but he derives his limit from that axis of revelation-redemption-faith which distinguishes his position from pure Hegelianism. His account of this limit finds him, curiously, closer to Kierkegaard than to Hegel: 'Art is not life, and faith is. Art does not prescribe a morality, and faith does. Christ did not come as a subject for Art, but as an object of faith and a giver of life' (*CP*, p. 293). Personal faith has an unsurpassable priority over art. Yet this does not mean that he wants to draw art back under the wing of ecclesiastical hegemony. Faith has priority: 'Fantasy is one thing, and faith is another; and it is faith that guides life; and it guides art as part of life' (*CP*, p. 289). But it is individual conscience and not the authority of the Church that provides the ultimate rule of faith itself. 'If we are to have guidance for art, faith in Christ must give it at last. A Church cannot' (*CP*, p. 280).

Yet it was perhaps precisely this emphasis which enabled him to allow a greater autonomy to nature and to predict a still open future for art. Hegel's totalising approach implied that we could reach a final judgement on the place of art in human life and recognise it to be a 'thing of the past', whilst his logical principles required us to look at art as exhaustively 'readable'. Forsyth however cannot regard history as finished in that way. The finality of faith operates on a different level and, as rooted in the action of a transcendent deity, can never be absolutely objectified within the limitations of human consciousness and language. The openness of history to new developments and configurations of events is secured by the transcendence of the God who is the ultimate goal of history. This openness includes the possibility of new developments in the relationship between nature, art and religion. If it does not concede to art the absolute autonomy that some forms of modernism might require it does allow considerable freedom to art to develop a religious meaning out of its own natural resources. It does not reduce art to a mere cipher for pre-ordained religious meanings. Such meaning is to be pursued and developed within what is essentially an open and flexible system. If Forsyth does – and I think it must be conceded that he does – all too often treat art as allegory, as a kind of text, that is not an immediate or obvious consequence of his system but of the way in which he applies it.

But can the thoroughly individualised faith which he commends, without the support of the solid ecclesiastical tradition on which, for instance, Neo-Thomism draws, weather the historical, cultural and intellectual storms of modernism?

Let us look at it like this. It is often said that the First World War signalled the collapse of the nineteenth century belief in progress, an event reflected theologically in Karl Barth's repudiation of liberal theology with its marriage of religion and culture. Drawing on Kierkegaard, Barth declared there to be an 'infinite qualitative difference' between God and humanity. But if Forsyth had hoped to integrate Kierkegaardian emphases on individual faith and divine transcendence into a broadly optimistic Hegelian view of history, didn't Barth's return to a strict Either/Or finally demolish such hopes? Wasn't it now a question of Either: culture – and the Somme/Or: faith – and Christ? In such hours of decision doesn't a purely individual faith need to let go of its cultural baggage? Forsyth, we may recall, wrote his books on art in the early 1900s, in the golden sunset of the nineteenth century whose 'soul-weariness' was to seem a relatively gentle thing when set against the harsher discords of the war and post-war world. Didn't the war mean 'goodbye to all that'?

Forsyth had courageously pushed dialectical idealism to its very limits in finding a religious meaning in the dark corners of late-nineteenth century pessimism and 'soul-weariness'. But would it be possible to go even further and find a meaning in the greater darkness which was now falling over European civilisation? Those theologies of art which we have been examining in these chapters diverge at many points, yet they have one thing in common: they hold to the ultimate convergence of human sensibility, nature and divine truth; for all of them the pattern of grace-perfecting-nature holds good in some measure. But what happens when this complex edifice begins to crumble? What is left for religion and art when the 'storm-cloud' of modernism threatens to sweep everything away? Is this not, after all, the vindication of Kierkegaard's call for the severance of the bonds uniting religion and culture? Is it not time to rediscover and reassert more clearly than ever that great tradition of Christian iconoclasm? Or can theology – even in this extremity – go with art into the abyss and find there the beginnings of a new relationship? Can art and religion perhaps find common cause in the assault on all premature consolations and, beyond all ideals of nature and of beauty, join in charting that dark wasteland which is the new landscape of the human pilgrimage? One man, at least, was to suggest that such a move was both possible and desirable: Paul Tillich. Let us then turn to his unique and disturbing theology of art.

6

Into the Abyss

Paul Tillich was one of the outstanding modernist theologians of the twentieth century and, in the words of John Dillenberger, 'of all the theologians of our century, he alone set the agenda for the role of the arts in theological work'.[1] Dillenberger is by no means uncritical of what he sees as the limitations of Tillich's views, but he is unequivocal as to their significance for the theology of art.

In various autobiographical remarks Tillich described how he discovered the power and the significance of art. This is of more than personal interest, however, since it was experienced by Tillich as directly relating to the epochal events taking place in the world about him. In the First World War he served as an army padre on the Western Front and in his experiences in the trenches he saw what he believed to be the literal end of a world taking place. By 1918 the impending defeat of German arms could no longer be seen simply as the failure of a particular imperial ambition: it was the end of a world in which it could be believed that history was progressing more or less harmoniously towards a triumphant conclusion. From now on nothing could be taken for granted since it had been demonstrated that history could go backwards into barbarism as well as forwards towards a social and moral utopia. Not only in the trenches but in Germany itself chaos seemed to be asserting itself as the country was plunged into in a state of virtual civil war with gun-battles between the paramilitary forces of right and left raging on the streets. This was the context in which he 'discovered' art. He had for some time been interested in painting, but his knowledge had been limited to the poor-quality reproductions available at the front. Then in his last leave of the war, something happened. In the Kaiser Friedrich Museum in Berlin he found himself face to face with a painting by Botticelli, 'Madonna with Singing Angels'. [Plate 7]

Gazing up at it, I felt a state approaching ecstasy. In the beauty of the painting there was Beauty itself. It shone through the colors of the paint as the light of day shines through the stained-glass windows of a medieval Church.

As I stood there, bathed in the beauty its painter had envisioned so long ago, something of the divine source of all things came through to me. I turned away shaken.

That moment has affected my whole life . . . I compare it with what is usually called revelation in the language of religion. I know that no artistic experience can match the moments in which prophets were grasped in the power of the Divine Presence, but I believe there is an analogy between revelation and what I felt. In both cases, the experience goes beyond the way we encounter reality in our daily lives. It opens up depths experienced in no other way. (*AA*, p. 230)

This experience anticipates much of what Tillich was to say about art in the future, in particular the link between aesthetic experience and revelation. However, Tillich was soon to turn away from the humanist ideals represented by Botticelli and to look instead at the contemporary art situation, finding there a more appropriate starting point for the dialogue between theology and art which he was to initiate. If the powerful impact of Botticelli's 'Madonna' was due in part to the utter contrast between the ideal of beauty made visible in the picture and the squalor and horror of the trenches from which Tillich had come, he was soon to become fascinated with those forms of contemporary art in which the dark and elemental forces of the present were, in his view, finding a direct expression: above all the art of expressionism. [Plate 9]

Expressionism was to have a decisive impact on Tillich's whole theory of art. Here too there was something like a revelation, but a revelation of a different kind. What was made visible in expressionism was the collapse of the whole realm of bourgeois values and ideals which had inspired the nineteenth century in its false pursuit of progress. It is, perhaps, worth noting that in the same period immediately after the war in which Tillich was developing his theory of art he was also working out a radical fusion of Christian and Marxist ideas under the banner of 'religious socialism' and was strongly committed to the cause of the far left in Germany, an aspect of his work which has rarely been highlighted in English-speaking interpretations. His political and social concerns were directly linked by Tillich himself to his perception of the value

of expressionism in art. Tracing the origins of expressionism back to
such artists as Van Gogh and Eduard Munch he claims that

> On this basis new forces developed everywhere, in Italy, in France,
> in Germany and in Russia. Expressionism proper arose with
> a revolutionary consciousness and revolutionary force . . . The
> abyss of Being was to be evoked in lines, colors and plastic
> forms . . . The discovery of primitive and Asiatic art came to be
> the symbol of revolt against the spirit of capitalist society. (*AA*,
> p. 68)

The anti-bourgeois, anti-capitalist aspect of expressionism was particularly sharply brought out in an extraordinary essay published in
1922 called *Mass and Personality*. 'Mass' here relates to the image of
the mass in the sense of the crowd, or mass movement. Whereas
many Christian thinkers saw the power of the masses – a controversial theme throughout the interwar years – as a sign of the
dissolution of moral responsibility and the capitulation to demo-
cratic levelling which characterised the modern world (and therefore to be rejected) Tillich, writing as a Marxist (of sorts) saw
the role of the masses as at least potentially innovative and creative. Let us, he says, look at how art has portrayed masses and
crowds in different periods of art history. He starts with some
observations on the depiction of crowds in mediaeval art. Here
'The crowd is completely dominated by the overarching idea that
it represents . . . Everything individual is erased' (*AA*, p. 59). The
figures all look the same and the dominant figure – the Christ,
the Madonna or a King – is distinguished not by any individual
characterisation, but by what Tillich calls his 'formal position',
'that he is in the centre, not transsected by other bodies, that he
is larger than the others, more richly adorned' (*AA*, p. 59). Tillich
calls the concept of the mass revealed in such pictures the 'mystical
concept of mass'. In it, he suggests, there is no tension, no distinction
between the individual personality and the crowd. The individual
is what he is only in and through his place in a hierarchically
ordered whole, and the particular is what it is only by virtue
of its participation in the universal. From here, he passes on to
what he calls the late Gothic or early Renaissance situation, to
the sort of crowd scene depicted by the Brueghels. The mass here
is no longer mystical but realistic: 'the composition is dissolved,
the paintings fall apart into unorganised singularities; the leaders

have lost their position of leadership; even Christ has become one among the realistic throng' (*AA*, p. 60). The crowd had become a multitude of individuals: its leader is no longer distinguished by his size or some other equally external emblematic device but by the fact that he expresses most forcefully the psychological feeling which animates each member of the crowd individually. With the Baroque period, in Rubens, for example, we find something new again, a 'flooding life' which unites all the members of the crowd:

> It is the inner, raging life, joining nature and man, that makes the throng too a dynamic unity and which embraces the leader as well, although it does so in such a way that the leader is lifted out of the flood of bodies and movements, the raging and swirling lines and is, as it were, the crest of the wave, the point at which it towers up to its strongest, most sparkling life . . .

This he calls 'the dynamic mass with an aristocratic culmination' (*AA*, p. 61). From here he moves on to the threshold of the present situation. Here he looks firstly at the portrayal of the crowd in the art of the French impressionists. Impressionism, he declares, 'is the form of style of the individualistic bourgeoisie of the second half of the nineteenth century' (*AA*, p. 61).

The impressionist may show us scenes of contemporary urban life, a thronged boulevard or café, a scene from industrial or working-class life, but 'for him it is no substantiality; it is for him a study of light or color or movement; it is for him a piece of the surface of nature which he intuitively experiences in a new impression, a vision of the moment, interesting, piquant, basically a piece of landscape' (*AA*, pp. 61f). There is no depth, no critique in such art: 'Form is everything, the form that has become supreme technique and rationality, bright, cool, dwelling at the surface despite all the fireworks of color'. The mass exists here 'only as a surface . . . only as an object of formal technique'. Thus it is, he concludes, 'the technical mass that impressionism reveals' (*AA*, p. 62). By way of contrast he comes at last to the expressionists. The expressionist artist does not look at the mass merely from the outside. In some ways like the mediaeval, mystical artist or like the baroque, dynamic artist, he enters into the inner unitary substance of the crowd. It is part of 'a new mysticism . . . a new inner experience of things' (*AA*, p. 63). Like the impressionist the expressionist shows the dissolution of external lines and contours, but whereas the impressionist does so merely in order to capture even more intimately the fleeting surface appearance of things, the expressionist goes through the surface into the heart of his subject. He is not merely recording his response, not merely showing us a subjective vision: his report carries with it a metaphysical objectivity. He discerns and 'expresses' 'a metaphysical lack of redemption and longing for redemption. For that reason they are sometimes approximated to animals, then again elevated beyond humanity to ecstatically visionary heights' (*AA*, p. 63). This is, he says, 'the mass of immanent mysticism' reflecting the age of the World War, and of the Russian Revolution. In disturbingly prophetic words he notes that in distinction from all the other portrayals of the mass which he has examined up to this point this modern mass lacks a leader or redeemer 'and one feels that he cannot come from above. He must be born from the depth of the mass longing' (*AA*, pp. 63f). Germany was, of course, to give birth to just such a leader, a man from the people, but a man whose political goals were to be diametrically opposed to those which Tillich saw as the 'answer' to the needs of the age.

This essay shows us several of the key features of Tillich's writings on art. Certainly at this period he sees art as standing in the closest possible relation to the overall crisis of society and as revelatory both of that crisis itself and of the resolution of the crisis. The typical characteristics of such expressionist art are spelt out in contrast to what he sees as the ultimate failure of impressionism, which 'despite all the fireworks of color' remains trapped in an empty and uncritical superficiality, whilst the expressionist penetrates and reveals the heart of things. This contrast is, in fact, highly typical of German writing of this period. Many Germans, including such writers as Thomas Mann, had seen the war itself as precisely a conflict between the sort of values which Tillich sees in impressionism (associated, of course, with France) and those which come to the fore in expressionism (always, inevitably, identified with Germany).

Tillich wants to emphasise what he regards as the objectivity and the metaphysical truth of expressionist art. This might be regarded as somewhat surprising, given that his thought as a whole can easily be read as highly subjectivist, but the prominent role which he does indeed give to the subject is always conceived within an over-arching metaphysical framework and seen as revelatory of Being. Thus, the unique historical crisis of Germany in the immediate post-war years is interpreted as a particular reflection at a particular point of time of an eschatological crisis which is determinative for all of history. Tillich was at this time developing his doctrine of the '*Kairos*', the term used in the gospels' summary of Jesus' preaching 'The time is fulfilled'. *Kairos* is time in the sense of fulfilled, meaningful time as opposed to the mere mechanical seriality of clock time. For Tillich there was a once-for-all *kairos* in the actual appearance in time of the Christ, but this once-for-all *kairos* did not reduce the rest of history to uniform indifference. Within history, Tillich believed, there are unique moments of fulfilment which correspond to the once-for-all *kairos*, moments when action and decision become charged with a more than momentary significance. The realisation of such *kairoi* can never be judged in abstraction from the actual situation of historical existence. 'It is a matter of the faith of those who act in a special situation'.[2] In this sense the crisis of Germany was a special *kairos*, a moment when the ultimate, metaphysical dimension of the human situation was uniquely 'at hand' – if those who experienced that situation chose to realise it and seize the time, making the decision in favour of faith (which, for Tillich at this time was also 'the socialist decision'). Expressionist art is the prophetic revelation which reveals this ultimate content of the contemporary moment, and puts that metaphysical choice before those who are living it.

Mass and Personality also raises a theme which was to run throughout Tillich's thought: the dialectic of heteronomy, autonomy and theonomy. Tillich sees the significance of the bourgeois revolution as consisting in its championing of the cause of autonomous this-worldly rationality over against the dogmatic claims of the Churches (principally the Roman Catholic Church). Autonomy is the rational subject's attempt to live its life solely by the light of reason, a principle which Tillich sees as operating not merely in the sphere of personal values but in the whole process of social and technological rationalisation. Capitalism is the particular economic system which has enabled this process to take place. Heteronomy, on the other hand, is the attempt to direct reason from the 'outside'. Although the principle of autonomy is rooted in the structure of reason itself, insofar as reason itself necessarily contains a dimension of depth, pointing beyond itself to the reality which it seeks to interpret or represent, it is typical of the modern world that the dictates of heteronomous authority are at odds with the interests of autonomous reason. A principal example is the wilful and arbitrary attempt by ecclesiastical authority to impose constraints on the discoveries of reason and science – and, as we have seen, on art. Against such an exercise of heteronomy Tillich wishes to take the part of autonomy. In the context of *Mass and Personality* this movement from heteronomy to autonomy is reflected in the break up of the mediaevel mystical crowd into the utterly individualised crowd of the early Renaissance. On the other hand the autonomous principle itself cannot create reality and its critical thrust can lead to the complete evacuation of meaning unless restrained by a higher principle. But what can such a higher principle be, if it is not to involve a return to the purely external authority of the heteronomous principle? It is, Tillich says, to be looked for in the advent of a situation of *theonomy*. Theonomy, divine law, does not negate the principle of autonomy but accepts and deepens it until it becomes transparent to its divine ground; it is the discovery of new substance, new content, on the ground of autonomous existence, but with no weakening of the principle of autonomy; it is the unity of the horizontal (autonomous) and vertical (heteronomous) dimensions of life. Such a situation is, Tillich admits, seemingly utopian, but this does not embarrass him: the spirit of Utopia, he states, is 'the power which changes reality. It is the spring of all great historical movements; it is the tension which impels man beyond everything reassuring and safe to a new uncertainty and unrest . . . Utopia is the power of renewal'.[3] The anticipation of such a theonomous, utopian situation can be seen in expressionistic art in its evocation of the metaphysical longing for a new mysticism; the longing of the crowd for a new leader, a new principle of reality which will not be imposed on it from above or from outside but will arise out of the life of the crowd itself.

Expressionist art, then, points to the human quest to snatch out of the catastrophic shipwreck of culture and society a new religious basis, to seize the time and fulfil the meaning of the present *kairos*, to root the shallow self-assertion of bourgeois society in the deep soil of theonomy. It is not however itself that new basis or that theonomy. It is *miserere* and not *gloria*; the cry from the depths.

Although his original interest in expressionism was clearly bound up with his passionate involvement in the contemporary traumas of German history he increasingly comes to give the term a much wider usage, so that 'expressionism' is no longer the name for a particular school of art (let us say one which belongs to German-speaking culture *circa* 1910–30) but for a particular style of art which is not limited to any period. Style was to become a key to

Tillich's whole philosophy of art and it is therefore worth asking what exactly he meant by it. He himself offers various definitions: 'every style points to a self-interpretation of man, thus answering the question of the meaning of life. Whatever the subject-matter which an artist chooses . . . he cannot help but betray by his style his own ultimate concern as well as that of his group, and his period' (*AA*, p. 121). 'Style is that element of a work of art which qualifies its particular form by a more universal form principle' (*AA*, p. 128) ' . . . wherever ultimate reality is expressed through . . . artistic images . . . the medium through which this happens is the stylistic form of . . . an image' (*AA*, p. 142). Style, then, is the particular way in which an encounter with ultimate reality or an ultimate concern becomes embodied in thought or imagery: it is a peculiar kind of response to the revelation of reality and it is to be found in the peculiar way in which an individual, group or age responds to reality at the deepest possible level and as such permeates every aspect of the life of an individual or community. 'If we now ask what is revealed by a style, the answer may be an encounter of man with his world, in which the whole man in all dimensions of his being is involved' (*AA*, p. 129). Tillich draws up various lists of stylistic 'types' (e.g. *AA*, pp. 143ff.) but the most important of these are the styles he refers to as 'naturalistic', 'idealistic' and 'expressive'. The first of these simply sees and represents things as they are according to their 'given' natural form. The second portrays reality as being more perfect than in fact it is, anticipating the ultimate union of divine and human, as in the art of the Renaissance. The last is said to be correlated with 'the ecstatic-spiritual type of religious experience' (*AA*, p. 150) and is regarded by Tillich as particularly significant from a religious point of view.

For although every style in some sense reveals the way in which an individual or an age experiences and responds to ultimate reality such revelation is peculiarly direct in the case of expressive style:

> The expressive element in a style implies a radical transformation of the ordinarily encountered reality . . . Expression disrupts the naturally given appearance of things . . . That which is expressed in the 'dimension of depth' in the encountered reality, the ground and abyss in which everything is rooted.   (*AA*, p. 123)

Thus, although (as we shall see) there is no absolutely unmediated encounter with ultimate reality, expressionistic or expressive style reveals such reality in a way which other styles fail to do. Naturalism and idealism tend to inculcate an attitude of contentment with this-worldly reality, they do not provoke us into the attempt to penetrate behind the 'mere' surface of things. Although some kind of relation to ultimate reality is never lacking in any work of art, naturalistic or idealistic art almost invariably tends towards one-dimensionality. This view has important consequences: 'the dominance of the expressive element in the style of all periods in which great religious art has been created and the directly religious effect of a style which is under the predominance of the expressive element, even if no material from any of the religious traditions is used' (*AA*, p. 123). In other words the presence of expressive elements is in itself religiously significant whatever the subject matter. As he put it in *The Religious Situation* (the first of his books to be translated into English): 'Expressionism . . . has a mystical, religious character, quite apart from its choice of subjects. It is not an exaggeration to ascribe more of the quality of sacredness to a still-life by Cézanne or a tree by Van Gogh than to a picture of Jesus by Uhde' (*AA*, p. 69). In this connection 'expressive style' can be seen in a wide range of periods and works: in mediaeval art, in Mathias Grünewald's 'Crucifixion', in Goya, and in Van Gogh and Cézanne as well as in the works of the expressionists in a narrow sense. But if expressive style reveals an encounter with reality which can be described as authentically religious, can we define this encounter still more closely?

In answering this question we may bring Tillich's remarks about expressive style into connection with his concept of existentialism. Again this is a term which he uses in the broadest possible sense covering not only the philosophical theories of such thinkers as Kierkegaard and Sartre but a basic orientation towards existence which Tillich sees pervading such diverse movements as Marxism (at least in some forms) and psychoanalysis. Writing for instance about the common roots of existentialism and psychoanalysis he declares that these are to be found in 'the protest against the increasing power of the philosophy of consciousness in modern industrial society'.[4] Again we may detect an implied critique of self-contained autonomy. But existentialism is also a protest against the kind of belief in harmony and reconciliation which typifies what Tillich calls the 'philosophy of consciousness', that is, the belief that the totality of history can be brought within the orbit of a single unifying idea or purpose, as in Hegel. Over against such reconciliatory systems existentialism draws attention to the finitude of the human situation, our inability to grasp the totality of Being and our consequent anxiety, loneliness, emptiness and fear of meaninglessness. Existentialism portrays the human subject in its alienation and separation from the deepest ground of its Being – but, paradoxically, at the same time says that it is precisely this situation of anxious separation which discloses the reality of our specifically human mode of being. To speak in the language of Christian theology: it is precisely by acknowledging our status as fallen creatures, alienated from God, that we enter into a right and truthful relationship to God; it is precisely as sinners that God's grace meets us and justifies us! As Martin Luther recognised, the situation of humanity before God can only be described as *simul peccator, simul iustus* (at once sinful and yet justified), a 'paradoxical formula' which Tillich describes as 'the core of the Lutheran revolution'.[5] Existentialism in this sense exists wherever the fundamental conflicts of human existence are expressed in philosophy or thought generally: in Plato and in Luther, as well as in those modern thinkers whose work deals with such conflicts. The link with Protestantism is especially striking, since Protestantism 'emphasizes man's finitude, his subjection to death, but above all, his estrangement from his true being and his bondage to demonic forces . . . ' (*AA*, p. 110)

These themes come together in Tillich's scattered comments on what he regarded as one of the great works of modern art: Picasso's *Guernica*, which he describes variously as a great Protestant painting, an existentialist painting and as a prime example of the expressive style. It shows, he said, 'the human situation without any cover' (*AA*, p. 96). Elsewhere he states that as '*the*' outstanding example of a contemporary artistic representation of the human situation it puts before us 'the question of man in a world of guilt, anxiety and despair . . . with tremendous power' (*AA*, p. 120). (Rookmaaker, however, whilst acknowledging Picasso's uniquely powerful genius, sees him as no more than a negative representative of consistent nihilism, as *the* anti-religious modern painter *par excellence*.) Protestantism, existentialism and expressionism alike focus on the negative aspects of the human situation: aspects which, for Tillich, are only too real and which must, albeit paradoxically, be affirmed as they are, without any false harmonisation. As such they are all suited to revealing the truth of the human situation in the modern world, a situation which in Tillich's views (and, we must add, in his experiences in the war and Nazi period) was continually overshadowed by uncontrollable and self-destructive demonic forces which threatened the loss of all established structures of meaning and coherence. 'Under the predominance of the expressive style in the last fifty years', he wrote in 1957,

> the attempts to recreate religious art have led mostly to a redis-covery of the symbols in which the negativity of man's pre-dicament is expressed: the Symbol of the Cross has become the subject matter of many works of art – often in the style which is represented by Picasso's *Guernica*. Symbols, such as resurrection, have not yet found any adequate artistic representation, and so it is with the other traditional 'symbols of glory'. (*AA*, p. 120)

The Protestant and existentialist character of the present age makes the production of a full-bloodedly religious art, an art which would be religious in subject matter as well as in style, problematic. Here Tillich is quite frank about his own uncertainty as to the extent to which attempts to create such an art have succeeded. Referring to the explicitly religious works of Graham Sutherland, Emil Nolde and Georges Rouault he comments 'Sometimes I am impressed by them – but in most cases I feel that they did not succeed' (*AA*, p. 99). This is because it does not lie within the power of the human subject to give the answer – artistically or intellectually – to the storms of the present day and the existential questioning which has arisen as an expression of the modern situation. Here a comment from the early work *The Religious Situation* remained normative for his thought as a whole. Creative art he says, 'can express metaphysical meanings; it cannot produce them' (*AA*, p. 70).

This, then, raises the question as to the limits of all art in plumbing the depths of the human predicament, in particular the limits of art over against religion. As we have seen copiously, art has an almost unparalleled power to express the human situation and to raise the question as to the meaning and coherence of existence as a whole. But it cannot create that situation and it cannot answer the question which it raises. Why is this?

The first part of the answer to this question touches on what is one of the central features of Tillich's theology: what he calls his 'method of correlation', which underpins the whole enterprise of his *Systematic Theology*. He defines correlation as 'interdependence of two independent factors',[6] and his method of correlation seeks to explain the meaning of theological statements by correlating them

with the human situation as disclosed, primarily, by existentialism
in the conviction that 'the revelatory answer is meaningless if there
is no question to which it is the answer. Man cannot receive an
answer to a question he has not asked'.[7] On the other hand he is
very aware of the criticism to which his use of this method might
be subjected: that the way in which the human question is asked
limits the scope of the theological answer and puts constraints on
what God can and cannot be said to do. As Barth was to put it in
another context, the humanistic tail comes to wag the theological
dog. Against such criticisms Tillich claims that the question and
answer are (as in the definition above) independent: the one cannot
be deduced or in any way derived from the other. This is part of
what his choice of the term correlation itself is meant to show:
correlation does not imply dependence one way or the other. He
is at pains to emphasise that 'The existential question . . . is not
the source for the revelatory answer formulated by theology. One
cannot derive the divine self-manifestation from an analysis of the
human predicament . . . Man is the question, not the answer'.[8] His
system therefore stands in an ambiguous relation to traditional
efforts in the direction of natural theology. Like those who practised
natural theology he wants to affirm that the human standpoint is
such that an intelligible and meaningful relationship can be established between the divine and the human. We are 'estranged, but
not cut off from God'.[9] On the other hand the attempt by the natural
theologians 'to derive theological affirmations from the analysis of
man's finitude' was 'an impossible task'.[10] This restriction on the
scope of the existential question remains normative for all forms
of human life, including the creation and reception of works of
art, which, as we have already seen, is itself 'correlated' with the
existential analysis of the human situation. Yet this still leaves the
question as to the precise boundary between aesthetic experience
and religious revelation undecided. Where does the artistic 'question' end and the religious 'answer' begin?

To pursue this question we must examine the complex relationship between image, symbol and language in Tillich's thought. In
the essay *Art and Ultimate Reality*, Tillich states that there are three
ways by which human beings can relate to reality: the indirect
ways of art and of philosophy and the direct way of religion. In
religion 'ultimate reality becomes manifest through ecstatic experiences of a concrete revelatory character and is expressed in symbols
and myths' (*AA*, p. 142). This is almost the language in which

he describes his Botticelli-experience and yet there is a contrast between 'direct' communication by means of 'symbols and myths' and 'indirect' communication by means of images. What, then, is the difference between images and symbols? Let us go back to 'Guernica'. This is said by Tillich to be a symbol of the Cross. Yet the painting contains no image of the Cross: it is not a 'Crucifixion'. 'The Cross' as symbol and 'The Cross' as image are not identical. Symbolism addresses a level of reality which mere images cannot attain and, as Tillich frequently says, symbols are never only symbols for the 'symbol participates in the reality which is symbolised'.[11] Whatever power images may have they have by virtue of their connection to the symbolic order. But even this symbolic order is not final. In relation to God a symbol is not unambiguous; the 'ordinary' meaning of its material content, its literal meaning, must be negated if it is not to mar its transcendent reference. Just as in the Catholic doctrine of analogy there is no unequivocal statement we can make about God, so every statement involves both likeness and unlikeness. Or, rather, there is only one statement we can make about God which is not symbolic: the statement that God is Being-Itself. This is the nearest thing we have to an unequivocal statement about God and, as such, all symbolic statements about God depend on the truth of this one non-symbolic statement. Without this, everything – including the images of artists and the words of theologians – is adrift in a sea of relativity.

Both images and words can transmit symbolic truth and the restrictions on the power of symbols to communicate the things of God apply to images and words alike. Yet language seems, ultimately, to provide a more appropriate medium of religious truth. Thus despite speaking of the revelatory power of art Tillich remarks on the 'superiority of words over lines and colours' (*AA*, p. 72). Some comments in the *Systematic Theology* on the relationship between Word and Sacrament are also relevant in this connection: Sacraments, like works of art, mediate the spiritual presence by means of material, sensuous objects. Without the Word, however, sacraments cannot exist: 'the word is implicit in the completely silent sacramental material'.[12] Sacraments 'are not without words even if voiceless, because language is the fundamental expression of man's spirit. Therefore the Word is the other and ultimately more important medium'.[13]

This prioritising of the Word and of language in general is not diminished by Tillich's bold use of an aesthetic analogy by which he hopes to resolve one of the most vexed questions of modern theology, the question of the relationship between 'the Jesus of history' and 'the Christ of faith'. Indeed this only serves to confirm and, to some extent, explain his final preference for word over image. What the gospels give us, he says, is not a factual account of the life and times of Jesus of Nazareth. What they give is actually 'an "expressionist" portrait' of Jesus.[14] Their impact is more like that of a work of art than of a photograph or a piece of historical writing. The approach of the gospel writer is like that of a painter who 'would try to enter into the deepest levels of the person with whom he deals. And he could do so only by a profound participation in the reality and meaning of his subject matter'.[15] At first glance it would appear that Tillich is almost reducing the gospel to an aesthetic or artistic model, but in fact it turns out to be only a model. There is nothing to suggest that the gospels have ceased to be composed of words. Indeed it is precisely because of its word-character that the gospel can be heard as the Word of God: '"Word of God" is a term which qualifies human words as media of the Spiritual Presence . . . the Bible . . . is the Spirit's most important medium in the Western tradition'.[16] If the gospel were only an expressionist portrait of Jesus then it would be bound by the same limitations which apply to all other expressionist portraits. It could reveal the estrangement and abandonment of the Crucified One, who, in Tillich's view, is 'man as such', but it could not give 'an adequate expression of the transforming power of the New Being in Jesus as the Christ'.[17] To do that we must cross the line which separates vision and word, symbol and reality, art and religion, existential question and theological answer. Tillich, it would seem, remains true to his vocation as a Lutheran 'minister of the Word' and it is as true for him as it is, for example, for Bultmann, that the actual preaching of the Word remains the most potent and the most direct way of eliciting the response of faith. Art 'works' by referring us to a symbolic order which is more-than-aesthetic, an order whose 'reality' lies beyond the scope of images as such. It is only in relation to this reality that we can receive the 'answer' to the question with which art, at its most profound, confronts us.

What, in conclusion, is the view of nature presupposed in Tillich's theology of art? This theme, which has featured so prominently in other views we have been examining, seems to be almost entirely lacking here. Tillich scarcely seems to allow the artistic style he calls 'naturalistic' any significant degree of religious value. Thus, in *The*

Religious Situation, he charges both naturalism and impressionism
with representing 'the metaphysics of a finitude which postulates its
own absoluteness' (*AA*, p. 68). Naturalism embodies the objective
and impressionism the subjective pole of such a metaphysics. In
this sense naturalism in art forecloses on possibilities of religious
expression, since this can only occur when the surface of the visible
world gives way to a disclosure of deeper dimensions of reality. Naturalism subjects man to nature: 'Nature, not man, is the
embracing reality . . . nature is decisive' (*AA*, p. 35). The breakthrough to existential meaning is impossible in such a situation.
The very plenitude of nature in which Ruskin found a witness to
divinity becomes a theological obstacle. This is especially true when
it is precisely the absence or lack of God which is experienced as the
motor-force impelling human beings to seek God and to express that
seeking in art. And yet Tillich does not want to exclude the depiction
of nature from art. The question for him is rather what sort of relation to nature comes to expression in art. In his sermon 'Nature also,
mourns for a lost good' he examines the silence of nature in an age
of technological domination and exploitation of nature.[18] Nature, he
says, is not simply plenitude; nature too is subjected to vanity and
melancholy; nature confronts us with tragedy as well as harmony,
beauty and peace. To the extent that art is able to reach into this
tragic dimension it can find a religious significance in nature. In art
nature can be made to reveal its tragedy. Nature too can become
existential, as in Munch's evocation of 'cosmic dread'. Despite the
great distance separating Tillich's whole approach from that of
Ruskin we might just detect the possibility of some kind of dialogue
at this point. We might, for instance, compare Tillich's comments on
nature with Forsyth's interpretation of 'The Scapegoat' (and Peter
Fuller's comments on that interpretation). For Forsyth had argued
that precisely by means of its loyalty to nature art could disclose the
subjection and suffering of nature as being both a symbol of human
suffering and a revelation of the desecration of nature by a rapacious
and alienated humanity.

Throughout the 1950s and 60s Tillich was perhaps the nearest
thing this century has known to a fashionable theologian. His views
on art were published in popular magazines or delivered in lectures
at museums and galleries as well as in the more conventional media
of theological discourse. There is little doubt that they caught a particular current in contemporary American life, when existentialism
was, as Walter Kaufmann put it, a matter of 'fashion, chatter and

1. Rothko: *Light Red on Black.*

2. Sir Stanley Spencer: *The Resurrection, Cookham.*

3. Pieter Sanraedam: *The Interior of Buurkerk, Utrecht.*

4. Tintoretto: *Crucifixion*

5. Terborch: *The Peace of Munster.*

6. George Frederick Watts: *Hope.*

7. Botticelli: *Madonna with Angels.*

8. (*above*) Holman Hunt: *The Scapegoat*.

9. (*below*) Franz Marc: *Tierschicksale* (The Fate of Animals).

10. Andrei Rubliev: *The Holy Trinity.*

11. Claude Monet: *Waterlilies.*

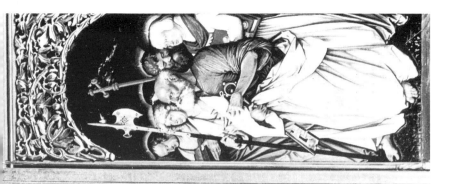

12. Hans Baldung: (Grien). *Krönung Mariä.*

13. L'iang K'au: *Sakyamuni Descending the Mountains.*

14.   Glynn Williams: *Pietà*

15. Antony Gormley: *Sound II*

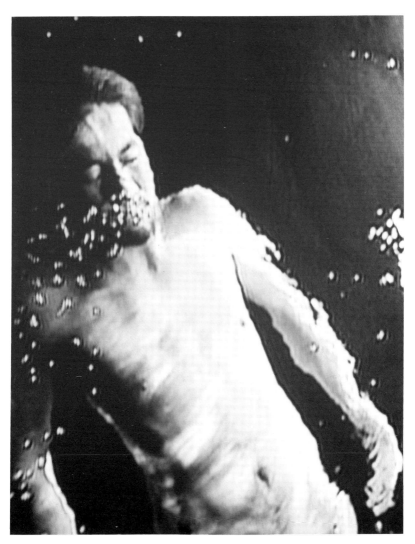

16. Bill Viola: *The Messenger*

17. Craigie Aichison: *Crucifixion 1994*

journalism'[19] as well as of more serious scholarly and cultural reception. The themes of angst and alienation struck chords at least in those levels of American society caught between a bewildering choice of identities in the post-war world, with nationalistic anticommunism at one extreme and the emergence of the 'beat generation' at the other. Although Tillich himself wrote relatively little about the abstract expressionism which became a significant movement in American art at this time, his theory of expressionistic style had a certain applicability to the task which such painters were setting themselves. John Dillenberger notes this parallel and comments that like Tillich 'these artists were striving for a view of the world and of art as a single, life-and-death issue. The question of art was a question of life; and life, of art'.[20] Arshile Gorky, for instance, took the theme for one of his paintings, *The Diary of a Seducer*, from Kierkegaard's work, and, as we shall see, Mark Rothko was to find support in Kierkegaard's writing for his own view of art.

Before Rothko turned to completely abstract painting several of his earlier works had evoked explicitly religious and tragic themes from antiquity: *Antigone, The Omen of the Eagle, Hierarchical Birds*. As Tillich had said of the first generation of expressionists this return to 'older, more primitive forms' was a deliberate attempt to draw on archaic powers with which to overthrow the complacency of a self-satisfied 'naturalism'. Rothko said that

> If our title recall the known myths of antiquity, we have used them again because they are the eternal symbols upon which we must fall back to express basic psychological ideas. They are the eternal symbols of man's primitive fears and motivations, no matter in which land or what time . . . Those who think that the world of today is more gentle and graceful than the primeval and predatory passions from which these myths spring, are either not aware of reality or do not wish to see it in art.[21]

'All primitive expression', his close fellow artist Adolph Gottlieb added, 'reveals the constant awareness of powerful forces, the immediate presence of terror and fear, a recognition and acceptance of the brutality of the natural world as well as the eternal insecurity of life'.[22] In line with Tillich's theological prescription these artists set out to plumb the darker depths of the human situation and only in and through such depths to reaffirm the fundamental religious truth of the situation. Gottlieb's *Evil Omen*, Robert Motherwell's striking *Elegies*, evocative of the cruelty and horror of the Spanish Civil War, and Rothko's black, grey and maroon abstracts all strike a dark and sombre chord. Speaking at the Pratt Institute in 1958, Rothko said that art should have 'A clear preoccupation with death. All art deals with intimations of mortality' with 'About 10 percent of hope . . . If you need that sort of thing: the Greeks never mentioned it'.[23] In a joint letter to the *'New York Times'* he and Gottlieb stated that 'only that subject matter is valid which is tragic and timeless'.[24] In the lecture at Pratt, Rothko referred to Kierkegaard's *Fear and Trembling* as containing a pertinent account of the artist's destiny in the modern world. *Fear and Trembling* centres on the predicament of Abraham, called on by God to sacrifice his only son, an act against all human reason and conscience. 'Abraham's act was absolutely unique', comments Rothko, ' . . . what Abraham was prepared to do was beyond understanding. There was no universal that condoned such an act. This is like the role of the artist'.[25] The artist must go beyond convention, beyond the given, beyond the accepted; he must break with tradition and expectation and venture alone, like Abraham, with fear and trembling into the dark places of the psyche, because it is only there that he will come face to face with the sources of transcendental experience. Rothko's appeal to Kierkegaard is striking, not least because he thereby effectively reverses Kierkegaard's own judgement on art. For Kierkegaard Abraham was specifically a religious hero, confronted with a religious problem, which aesthetics could not handle. To deal with such things we must leave art behind. Now, however, in the twentieth century art has taken on the religious task in the very terms defined by Kierkegaard. As the critic Stanley Cavell put it:

> both his and our concepts of aesthetics are historically condi-
> tioned; that the concepts of beauty and sublimity which he had
> in mind (in deploring the confusion between art and religion) are
> ones which our art either repudiates or is determined to win in
> new ways; that, in particular, our serious art is produced under
> conditions which Kierkegaard announces as those of apostleship,
> not genius . . . the activity of modern art, both in production and
> reception, is to be understood in categories which are, or were,
> religious.[26]

Rothko's final work was a commission for a series of paintings in what has come to be known as the Rothko Chapel in Rice University, Houston, Texas. His scheme consisted of fourteen paintings, each approx 10 feet by 15 feet, described as 'two triptychs with black geometric forms floating on a plum background . . . seven mono-chrome plum-coloured paintings and one solitary painting with a black form on a plum background'.[27] It is a sombre achievement and our reaction to it is inevitably coloured by the artist's suicide shortly after the completion of the work. Robert Hughes writes that 'It is hard to enter the Rothko Chapel without emotion, for its huge obscure paintings . . . have had the memorial dignity of funeral stelae given them by Rothko's death'. It is, he adds, 'The last silence of Romanticism'.[28] Here art itself eerily takes on the iconoclastic programme of religious existentialism. Is this, then, the culmination of a century and a half of artistic modernism and of the assault on what Tillich called the self-satisfied finitude of the bourgeois mind?

But, whilst recognising the dignity and even the grandeur of the achievement (words not often applicable to modern art), must we say with Rothko and Tillich that all attempts to depict the plenitude and the delight of the visible world are sentimental evasions of existential truth? Is this dark holy of holies the shrine at which a contemporary theology of art must consecrate itself? Is all art which would be religiously significant summonsed to such tragic seriousness? And may the bridge which leads from humanity to God henceforth be ventured only by such Abrahamic individuals as can brave its fear and trembling?

A theology of art forged in such an atmosphere may hold out a salutary 'discipline of the Void' (Don Cupitt) – but does it all end here? Without shrinking from such a discipline is it not possible to conceive of some kind of new beginning for art and religion 'beyond' the void? Is there to be no tenderness, no gaiety, no delight, no laughter, no transcendence of tragedy for art? Or must an art which once again finds a footing in the natural world and the great 'givens' of human life, be henceforth, as Peter Fuller requires, without God?

7
Icons of Glory

At this point our enquiry takes a sudden change of course. From the dark abysses of existentialism we turn to the luminous metaphysical confidence of the iconography of the Eastern Churches. This might seem to be a totally inconsequential step, since the whole ethos of icons is far removed from any of the views we have examined so far and stands altogether outside the line of that Western development, culminating in the modernist crisis, which is the context of this study. In addition it means taking a leap back in time from the twentieth century with its angst and tragedy to the Byzantine world and to that great flowering of Russian iconography in the fourteenth and fifteenth centuries.

But this sudden turn is by no means unpremeditated. For both the icons themselves and the theology of icons open up certain possibilities for a theology of art which are lacking or undeveloped in the Western tradition. In particular the Eastern tradition was able to provide a far more robust, yet highly theological, defence of the visual image than anything we have yet encountered in Western theologies of art. It is also distinctive in that it does not in any obvious way follow the pattern of 'natural theology' which characterises most Western approaches to art. The theology of icons does not start from the human subject of the natural world and then attempt to progress by a mixture of analogy and negation to the knowledge of God, but places the production and reception of icons themselves clearly within the economy of the divinely-initiated redemptive action. Neither of these contributions are without problems for a workable contemporary theological aesthetic and I shall be offering reasons why I do not believe that we can simply take the Eastern doctrine on board without qualification. Nonetheless the theology of icons can contribute to our own search for a new relationship between art and religion.

The introduction of this new theme at this point is quite easily justified. We have, very roughly, been following a line of development from the mediaevalism of Jacques Maritain through to the existentialism of Paul Tillich. But, from the point of view of the West, the impact of icons, as of Eastern theology generally, has been a very recent event. Moreover their positive reception in many quarters has often been related to the contrast between the world of icons and the decay and desolation of late modernism. Over against the fragmented values of Western materialism, Orthodox spirituality seems to offer the promise of deeply stable tradition enshrining spiritual values capable of resisting the ever more rapid and ever more vacuous pursuit of the new. In this connection the discovery of icons is very much a contemporary issue.

Orthodoxy maintains a strongly held tradition which traces the origin of icons back to the time of Christ. Such a view, of course, is in clear contrast to those Protestant and art-historical views which see the Early Church as having been entirely aniconic and which regard the introduction of visual art as a corruption of its original purity. A prominent place is given to the legend of Abgar, the ruler of the city of Edessa in the first century. Details of the story vary, but the general drift is similar. Abgar suffered from leprosy and, hearing news of the great miracle-worker in Palestine, sent his servant Ananias to persuade Jesus to come and heal him. Ananias attempted to draw a portrait of Jesus but was prevented from doing so by the dazzling light which radiated from him. Seeing Ananias' predicament Jesus provided an original solution. After washing himself he dried his face on a cloth and – lo and behold! – an image of his face was found to be imprinted on it. Although Jesus declined to journey to Edessa the cloth alone proved efficacious in healing Abgar and, displayed above the city gates, became the city's most treasured relic, known as the *mandylion*. This was later transferred to Constantinople where, in 944, the Emperor commissioned an official report on its origin. It was processed and displayed publicly on various occasions, one of the last of these being witnessed by the crusader Robert de Clari in 1203. Shortly after this it disappeared, although many copies had been made by this time. Some of these came to Europe, such as an icon painted *circa* 1200 in the Balkans and purchased in the mid-thirteenth century by the Archdeacon of Laon Cathedral, later Pope Urban IV. It is possible that the *mandylion* played a role in establishing iconographical norms for the representation of Christ, being, as it was supposed, a likeness from life. (In this respect the Orthodox would therefore reject the argument of the Elizabethan homilist that we simply do not know what Christ looked like as a human being.)

The story of the origin of the *mandylion* is plainly legendary, but that should not lead us to overlook its theological significance. For it highlights the Orthodox conviction that icons of Christ are not merely subjective artists' impressions of what Christ might have looked like but are reproductions of a true and objective model. It also points towards the key role which Christology plays in the doctrine of icons.

The place of icons in the Eastern Church was not secured without bitter and even violent controversy. Whatever the exact extent of the visual arts in the Church prior to the fourth century there can be little doubt that Constantine's endorsement of Christianity as the official religion of the Empire gave considerably greater scope to architects, sculptors, painters and other artists than had previously been the case. From this time onwards there is increasing evidence relating to the greater aesthetic ambience of the Church. Not all of this is favourable. One of the 'proof texts' used by iconaclasts in the Byzantine period itself and in the Reformation (it is found in the Homily *Against Peril of Idolatry*) is the description by the fourth century Bishop Epiphanius of Salamis of how he came across a Church in which the curtain hanging on the door

> bore an image either of Christ or of one of the saints; I do not rightly remember whose the image was. Seeing this, and being loth that an image of a man should be hung up in Christ's Church contrary to the teaching of the Scriptures, I tore it asunder and advised the custodians of the place to use it as a winding sheet for some poor person.[1]

It has recently been argued that this passage is not as obviously iconoclastic as a first reading would suggest, but whatever the meaning of Epiphanius's vigorous action the making and use of images continued to spread. From the seventh century onwards, however, the Eastern Empire was increasingly under pressure from the new faith of Islam, which was, of course, fiercely iconoclastic. Regions involved in subsequent controversies over images had often experienced Muslim as well as Christian rule and it is possible that the indirect influence of Islam helped to stir those controversies. Whatever the (doubtless complex) causes of Eastern iconoclasm the first official enactments against images were instituted by the Emperor Leo II between 726 and 730. As in the Protestant Reformation innumerable images of various kinds were destroyed, often with considerable violence and many iconodules (as supporters of the cause of icons are called) became martyrs. Over the next century the balance of power between the two parties was in a state of flux, until the final triumph of the iconodules in 843. The veneration of icons was re-admitted to the Church on terms drawn up by an Ecumenical Council of 787, under the protection of the pro-icon Empress Irene. (She was the particular target of the Elizabethan homilist in his lament over 'these Tragedies about images'.) The council declared that

> matter consisting of colours and pebbles and other material is appropriate in the holy Church of God, as sacred vessels and vestments, walls and panels, in houses and on the roads, as well as the images of our Lord and God and Saviour Jesus Christ, of our undefiled Lady, the Holy Mother of God, of the angels worthy of honour and of all holy and pious men. For the more frequently they are seen by means of pictorial representation the more those who behold them are aroused to remember and desire the prototypes and to give them greeting and the worship of honour . . . [2]

This final 'Triumph of Orthodoxy' (as the vindication of icons is called) is celebrated on the first Sunday in Lent in the Orthodox Churches, its very title providing a telling commentary on the status given to icons in those Churches.

In the later Byzantine period the cult of icons proliferated throughout the Eastern Churches, each region developing its own distinctive schools and styles. There are, for instance, immediate and striking differences between the icons of Greece, Constantinople and the various Russian schools such as Georgia, Novgorod and Moscow. Nor does the relative continuity of the tradition of of icon-painting mean that all historical development was prevented. Later Greek icons, for instance, show the clear influence of western, Renaissance technique and ideals.

Icon-painting was in many respects a highly *popular* art-form, an 'art of the tribe'. Many of the icons of saints, for example, have a surround depicting a variety of scenes from the life of the saint in question, very much along the lines of a strip cartoon. These set out unashamedly to tell a story, which they do dramatically, not sparing either grisly or humorous details.

One of the most significant developments in the history of icons was the emergence of the Russian schools of Novgorod and, especially, Moscow. Novgorod was an independent city ruled by a Boyar oligarchy which was already an important economic and cultural centre by the eleventh century, when the first icons were produced there. The Soviet historian of icons V. N. Lazarev emphasises the distinctive character of this new development:

> The artists of Novgorod did not favour complicated, intricate subjects. The involved symbolism of both Byzantine theologians and West European scholastics was alien to them. They preferred to depict the most venerated local saints . . . on whom they counted to help them in their farming and their trade. Lining the saints up in a row, beneath the image of the Virgin of the Sign, which came to be regarded as the city's emblem, Novgorodians treated the icon without undue ceremony, as an old friend. They confided their innermost thoughts to it, and they fully expected it to help them in everything that they regarded as important and urgent.[3]

Not, he goes on to say, that visionary or symbolic elements were lacking, but simply that the Novgorodians' metaphysical aspirations were firmly rooted in the everydayness of their economic, social and cultural life. This tradition reached its zenith in the fourteenth and fifteenth centuries by which time an equally significant school was coming into prominence in Muscovy, a school particularly associated with St. Andrei Rublev. Rublev's encounter, via Theophanes the Greek, with Byzantine traditions of icon-painting led to the inauguration of a new yet typically Russian development. Even though icon-painters operated in a workshop tradition with little or no emphasis on individual creativity – according to 'hieratic canon' as Eric Gill might have put it – and though there is no firm agreement on a number of works attributed to Rublev, commentators are united in praise of his achievement. As Leonid Ouspensky put it 'All the beauty of antique art here comes to life . . . His art is distinguished by a youthful freshness, a sense of measure, a supreme harmony of colours, enchanting rhythm and music of line'.[4] Rublev, like a number of other icon-painters, is customarily regarded as a 'saint' (itself a telling comment on the different status of art in the Eastern Churches), and his stature is indicated by the fact that he was chosen as the subject of a film by the Russian film maker Andrei Tarkovsky, who saw in Rublev a symbol of the artistic commitment to truth in a world of brutality and violence.

Bearing in mind the historical and regional variations in icon-painting, let us now move on to the theological understanding of them.

A first point arises directly from the practical eminence of icons in the Eastern churches. For good or ill the visual image is no longer subordinated to the *logos* or word. This closing of the gap between words and images, between theology in the narrow sense and iconography is expressed in various ways. Constantine Scouteris, for example, has written that 'icons are words in painting', ' . . . a visible gospel . . . ' and speaks of icons as themselves an aspect of proclamation rather than mere illustrations of it, referring to 'the iconic dimension of scripture and the scriptural dimension of icons'.[5] In a subtle and complex argument Vladimir Lossky distinguishes iconographical practices from scripture but not in any way in order to diminish their stature. For he argues that Orthodoxy maintains the irreducible status of Tradition alongside Scripture as a primary source of revelation. The key characteristic of Tradition in this sense is its manner of transmission. Assigning to 'Scripture' all those 'traditions' (with a small 't') which fall within the scope of the word, he claims that the reality of Tradition (capital 'T') is Silence. Citing the saying of Ignatius of Antioch that 'He who possesses in truth the word of Jesus can hear even its silence'[6], he claims that whilst Scripture is the proper realm of the Word, Tradition is the realm of the Spirit, comprising a unique mode of receiving revelation. It is within this realm of the Spirit, and therefore as a truly Spiritual and Trinitarian mode of receiving revelation, that iconographical practices find their proper place – within 'the Tradition of the Holy Spirit'.[7] 'Just as much as dogmatic definitions it has been possible for the icons of Christ to be allied with the Holy Scriptures, to receive the same veneration, since iconography sets forth in colours what the Word announces in written letters'.[8] His co-author, Leonid Ouspensky, does not pursue all the subtleties of Lossky's argument, but reaches a similar conclusion: 'that the Church sees in the icon not a simple art, serving to illustrate the Holy Scriptures, but a complete correspondence of the one to the other, and therefore attributes to the icon the same dogmatic, liturgic and educational significance as it does to the Holy Scriptures'.[9] Iconography, then, is visual theology, revelation in visual form.

I should now like to concentrate on three of the typical theological emphases which recur in Orthodox accounts of the theology of icons: the roles of Christology, of the Transfiguration (together with the theme of light) and of Eschatology.

All Orthodox writing on icons agrees in giving Christology a central place in the doctrine of icons. In this context the stance taken towards icons may even become a test of true Christological understanding such that the denial of the role of icons is a denial of the Incarnation. For, it is claimed, the Incarnation, as the assumption by the Second Person of the Trinity of a specific, visible, individual human form, makes the representation of Christ not merely possible but necessary. As we have seen, the legend of the *mandylion* encourages the confidence that such representation is no mere play of the imagination but a faithful representation of a divinely bestowed image. Thus the ninth century patriarch St. Nicephorus states that 'The humanity of Christ, if bereft of one of its properties, is a defective nature, and Christ not a perfect man, or rather not Christ at all. He is lost altogether if he cannot be circumscribed and represented in art'.[10]

A pictorial comment on the extent to which the doctrine of icons involves affirming the physical aspect of the Incarnation is provided by the difference between Eastern and Western conventions regarding the depiction of the baptism of Christ. In the West Christ is invariably shown in a loincloth. In the East, however, he is seen entering the river fully (though modestly) naked. This is a deliberate theological move relating to two complementary aspects of incarnational theology. Firstly it alludes to the *kenosis* or emptying of the divine nature according to the model of the Christological hymn of Philippians 2, vv. 5–11. Secondly, it points to the fact that this *kenosis* leads to a complete affirmation of the commensurability of the divine person and human flesh – 'by stripping His body, He thereby clothes the nakedness of Adam, and with him that of the whole of mankind, in the garment of glory and incorruptibility'.[11] One might add that the reticence of the West at this point says something both about its attitude to the reality of the Incarnation and about its attitude to art – both perhaps connected to deep-seated suspicions concerning the life of the body.

But what is the relationship between Christ and the icon with regard to the work of salvation? In order to answer this question we need to take note of the fact that Orthodoxy, because of its distinctive metaphysical thought, operates with a quite different concept of representation from that which has prevailed in the West. In the Orthodox doctrine of the Trinity, the Trinity is described in terms of the three hypostases (persons) and the one divine being (GK. = *ousia*). This is how the Byzantine theologian Theodore of Studios applies this vocabulary to the icon: 'In the icon of Christ there is no other hypostasis than that of Christ himself. It is the same hypostasis of Christ, the same character, which appears in the icon in its visible form'.[12] And, elsewhere, 'As there [in the Trinity] Christ differs from the Father in hypostasis, so here he differs from his own image in nature'.[13] What this means is that whereas the three hypostases of the Holy Trinity are united by virtue of the one divine *ousia* or being (which makes them divine!), the icon, whilst being hypostatically identical with Christ (i.e. representing the *same person/hypostasis*) will nonetheless have a different kind of *ousia* (being or nature) – namely, that which is proper to a created thing. On this understanding there can be no question of ascribing a false divinity to the icon – that is, idolising it – since it is never in doubt that its *being* is that appropriate to a creaturely, finite, limited object. The icon is identical with that which it represents in terms of *hypostasis* only, in a manner similar to that whereby the divine and human natures are, in the Incarnation, united in the one *hypostasis* of Christ.

In all this we should note that the whole theology of the icon is grounded specifically on the second person of the Trinity. Its exclusive association with his *hypostasis* rules out any thought that it might be possible in some way to represent the Father, who is separated from the realm of pictorial representation not only by virtue of his divine being, but also by virtue of his separate personhood. The Council of 787 which provided the standard definitions ordering the cult of icons specifically rejected the possibility of depicting God the Father.

The first part of our answer to the question as to the role of the icon in Christ's work of salvation is, then, that it is related to this work to the extent that its hypostatic union with Him makes possible.

We may, however, learn more by proceeding to our next theme: that of transfiguration. If the second person of the Trinity, incarnate in human form, is the source and justification of all iconography there are special moments in his earthly life which point to further ramifications of the theology of icons. His baptism, to which we have already alluded, is one. Another is the story of the Transfiguration, when his human form was seen by Peter, James and John as irradiated by a light brighter than any created light. This story plays a far more prominent role in the East generally than it does in the West. In Orthodoxy it is taken to be not just a revelation to the disciples of the 'secret identity' of Christ but also a revelation of what we ourselves are destined to become. Orthodox theology speaks quite frankly about *theōsis*, deification, the ultimate union of the human person with the Godhead. Whilst the language of redemption and salvation relates to the negative aspect of our fallen condition, deification points to the positive aspect of the same process. 'Man is thus to reunite by grace two natures in his created hypostasis, to become a "created god", a "god by grace", in contrast to Christ who being a divine person assumed human nature'.[14] In the Transfiguration the disciples saw (as we can literally see in the icon) the actuality of the co-existence in one person of the divine and the human. In the words of the nineteenth century Bishop Philaret, quoted by Ouspensky, 'On Mount Tabor not only does the divinity appear to men, but manhood appears in Divine glory'.[15] In Ouspensky's own words, the Lord's body is seen to become 'a radiant raiment of the Deity'.[16] But the key point is that all of this is not merely a historic occurrence in the human life of Christ but is an anticipation of our own future glory. It is what we too may become.

The story of the Transfiguration plays particularly strongly, of course, on the imagery of light, perhaps one of the most universal symbols of divinity (cf. Ruskin's 'golden rule' regarding light backgrounds). Many Eastern theologians would wish to affirm with St. Gregory Palamas, whose theology of light is particularly boldly expressed, that 'the theology of Light is not a metaphor, a literary fiction lending an affected disguise to some abstract truth'.[17] Light is not merely a symbol or image of the divinity: it is divinity. Thus, in the Transfiguration, what the disciples saw was not simply an illumination of Christ's body from some external source; what they saw was the divine light itself, totally identical with the singular divine person in human form whom they beheld with their bodily eyes. Ouspensky, commenting on the definition of the Seventh Ecumenical Council adds that the icon itself is an image 'not of corruptible flesh, but of flesh transfigured, radiant with divine light'.[18]

This in turn relates to the justification for what Western viewers might be tempted to regard as the conventionalism of icons and their general lack of realism. But the aim of the icon-painter is not to portray a physical likeness according to our limited understanding of what a physical body is. It is rather to represent the divine prototype of the human person, either directly (as in icons of Christ) or indirectly (as in icons of the saints, who share in some measure in the transfiguring light of Christ). It is the divine aspect of the person which the icon-painter aims to show, and his task is not falsified by what Ouspensky refers to as any 'defect of resemblance'. The artist seeks to portray the spiritual aspect of the scene or person, not 'what it was like'. In accordance with this principle the details of a saint's appearance 'lose the sensory aspect of corruptible flesh and become spiritualised . . . this . . . is the visible expression of the dogma of transfiguration'.[19] This spiritualisation manifests itself in some of the standard conventions of Eastern iconography: the thin nose, the small mouth and the large eyes are all marks of a nature which is growing towards its destiny of beholding and adoring for eternity the radiance of the divine glory.

As far as the eschatological aspect of icons is concerned much has already been said, at least by implication. The icon anticipates that destiny which all the faithful are to attain, when our human nature is transfigured and deified by the eternal and uncreated divine light. A final comment may be added however. This is that the representative function of the icon is once more seen in a quite different way in the East than in the West. John Zizioulas has argued that the Augustinian-Platonic notion of representation sees the image as the reflection or copy of some pre-existent thing. On such an understanding it is inevitable that iconographical symbolism is seen as determined by a reality which exists otherwise than and 'outside' of its image. The image is a kind of memory trace. In the Eastern tradition, however, there is 'no tendency to understand the εικών in a retrospective psychological sense'.[20] The truth of the icon is seen rather as the truth of what we are to become as it opens up 'a new set of relationships, a new "world" adopted by the community as its final destiny'.[21]

In the proper liturgical and devotional contexts then the wor-shipper is not seeking (as a Catholic worshipper kneeling before a holy picture might seek) to raise her mind above the level of her eyes. There is a plenitude of divine truth working transfiguratively as part of the process of deification in the icon itself. The icon makes the fulness of what is to come, the fulness of things hoped for, concretely present.

All this would seem to have implications for the actual practice of icon-painting itself, the way in which the icon is visually constructed. Thus, for example, it would seem that any crude sort of allegorising or symbolisation which might suggest that the truth of the icon was actually elsewhere than in the picture itself is 'out'. The material element, the actual configuration of space, form and colour, must be treated in such a way as to meet the requirement that it is completely congruent with its religious meaning. It may not allow itself to subserve other – ecclesiastical, idealistic or historical – levels of meaning.

This is, of course, a prodigious challenge, but the claim has been made that this is what is in fact achieved. Aidan Nichols, for instance, holds it to be true of all genuine artworks that 'the meaning embodied in the artwork is communicated, then, in a unique *sui generis* manner. It is found in the very organization of the sensuous and lies in the spatial schemata of the canvas'.[22] This holds good, he believes, of icons, whose iconology, he says, 'is not . . . purely an affair of themes superimposed on the painterly techniques of artists to give art a theological coherence. It is partly achieved by the distinctively painterly means of colour and line'.[23] Indeed, if the theology of icons is developed along the lines I have been suggesting, this must be so, since such a theology requires the elimination, as far as this is possible, of the gap between representation and that which is represented. Let us now test this out with regard to a specific example, taking what is perhaps the best-known of all Russian icons, the 'Old Testament Trinity' by Andrei Rublev. [Plate 10]

Painted sometime between 1408 and 1425 this icon depicts the three angels said to have been entertained by Abraham at his dwelling at Mamre (Genesis 18). This episode had from early times been seen in Christian circles as a prophetic anticipation of the revelation of God in Trinity and the angels identified as the three persons of the Godhead. The subject-matter therefore offers the painter the possibility of depicting a scene which belongs fully to the visible world yet which can also be seen as involving a direct encounter with the divine *and* without transgressing the dogmatic ban on the representation of the supreme divinity of the Father.

Rublev's construction is geometrically balanced. The 'angels' sit round a table in the foreground of the picture, one on the right, one on the left and one in the middle, sitting on the far side of the picture from ourselves. They are inscribed within an almost visible circle, which is in itself a potent symbol of unity-in-multiplicity.

From left to right these figures represent the Father, the Son and the Holy Spirit respectively. The two right-hand figures (the Son and the Spirit) are inclined towards the figure on the left, thereby indicating his eminence, whilst the middle figure (the Son) occupies both the central position and highest position on a vertical axis, thus establishing another kind of eminence. The greater clarity and precision with which his robes are painted suggests, according to Ouspensky, that he is a historically specific individual. The colours of the robes also serve to differentiate the three persons according to established iconographical conventions. At the same time the strong facial similarity of the three, as well as their enclosure within a common circle, strengthen our sense of their fundamental unity.

Turning to other aspects of the picture we see in the background (again moving from left to right) a house, a tree and a mountain. These all relate to elements in the biblical narrative. The house is that of Abraham himself, the tree the oak of Mamre mentioned in the text, and the mountain is the mountain of Moriah where Abraham was to go in order to sacrifice Isaac. But the associations of these images have an intrinsic value apart from that which they derive from the text. John Baggley comments that the house is a symbol of 'our own inner world', the self; the tree, 'a symbol of the Tree of life and spiritual growth'; the mountain, 'a symbol of an event of profound significance'.[24] These are not simply arbitrary associations but correspond to the very basic, bodily way in which we experience these realities. The house is that which encloses us, that in which we feel ourselves secure, the 'parental home'. The tree is a form of life which thrust up from the darkness of enclosure in the earth to spread out in the warmth and light, developing a rich foliage, yet remaining firmly rooted. The mountain (quite bare in Rublev's picture) is that up which we must ascend slowly, painfully, having left behind the natural vitality of the sap which flows up from the ground – yet in the journey upward we are still following the same direction as that of the life force of the tree, up towards the summit as an open space of clarity, vision, light. In these images then there is a communication of a very basic pattern of spiritual life and growth.

The colour and tone of the picture also deserves comment. Lazarev:

Perhaps the most remarkable thing about the icon is the colouring. The viewer is primarily impressed with the unparalleled 'singing' quality of the hues . . . The choice of colours, which could be

described as 'sympathetic' to one another, conveys . . . the feeling
of accord amongst the three angels . . . Combining three shades of
blue, the painter weaves subtle harmonies which supplement and
enhance each other producing an effect of exquisite purity.[25]

Lazarev also speaks of the 'extreme luminosity and exceptional
transparency' of the colours in the painting. This delicacy, tenderness
and harmony of colour corresponds, in Lazarev's view, to Rublev's
essential concept of God. 'To Rublyov God was not the terrifying,
blind and merciless force He was to the ordinary mediaeval mind.
Rublyov humanised God and made Him seem closer to the world.
There is nothing in the painter's icons to inspire fear or to demand
mortification of the flesh'.[26]

There is one more feature of the icon which requires comment at this stage, a feature found in many icons. It is the
strange distortion and even reversal of perspective to be found
in it – in, for instance, the construction of Abraham's house and
the chairs (or thrones) on which the angels are seated. It is not,
as interpreters of icons insist, a result of the painter simply not
understanding the laws of perspective. It is rather a deliberate
disruption of our 'normal' visual expectations. We no longer
find ourselves in the position of spectators who dominate the
scene by our sovereign glance, enclosing it within our 'point of
view'. It is more as if we ourselves were being looked at! As
Ouspensky put it

> A man stands, as it were, at the start of a pathway which is not
> concentrated on some point in depth, but which unfolds itself
> before him in all its immensity. Inverse perspective does not
> draw in the eye of the spectator . . . it concentrates the attention
> on the image itself.[27]

It is, we may say, a manifestation of the eschatological world, the
redeemed and deified world, the divine life itself, reaching out into
the world of the 'spectator', transforming and transfiguring it into
the reality which is 'represented' there.

To a considerable extent then the claim is justified that the
painterly technique is throughout determined by its theological
conception, or, rather, that the method of painting itself is theologically conceived, without the use of allegory or extrinsic and
obtrusive symbolism.

Yet there is a paradox here. Although the tradition and practice of eastern iconography may in this way offer a more immediate blending of visual form and theological meaning than in much of the religious art of the West (and therewith a more robust affirmation of the theophanous potentialities of matter) it nonetheless treats its material, visual element in a distinctive way. The icon in one sense deconstructs the given sensuous, material world. In particular the use of inverse perspective and stylisation ('spiritualisation') of figure and gesture seems to imply an abstract rather than a concrete engagement with the world of matter and sense. The 'matter' of the icon is not the 'matter' of the world of sensuous experience and activity. It is not the world as seen by the physical eye but the world as seen by the spiritual eye. Its matter is a different kind of matter. Matter is reassembled on a different plane, within the horizon of another (eschatological) plane. The flesh which it reveals is a flesh whose desires and passions have been vanquished and subjugated. Despite Lazarev's comment that there is no call for the mortification of the flesh in Rublev's work, and despite the claims made by commentators that there is nothing here of the kind of world-denying 'spiritualism' of the Augustinian-Platonic tradition of ascetic spirituality, there is nonetheless a kind of Platonism and a kind of asceticism in these pictures.

We may recall, as John Baggley emphasises, that this is essentially a monastic art produced under strict ascetical traditions. Its spiritual context is that of the *Philokalia* (a collection of monastic and eremetical texts collected in the eighteenth century) and of the hesychasts (practitioners of the mantra-like repetition of the sacred name of Jesus). Baggley gives many extracts from the *Philokalia* which give something of the flavour of its spiritual attitude. For example: 'If, then, you wish to behold and commune with Him who is beyond sense-perception and beyond concept, you must free yourself from every impassioned thought'.[28] And: 'You cannot attain pure prayer while entangled in natural things and agitated by constant cares'.[29] It is, in short, a spirituality of ascesis, of solitude, of the celibate, undistracted life, of a life of total conversion and sanctification. It is in this context that the tendency towards abstraction, the stylisation and the conventionalism of much icon-painting is to be understood. The icon-painters and their defenders are, at the end of the day, no less – perhaps more – suspicious of the body and the visible world than their western counterparts. It is perhaps simply that they have ascended so far up the ascetical ladder that they are confident of being able to re-order matter on their own terms. I do not mean to suggest that such a spirituality is worthless and I certainly do not want to imply that its art is devoid of beauty or sublimity. But there are dimensions which are totally absent from it. Its world is a thoroughly religious world. There is no attention to the human figure, to worldly situations, to natural forms and colours as being of interest and value in themselves. Its world is a sacred world, turned away from the concerns of secular living and the common life in the world. There is no sign of either artistic or spiritual existence having been risked in the dangers and delights of the sensuous phenomenality of life.

But all this is precisely the starting-point for the theology of art which we are seeking here, since our theology respects (because it knows in the experience of those who write it) the truth of the modern affirmation of autonomy and worldliness both in life and in art. And our theology knows that it cannot hope to respond to the crisis of modernism and post-modernism by simply turning its back on the whole development which has led us to this point.

There has been an astonishing flowering of interest in icons over the last twenty years. This may simply be an accident resulting from the opening up of previously little-known cultural traditions. Yet, as Sartre said, there are no accidents in life. If this interest has flowered at this time it may be precisely because the world of icons seems to offer one kind of way out from the present confusion of religious and cultural values, a way out of the complexity, darkness and flux of human affairs into the abstract clarity of a heavenly order. But it is unlikely that any theological response to the present will stick unless it addresses the concrete historical form of the present. It may be both refreshing and stimulating to step sideways out of our own situation into the realm of another cultural tradition but neither Orthodoxy (nor any other tradition) can resolve questions which have arisen within the very specific horizons of western thought and culture. Yet as we return to the West and its concern for 'creation's images . . . in their sensuousness'[30] we may take with us something of the Orthodox conviction that images may attain an equal dignity with words in the communicating of divine things, and, following from this, that in doing so they do not need to be reduced to symbols or allegories.

As a footnote it might be remarked that much that has been said here would support the view that Kandinsky's path to abstraction was influenced by his own Orthodox background.

Although he himself referred to theosophy as a main force in this there is in icon-painting itself a tendency towards abstraction (as in Rublev's noticeable use of geometrical shapes, both in the 'Trinity' and elsewhere). It may also have influenced his strongly spiritual conception of the task of the artist. But this only further highlights the problem of the tradition of icons in relation to a quest for an art which finds itself at home amidst the forms, structures and colours of the natural world.[31]

8

Restoring the Image

The Western Christian tradition is, as we have seen at many points, pervaded by a consensual suspicion concerning the visual. The meaning or value of simply *seeing* is almost invariably justified by referring our acts of seeing to another 'higher' level of meaning. The extreme form of such suspicion is to be found in the iconoclastic movements and theologies which have remained a persistent feature of the tradition. But even those theologies which seem to offer greater scope for art often turn out to maintain a considerable reserve with regard to the material, visible world. Much of this is connected with the Christian appropriation of platonic and other metaphysical themes derived from classical culture, as well as from the iconoclastic thrust of the second commandment and other biblical texts. It is in this respect notable that even the Orthodox veneration of icons, whilst affirming the theophanous possibilities of icons, distances itself from an unrestrained affirmation of the visual realm as such, a realm which gives itself to an eye which is both sensuous and carnal.

Another characteristic of the tradition is the location of theological discussions of art in the realm of natural theology. Artistic practices, together with that realm of visibility from which they arise and in which they take on form, are discussed in terms of humanity's 'natural' endowments and capacities. They are not seen – except in certain specific cases – in the context of redemption. As such they are therefore regarded as being by definition outside the sphere of grace, even if grace is understood as having a positive relation to the natural world. The Eastern Church is perhaps distinctive at this point, but Calvin is paradigmatic of western theology when he treats art under the rubric of 'the knowledge of God the Creator', finding no place for it in relation to 'our knowledge of God the Redeemer'.

In this chapter I wish to question both these assumptions: that the visual is not capable of communicating meaning in and of itself and that the theological context of a theology of art lies outside the

134

sphere of a theology of redemption. More positively, I wish to argue that a theology of art which is to be of service in the context of the present relationship between art and religion will need to affirm that the processes of *seeing* are of irreducible value in human life and that they must on this account continue to be characteristic of the human subject when he or she is caught up into the processes of redemption. This involves moving away from traditional metaphysical perspectives towards a more dynamic, relational and historical way of looking at things, which can, arguably, be said to represent better the characteristic language of the Bible itself. From this point of view the meaning of the work of art (or, perhaps better, the presence of the work of art) is not reducible to the play within it of some higher level of meaning or being. It is rather an aspect of the concrete *prolepsis*, or irruption into presence, of an act of redemption whose fulness lies in the future which is nonetheless completely itself in its every manifestation. The familiar dualities of image and idea, natural form and transcendent truth are no longer relevant in this context. What is more to the point is whether what we think, feel, see, say, do or make enhances our capacity to affirm ourselves, our fellow human-beings and our world as 'God's good gifts in creation'. To the extent that we are able to make such affirmations we stand already within the circle of redemption and of the fulfilment of the original judgement on creation: that God saw that it was good. Such movements of aesthetic enhancement of life constitute an awakening of the lure to participate in the divine dance 'from glory to glory advancing' – and this is no less so when the content of such a movement is predominantly sensuous and material.

The requirement for a contemporary theology of art to be unashamedly sensuous has been noted both by Nicholas Wolterstorff and John Dillenberger, two major contributors to current discussions of religion and aesthetics. Wolterstorff (whose work is not exclusively concerned with the visual arts) sees all significant art as located at the point where the earthliness of human existence on the one hand and the dialectic of fall-and-redemption on the other intersect. But this does not mean that the artist's religious 'beliefs and goals, convictions and concerns'[1] are simply stamped on to an indifferent matter. The artist must work with the grain of the material itself: 'her material is not some infinitely protean stuff. It has a nature. There are laws holding for it. The stage of actuality is God's structured creation'.[2] What counts, then, is what Wolterstorff calls 'fittingness', that is, getting the right fit between the matter and that which is represented

in it. The matter of art itself matters. Wolterstorff is convinced (in
my view rightly) that 'Earthly existence is one of God's favours to
us',[3] with the result that 'when you and I carve wood, apply paint
to canvas, pile stone on stone, or inscribe marks on paper, we are
dealing with things which bear to us the most intimate of relations.
To an angel art must seem a very foreign thing indeed. With us it
shares its substance'.[4] (We may note that there are interesting points
of contact here with Gilson's conception of the material element in
art and the way in which matter itself requires a certain form.[5])
Dillenberger, whose overriding concern is with visual art, pleads
for a 'theology of artistic sensibilities' and makes it clear that it is
not just an 'aesthetic' sensibility in the narrow sense that is at stake
here. For this is only a part of 'a theology of wider sensibilities'.[6]
Against 'the alleged purity of intellect and the seductiveness of the
sensual' he affirms that 'the emotional, which is related to the senses,
is a pervasive part of existence'.[7] Whilst not denying the value of
rationality or language he confesses himself to be uneasy at the 'total
victory' of these 'higher' elements over touch, sight and hearing.
In this context the triumph of a logocentric civilisation becomes
'oppressive as well as liberating'.[8] But, it seems, this victory is not
yet final: 'There is, however, a residual, almost magical power to
the visual, which has not lent itself to exorcism by a reading, verbal
culture'.[9] It is to the rescue and rehabilitation of this residual vision
that Dillenberger's work is devoted and to the recognition that it
requires of us a definite discipline, however different that may be
from the customary verbal disciplines of the humanities. 'Precisely
because art has a seductive character, sensuous to the core', he says, 'a
discipline of seeing . . . learned by repeated seeing and essentially in
no other way, forms the seductive into a discriminating sensuousness
that is more than itself'.[10]

But isn't all this little more than a re-hash of familiar (and discred-
ited) Romantic theories? I do not think so. For a start Romanticism
in many ways remained within the paradigms of metaphysical
knowledge, only, instead of seeing reason and intellect as the paths
to absolute knowledge (or knowledge of the absolute), it preferred
the claims of intuition and imagination. The yield of intuitive experience (including aesthetic experience) was seen as superior to that of
the discursive intellect – but both were nonetheless conceived as
different ways of reaching the same end. Against such Romanticism
I am not claiming epistemological finality, or absoluteness of any
kind, for the sensuous vision which inheres in the core processes

of artistic making and reception. The religious significance of such seeing is in its being just what it is and no more – no key to universal mysteries, no glimpse of a reality behind or beyond the veil of sense. Although I call for a distinction between the realms of such seeing and of language this is not in order to establish any kind of hierarchy between them. It is in this respect curious that whilst metaphysical thought betrays a consistent suspicion of the sensuously visible it nonetheless speaks of its own project in highly visual terms. 'Vision' itself, along with contemplation, intuition, idea and cognate terms are used throughout the tradition to describe mental acts which are in fact far removed from the context of sensuous visibility in which these words have their *sitz-im-leben*. Part of the programme of restoring the image must also be to re-examine those linguistic confusions which allow the metaphysician to imagine that he is taking the real essence of vision along with him in his journey towards the metaphysical heights. As opposed to Romantic aesthetics, then, the project of *this* theology of art is both modest and chaste. It is, in this respect, simply to call things by their right names.

An initial step in re-evaluating vision along the lines I have suggested might be to re-examine the concept of representation itself. For one aspect of the demotion of art to a kind of second-order activity is the way in which the truth of art is persistently understood as being somewhere other than in the art-work itself. It might, for instance, be 'in' the scene or figure of which the art-work is a copy or imitation. Or it might be 'in' the intellectual or emotional life of the artist which the work 'expresses'. In both cases, however, the meaning of the work of art is seriously dislocated. A classical example of this is Hegel's distinction between representation and concept. Representation is the appearance, the phenomenal surface which shows itself to vision and is bound by the limits of the external, material world. The concept is the inner truth or idea which, though it has the same ultimate content as representation *knows* exhaustively that which is only 'represented' in representation itself. Art operates on the level of representation, picturing the surface appearance – even the arts of language are constrained by their figurative, representational character. Philosophy, however, penetrates behind the surface and grasps the concept or idea which is 'only' intuited in art. (Religion is seen as occupying a kind of middle ground which Hegel refers to as 'picture-thinking'.[11]) Hegel, as usual, betrays his own distinctive emphases in all this, yet he does in many ways also reveal an underlying theme in the Western tradition of thinking about art. For it suggests, as philosophers as diverse as Plato and Kierkegaard have maintained, that art is somehow a 'lie', a 'ghost story', as Derrida has put it,[12] in which it is far from obvious who the real 'owner' of the work is.

In his thoughtful essay *The Art of God Incarnate* Aidan Nichols has stipulated that we should learn to take artistic experience 'as a unique form of communication not to be reduced to some more general category less than itself'.[13] Nichols is in particular concerned to rescue aesthetic experience from being reduced to a function of the inner psychological states either of the artist herself or of the recipient of the work. The judgement that a work of art is beautiful or of value is not, he says, simply a matter of the sensations it awakens in us (as Ruskin had already insisted on by distinguishing theoria from aesthesis). Yet, like Wolterstorff and Dillenberger, he emphatically affirms what he calls the 'sensory matrix' of the art-work as 'an integral aspect of its being and its value to the perceiver'.[14] As well as calling for a fuller recognition of the value of the Orthodox doctrine of icons he appeals to Heidegger's phenomenological approach to art as embodying precisely the sort of respect for the proper autonomy of the art-work. He does not himself develop this suggestion, but, I believe, Heidegger does offer an important attempt to rethink the basis on which we look at the art-work and, in particular, at the kind of concept of representation which is presupposed in conventional aesthetics. His phenomenological approach also allows us to integrate into our thinking that subjective element which Ruskin recognised but which Peter Fuller's empiricist reinterpretation of Ruskin notably neglects.

Heidegger saw the crux of the Western tradition of thinking about art in the distinction between matter and form, according to which the material, sensory surface or objective structure is conceived as a 'vehicle' for the expression of form. In this respect it makes little difference whether that form is thought of metaphysically (as an objective, transcendent idea) or whether it is seen as an idea or a feeling in the mind of the artist. Either way the art-work is being torn apart and the material element in it downgraded. But this, Heidegger says, is 'the conceptual schema which is used, in the greatest variety of ways, quite generally for all art theory and aesthetics'.[15]

Instead Heidegger sets out to look at art from the standpoint of its 'thingly' element.[16] What is the 'thingliness' of the work of art? It has, for instance, been conceived of as 'the core' of an object 'around which the properties have assembled', corresponding to the Greek concept of the *hypokeimenon* and (in what for Heidegger is a fateful translation) the Latin *substantia* (substance).[17] Or, it may be regarded as 'that which is perceptible be sensations in the senses belonging to sensibility', corresponding to the Greek *aesthesis*, that is, that which is immediately present to the senses of sight, hearing and touch.[18] Or, again, 'the thing is formed matter', a synthesis of matter (*hylē*) and form (*morphē*). In this case the thingly element in the work of art 'is manifestly the matter of which it consists. Matter is the substrate and field for the artist's formative action'.[19] He is suspicious of all these interpretations, however, observing that in fact 'Form and content are the most hackneyed concepts under which anything and everything may be subsumed'.[20] When this pair of concepts is further correlated with such other pairs as rational-irrational, logical-alogical, then, he says, 'representation has at its command a conceptual machinery that nothing is capable of withstanding'.[21]

So where do the concepts of form and content/matter derive from? They belong, Heidegger says, to the domain of 'usefulness'. Whatever is properly designated as 'useful', however, 'is made as a piece of equipment for something'.[22] Consequently 'matter and form have their proper place in the essential nature of equipment'.[23] As a result of this the 'matter' side of the equation almost invariably becomes 'mere' matter, subordinated to the end (*telos*) which the form bestows on it. Thus, for example, the thingly element in a shotgun is the wood and the metal, shaped and worked according to a certain form in order to enable it to function as a shotgun. The material is chosen and worked entirely from the standpoint of its eventual use. But this way of understanding the thingly element of a product is customarily transferred to our understanding of the work of art. Thus the thingly element of the art-work comes to be seen as a 'mere' means, a material, visual means, by which to communicate something which essentially belongs to a quite different order of things. Heidegger also remarks that the Christian tradition of thinking of God as Creator reinforces the prevalent role of this matter/form distinction in Western thought. For it all too easily leads to us seeing the whole of creation, the whole of the material world, as being no more than a means by which God aims to accomplish his spiritual end. The whole creation is the matter on which the divine craftsman impresses the particular form he desires to give it. And if that is how things are with the

Creator and his world, what more can we expect from a human artist?

Heidegger's own example of a piece of equipment is a pair of boots such as might belong to a peasant woman. In a controversial move he asks us to visualise one of Van Gogh's paintings of such boots,[24] and then proceeds to show how the picture discloses to us the woman's relation to the earth and to her world as that is given in and with this essential piece of equipment. The painting, he says, discloses 'what the equipment, the pair of peasant shoes, is in truth'.[25] It does this, moreover, in a way which no technical or factual analysis could match.

Now Heidegger notoriously gives such terms as 'world' and 'truth' highly specific meanings. 'World' does not mean the sum-total of empirically-observable reality. To have a world or to exist in a world is 'to dwell in the overtness of beings'.[26] It is a uniquely human way of existing, standing out from the silent, self-enclosed reality of the earth. 'Truth' is similarly said to occur within 'the unconcealedness of beings' and Heidegger draws on his distinctive interpretation of the Greek word for truth, *alētheia*, to ground this conception. *A-Lētheia* is, he asserts, that which does not pass away into the water of forgetfulness (*Lēthē* in Greek mythology), hence that which can be said to be 'unconcealed'. What is 'at work in the work' of art, then, is 'the disclosure of the particular being in its Being, the happening of truth'.[27] In this perspective it is a complete mistake to talk about the thingly element as if it were a kind of substratum lying 'beneath' the form. That is once again to see the function of art in terms of equipment. But the truth of art is more fundamental than that. Work in general, and the art-work in particular, is the happening of truth in the sense of the opening up of an 'open region', a realm of 'unconcealedness' within which human values and decisions can, for the first time, come to articulation.

In order to secure this account Heidegger moves on to another work of art, a Greek Temple. Even less than Van Gogh's boots does such a work of art serve to give us any kind of insight into the thoughts and feelings of the artist. It is rather the Temple itself which first gives to a historical community its experience of itself as a distinctive community.

It is the temple-work that first fits together and at the same time gathers round itself the unity of those paths and relations in which birth and death, disaster and blessing, victory and disgrace, endurance and decline acquire the shape of destiny for a human being.[28]

Equally it is the temple-work, as a work of art, which first gives a specific shape to the earth itself, to the rock on which it stands, to the air which surrounds it and the creatures of the land whose destiny it reveals.

> Tree and grass, eagle and bull, snake and cricket first enter into their distinctive shapes and thus come to appear as what they are . . . The temple, in its standing there, first gives to things their look and to men their outlook on themselves.[29]

In short, 'to be a work means to set up a world'.[30]

Once more the contrast between the material element in a piece of equipment and the material element in a work of art is firmly drawn. In the case of the former, the material 'is used, and used up. It disappears into usefulness. The material is all the better and more suitable the less is resists perishing in the equipmental being of the equipment'.[31] And, of course, this is how the material element of the art-work has all too often been understood. The function of the material is simply to make way for the 'meaning' or 'idea' which the matter serves to represent. On Heidegger's account, however, the art-work, within which the 'world worlds' 'does not cause the material to disappear, but rather causes it to come forth for the very first time . . . metals come to glitter and shimmer, colors to glow, tones to sing, the word to say'.[32] This is no less the case with respect to religious works of art. Religious meaning too belongs to that world which the work of art can uniquely open up.

After all this it may perhaps be surprising that Heidegger gives clear priority to the arts of language, to poetry: 'language alone brings beings as beings into the open for the first time, first brings being to work and to appearance'.[33] Consequently 'the essence of art is poetry'.[34] Thus, although several of Heidegger's examples are taken from the plastic arts and although he provides considerable help towards preparing the ground for the kind of theology of art we are seeking here he does not himself offer a definitive basis for that theology.

Heinrich Rombach, a pupil of Heidegger's, has, however, extended the principles of Heideggerian analysis in the direction of a philosophy of vision. In his book *Life of the Spirit* (*Leben des*

Geistes) he sets out what he calls a 'concrete philosophy' elucidating humanity's constantly rediscovered and re-established relation to 'the basic structure of its existence'.[35] This is conceived as a history of those basic decisions, actions and conceptions which, in the sense of Heidegger's account of the Greek temple-work are foundational for the various epochs of human existence. In pursuing this task he draws on what he calls the 'tradition of images' (*Bildtradition*) which, he says, is 'older and more comprehensive than the written tradition'.[36] Thus

> Grasped as an image the basic character of a farmhouse says a great deal more about the 'spirit' of the country, and a style of building reveals more of the basic philosophy of a period than the carefully smoothed-out texts of the school-philosophy of that time . . . The images of [human] self-interpretation provide the only steps by which we may descend to the events of fundamental history with which we are here concerned.[37]

Images are not arbitrary or individually contrived. They embody the 'style' of an age outside which no thought and no philosophy is able to reach – although that 'style' is not necessarily what those who live within it are consciously aware of. Such fundamental images, he says, 'provide the ground for every kind of assertion, but are never themselves objects of our assertions'.[38] He does not, therefore, offer 'a text to read' but 'images to see' in an attempt to re-awaken his fellow philosophers and intellectuals to a dimension which they have largely overlooked.[39] The range of these images is vast: from documentary photographs of contemporary wars and news events, through the work of great artists of various traditions to artefacts and relics of ancient or primitive cultures.

His concluding remarks make it clear that he regards a philosophy of images as providing a unique mode of access to a hitherto unexplored dimension of history and of Being. He connects this project with a theme which also runs through much of Heidegger's thinking, the theme of the crisis of scientific knowledge and the search for the proper limits of such knowledge. In Rombach's view the history of science, as a history of successive scientific paradigms or epochs, is conceivable in its entirety as a single epoch, the epoch of scientific knowledge (*Wissenschaft*) which he believes is now being called radically into question. He regards the philosophy of images as a rigorous and disciplined path, leading thought in the direction of a post-scientific conception of spirit in which the ideal of a universalised knowledge, whether in the humanities or in the natural sciences, is no longer dominant. Images may prove able to guide us through fields where knowledge cannot go.[40] These reflections may be read as, in part, a commentary on the modernist/post-modernist crisis described in the first chapter of this book, and as the proposing of one way out of, or through, that crisis.

Another phenomenological approach which offers a promising philosophical defence of vision can be found in the work of the French phenomenonologist, Maurice Merleau-Ponty. Merleau-Ponty's description of human consciousness places a high value on vision, asserting that it is a distinctive mode of consciousness, irreducible either to knowledge or action. In addition he assumes a high degree of continuity between 'vision' – understood as a mode of perception – and 'vision' in the context of artistic activity: 'pictorial expression assumes and transcends the patterning of the world which begins in perception'.[41] He therefore uses the painter as a paradigm of what seeing and vision in the general perceptual sense involve. Vision, he says, 'learns only by seeing and only from itself . . . the painter's world is a visible world, nothing but visible'.[42]

Like Heidegger, Merleau-Ponty wants to free us from the kind of thinking about representation which has governed so much aesthetic theory in the past. He is committed to affirming the full integrity of vision, whether in perception or in art: there is no getting behind what takes place in vision since our perception of the world as a world itself takes place within vision. There is no 'ghost story' in art. In this spirit he repudiates the notion that the mental image is 'a tracing, a copy, a second thing'.[43] The world is not somehow given prior to or outside of its being seen in such a way that all we (or all the artists) have to do is to copy what is already there waiting for us. The artist's use of line, for instance, cannot possibly be justified by claiming that objects 'out there' are circumscribed and bordered by lines. Rather the line itself 'renders visible'.[44] Referring to the work of Henry Moore, Matisse and Klee, Merleau-Ponty comments that 'the line is no longer a thing or an imitation of a thing . . . it is a certain process of gouging within the in-itself . . . '[45] Matisse's 'Blue Nudes', for example create images of women from only the most essential curves and gestures, yet they are very distinctively women. Their contours are not recognisable 'in a "physical optical" way' (ie. as a faithful rendering of what is there) but 'as the axes of a corporeal system of activity and passivity'.[46] They are precisely *women* by virtue of the specific visual form which the painter makes. They are not things or imitations of things, but women *as they may be seen*.

The vision embodied in the picture is the essence of what each of us sees when we do actually *see* something. Citing Malraux Merleau-Ponty writes

> Perception already stylizes. A woman passing by is not first and foremost a corporeal contour for me, a coloured mannequin, a spectacle in a given spot. She is 'an individual, sentimental, sexual expression'. She is a flesh in its full presence, with its vigor and weakness there in her walk or the click of her heel on the ground. She is a unique way of varying the accent of feminine being and thus of human being, which I understand the way I understand a sentence, namely, because it finds in me the system of resonators that it needs.[47]

Visual perception is not just a matter of refining an initial blur of raw sense date into a decipherable image to which we can then attach a concept and a word. Vision is of a piece with itself and always already stylised, i.e., it sees things in a certain way. It is, in another expression of Malraux's a '"coherent deformation"' of the world – and only as such does the world become significant for us, indeed, only as such is the world *seen* by us at all.

A key aspect of Merleau-Ponty's account of perception is his distinctive emphasis on the role of the body, or what he calls 'the flesh' or 'carnality'. The seer's relation to the world is not that of a mind puzzledly trying to make contact through the senses with a world 'out there'. It is primarily a *bodily* contact. As a body the seer (you or I looking at the tree outside the window or the artist manifesting her vision in colour and line) has direct entry into the world which is seen. The bodily nature of vision corresponds to the experienced materiality (or, in Heidegger's expression, the thingly quality) of the world. There never are any 'mere' things, for the perceived world arises from the very beginning in and among things. 'Things', Merleau-Ponty says, 'are an annex or prolongation [of the body]; they are incrusted into its flesh, they are part of its full definition; the world is made of the same stuff as the body'.[48] Again this applies fully to the artist who in no way abstracts herself from the bodily specificity of seeing. On the contrary, Merleau-Ponty quotes Valery in asserting that 'the painter "takes his body with him" . . . It is by lending his body to the world that the artist changes the world into paintings . . . '[49] 'Flesh', in Merleau-Ponty's special sense, is not simply the objective, physiologically or biologically describable 'envelope' of our psychic experience; it is the concrete matrix or conjunction of self and world behind or beyond which we cannot go. It is the overlapping or intertwining of what is seen (as if it were out there) with the motor projects by which the subject launches himself out into the midst of a world of visible things. We have no access to or knowledge of either of these aspects apart from their coinherence in our actual fleshly, carnal existence.

In this sense, then, Merleau-Ponty's concept of the flesh enables us to make sense of that subjective element which, for instance, we found to be lacking in Fuller's empiricist approach. Yet his standpoint is not 'subjectivist'. Although he dismisses any phantasmagoric concept of pure objectivity his method is distinct from that of Sartre's account of human existence, which is suspicious of attempts to concede to the passivity of the body any ultimate influence over the self-determination of the free subject. Merleau-Ponty's carnal self is always in the world, as a thing among things, feeling them and seeing them. 'Sight', he says, 'is achieved and fulfils itself in the thing seen'.[50] He does not want to suggest that we impose our meanings on the world. We really do see them there. As in Bultmann's interpretation of St. Paul's concept of the body, existing as a body means to exist as a being who is from the ground up in relation to that which transcends it – and, in, and through that relatedness, acquiring a specific identity, character, or 'style'. We may add that Merleau-Ponty's account is not only intended to rebut charges of subjectivism in general. It is also specifically intended to rescue the seer from the seclusion of a mere 'knowing' mind. For as he sees it there can be no completely private vision, any more than Wittgenstein allows the existence of a private language. Bodily existence means inescapable involvement in every respect with others: ' . . . the *idios kosmos* private world opens by virtue of vision upon a *koinos kosmos* common world . . . '[51] Thus, 'It is the mountain itself which from out there makes itself seen by the painter; it is the mountain that he interrogates with his gaze'.[52]

Another aspect of this public and self-transcending character of vision is that vision (and visual 'representation' in art) does not require further explanation in order to make it meaningful.

It already is meaningful. We do not need a verbal commentary to understand the image. Vision itself interprets vision. Vision occurs out in the open, in a shared visual world, and is not to be explained by occult meanings which do not appear in vision itself. In the context of painting this has a further implication: that our 'understanding' of paintings takes place within a wide realm and history of images. This is above all true of the painter herself who, as a painter, participates in the historicity of painting, in a continuun of visual sensibility opened up by the first cave-painters.

There is also, and very importantly for the present study, a definite if elusive theological element in Merleau-Ponty's account of vision. Against Descartes' conception of an absolute space, containing all events but itself 'outside all points of view, beyond all latency and depth, having no true thickness',[53] Merleau-Ponty insists that there is *no space* outside seeing itself and therefore no space outside the fleshly, bodily event of visual perception. Descartes' space is regarded by Merleau-Ponty as a mental construct, called in to explain – literally, to make a place for – our perception of the world. But the perceptions of a carnal being are 'indices of an order of existence . . . about which we do not have to think'.[54] That is to say, the conviction as to the reality of the world does not have to rest on the guarantee of any *a priori* intellectual constructions. Perception itself opens out into reality. Vision itself has a voluminosity or depth which assures us of the being of what we see; 'a voluminosity we express in a word when we say that it is *there*'.[55] Depth in this sense is not a third dimension – it is the first dimension, 'a global "locality" . . . from which height, width and depth are abstracted . . . '[56] The 'truth' of depth in this sense does not only serve to validate (as Cartesian space validated) the intellectual perspicuousness of demonstrable truths. It grounds the 'obscurity' as well as the 'lights' of thoughts. The *theological* implications of all this are brought out in a footnote by Merleau-Ponty's translator who comments that 'the obscurity of the "existential" order [the order, that is, of a carnal being] is just as necessary, just as grounded in God, as is the clarity of true thoughts'.[57] In, with and under the act of carnal seeing we see also the inseparable but never objectified ground of that seeing, the unfathomable God of depth, 'the abyssal Being that Descartes opened up and so quickly closed again'.[58] God, to put it at its boldest, is not revealed otherwise than in the modes of bodily vision, colour, space, light. It is such a God of depth that the modern painter (Merleau-Ponty's favourite examples are Matisse and Klee) seeks when he assumes the role of 'artisan of Being'. This God, Merleau-Ponty claims, is fully compatible with the Christian God, since, he says, 'Christianity is for the most part the recognition of a mystery in the relation of man to God. This derives precisely from the Christian God's refusal of any vertical relation of subordination'.[59] That is to say, the Christian God does not require the so-called 'horizontal' realm of incarnate perception, action and knowledge to be justified in terms of some supposedly superior 'vertical' dimension. The Christian God is the God whose self-expression is altogether and utterly compatible with the flesh. Such a God may be palpated in the heart of colour and in our perceptions and our artistic visions may be for us 'another self in ourselves which dwells in and authenticates our darkness'.[60] It will, of course, be a surprise to many theologians to read that the West abandoned the horizontal/vertical way of construing the world's relation to God two thousand years ago!

It is once again curious that after all this Merleau-Ponty too seems ultimately to commend language as offering a more adequate medium for the self-expression of the flesh than vision. 'Man', he says, 'feels at home in language the way he never will in painting'.[61] Not that language operates on a different ontological plane from the life of the flesh. It is rather the continuation and 'the highest point of a tacit and implicit accumulation of the same kind as that of painting'.[62] But once this point has been reached language asserts its priority and offers vision the opportunity to 'emigrate' 'not outside of every body, but into another less heavy, more transparent body'.[63] Language too arises from the life of the body, but once it has established its sway the whole landscape of vision 'is overrun with words' and 'is henceforth but a variant of speech before our eyes'.[64]

Yet – once again – we do not have to make this move with Merleau-Ponty any more than we had to follow Heidegger in his final preference for language over against vision. Merleau-Ponty has been challenged at precisely this point by Jean-François Lyotard, a leading philosopher of post-modernism. Lyotard sets out to offer a vigorous defence of the world of perception 'against the imperialism of language'.[65] According to Lyotard, Western philosophy has through millennia made discourse, language, the special locus or site of truth. It is in language that truth gets established. But, he asks, is the alignment Discourse/Logos/Knowledge/Truth on the one side and Image/Illusion on the other beyond question?

He suggests that figural space can never be entirely assimilated into the realm of language and knowledge without loss. There is always a remainder which does not get put into words. The point of view of philosophy has always been dominated by the quest for a unitary system of meaning to which even Merleau-Ponty ultimately succumbed. But, he says, 'we have renounced the folly of unity, the folly of providing the first cause in a unitary discourse, the fantasm of a [common] origin'.[66] Instead he wants to defend the opacity of vision against the self-styled clarity of discourse. 'This book', he says 'protests that the given is not a text, that there is in it a thickness, or rather a difference, constitutive [of it], which is not for reading but for seeing'.[67]

But, and the point is important, this does not mean that we should attempt a crude prioritising of the one over the other. I have already suggested that the defence of vision and of art in this chapter is likewise intended to endorse the integrity and truthfulness of vision without, however, attempting to absolve the theology of art from an appropriate discipline of language and reflection. Otherwise, of course, it would be self-defeating even to attempt to *write a book* on such a subject. The point is not concerning the priority of either language or vision but of the sheer *difference*, the ultimately *irreducible* difference between them. But does this difference exclude all overlapping between them? Are there no points of contact? It would seem that there must be some convergence or we could never talk about pictures at all. Equally if visual reality did not in some way mesh in with other dimensions of life it would be hard to say what sort of significance it might have at all. It may well be, as Merleau-Ponty has suggested, that the grounds of such convergence spring at a very fundamental level from the shared bodily matrix of word and image alike. For they are both the words and the images of living, incarnate human beings. Yet I do not wish to pursue this convergence further in the direction of a fundamental philosophical analysis. I shall turn instead to the immediate practical problems which such questions throw up for a working theology of art, and by reference to these problems, to illuminate the same question from another angle.

I have been arguing for a theology of art in which the integrity of the visual image itself is respected as the principal ground of religious significance in art, as the visual image makes visible the invisible depth of the God who grounds the darkness, thickness and opacity of our bodily vision (as well, perhaps, as our intellectual 'lights'). Such a theology might, for example, help us to make sense of the numinous quality which suffuses many supposedly 'non-religious' works. Take Monet's many series of paintings of his garden at Giverny. [Plate 11] Here we find the same scenes and themes repeated and reworked again and again: trailing wisterias, irises and water lilies, the Japanese footbridge and the garden path. With each treatment of the subject Monet seems to be moving further and further away from conventional concepts of imitation into the pure play of col+oural presences. Yet, against the aesthetic theories of the impressionists themselves and against the sort of critique levelled at them by Tillich, these pictures elicit a response which is readily assimilable to the kind of response appropriate to the manifestation of grace in creation and redemption. These paintings assure us, in an irreducibly pictorial way, that the world is a good place to be, that it is holy ground, that we may trust ourselves to the particularity of our carnal situatedness and find in it a texture of meaning and value of the first order. There is no 'ghost story' here but the palpable assurance that the 'religious' response to existence resonates within a shared field of vision in which such responses as reverence, rapture, delight, trust and peace are thoroughly appropriate. These works provide an outstanding example – but only one of an almost innumerable range of more or less well-known paintings – in relation to which we may fruitfully practise that theoria which Ruskin saw as a key to the religious interpretation of art. The seeing of such art does not lift us out of the mire of material existence into some pure aesthetic aether: it transforms our bodily sense of being-in-the-world.[68]

But the theological 'vindication' of such works is one thing: and the theological response to what is generally called 'religious art' is another. Such art is typically shot through with narrative and allegorical elements which cannot be said to derive from or relate to a purely visual 'looking' in the way that Monet's work does. Are such elements simply excrescences on the surface of art, irrelevant to its real (visual) religious meaning? We may refer to Ruskin's somewhat devious praise of Charles Collins' painting 'Convent Thoughts', which is the starting point of Fuller's study *Theoria*. The picture shows a young nun, standing in an island in a pond set in a walled garden; she is surrounded by lilies and is considering the mysteries of the passion flower she holds in her right hand. Ruskin ignored the heavily laboured religious symbolism of the painting and concentrated his praise on the faithful and excellent depiction of the water plantain *alisma plantago*.[69] Similarly it might appear that my argument is tending in the direct of affirming a religious value only for that which belongs in a purely 'figural space' (Lyotard) and neglecting the whole issue of overt religious content. But that would be to render ninety per cent of what is generally taken to be religious art redundant! Aren't there religious pictures which *do* work, in which the religious symbolism does not destroy but enhances or extends the visual integrity of the work? And, if so, how is this achieved?

We have already looked at Forsyth's interpretation of G. F. Watts' picture 'Hope'. Forsyth's tendency is, as we saw, to find an almost directly literal or allegorical 'meaning' in this, as in the other pictures on which he commented. But is this just an allegorical or literary painting in which the painterly means are subordinated to the ideal 'truth' which it seeks to 'express'? This question is directly addressed by G. K. Chesterton in his study of Watts, and his remarks are still worth considering. Observing that – as was previously pointed out – one's first response to this picture of a bowed, almost inconsolable figure might be to call it 'despair', he goes on to argue that its meaning as a picture of 'hope' is not dependent on, let us say, the fact that we know that it is called 'Hope'. The title, he says,

> is not (as those think who call it 'literary') the reality behind the symbol, but another symbol for the same thing, or, to speak yet more strictly, another symbol describing another part or aspect of the same complex reality. Two men felt a swift, violent, invisible thing in the world: one said the word 'hope', the other painted a picture in blue and green paint. The picture is inadequate; the word 'hope' is inadequate; but between them, like two angles in the calculation of a distance, they almost locate a mystery . . . [70]

In other words, the fact that it is painted, as it is painted, is precisely its way of communicating what Chesterton describes as a 'mystery', 'something for which there is neither speech nor language, which has been too vast for any eye to see and too secret for any religion to utter . . . '[71] The painting, that is, reaches into that depth which is given with all vision and establishes its meaning within a properly figural space. The image does not 'mean' whatever we find ourselves able to say about it, nor is it simply a kind of presencing of undifferentiated being. But, by using the thoroughly material and thoroughly visual means of space, line and colour the artist finds his truth in the thickness and opacity of the bodily depth of existence – what Merleau-Ponty called 'the flesh' of human life.

In the light of this we cannot expect any direct reciprocal translatability of words and images, yet at the same time their common rootedness in bodily depth does enable a process of indirect translatability to occur. This process may go in either direction. Watts' painting (if, that is, it works in the way Chesterton claims it does) starts with the visual and from the visual opens a vista on language so that, as Chesterton says, 'the title is therefore not so much the substance of one of Watts' pictures, it is rather an epigram upon it'.[72] Conversely Rublev's icon of the Trinity starts with a verbal text (and also, of course, an iconographical tradition) but does not simply 'illustrate' the text. What he produces is, in the language of Orthodoxy itself, visual theology. We do not read it: we see it. It creates an 'open region' (Heidegger) in the depth of bodily life and it is in that open region that its meaning confronts us and engages us.

Wolterstorff called the artist a 'worker in fittingness' and we are now in a position to grasp the aptness of this remark. What is at stake in such pictures is precisely the 'fittingness' by which materials drawn either from the artist's own imaginative life (as in the case of Watts) or from an extant religious tradition (as in the case of Rublev) are worked into the figural space of the picture. If for one moment we suspect that the image is only a cipher for some other kind of meaning then 'fittingness' is lost. We must be able to see it as visual – therefore also sensuous and carnal – through and through. Such is the Church's neglect of the visual that we scarcely know where to begin in assessing such 'fittingness', yet it is just this process of assessment which will constitute the most extensive part of any future theology of art. (A theology of art, that is, which is concerned directly with the religious value of works of art rather than, as here, with the varieties of theological understanding of art.) In a sense many of the views we have been examining here have been arguments in favour of the 'fittingness' of certain works, movements or periods of art: Maritain and the mediaeval order, Gilson and still-life, Ruskin and Turner, Forsyth and the Pre-Raphaelites, Tillich and expressionism, and, lastly, the Eastern theology of icons. We might comment, in retrospect, that it is unfortunate that they mostly take up a strongly exclusive stance, and, in commending one artist, work or movement, denigrate others. Thus Tillich's concept of 'depth' in art is used to favour expressionism and to deny religious value to impressionism which, he says, remains on the surface. The view of 'depth' advocated by Merleau-Ponty and espoused in this chapter, however, can be used (as in the case of Monet) to articulate the religious value of impressionism just as much as it can be used to interpret the existential meaning of expressionism. The republic of art, as of human life, has open borders. There can be no *a priori* limit on what may or may not be welcome in it. The work of art and the work of appropriating art (including religious appropriating) is continuous and open-ended – and there is much to do!

It must, however, be stressed that the 'fittingness' which I have been discussing can only be achieved and received in the milieu of carnality. It cannot, therefore, be objectified as a form of knowledge. In this, thinkers as diverse as Gilson, Rombach and Lyotard agree. It is more appropriate to see in it a movement of desire. We have, for instance, noted Dillenberger's comments on the seductive character of art, a feature of which Christian iconoclasts in every age have been aware. Lyotard too comments forcefully on the 'connivance' between the figural and desire.[73] But even if we cannot follow Lyotard and other recent French philosophers in the direction of a totally utopian liberation of desire from the shackles of knowledge, to plead for a theology of art in which vision is affirmed in its essentially sensuous and carnal character is to plead for a theology in which desire is allowed to invade the domains of knowledge, and to shake the prevailing paradigms of 'theological science'.

The relationship between nature, desire and knowledge is complex and cannot be adequately discussed here.[74] As I have just suggested, there is much to question in the position of those recent French philosophers who wish to throw Freud's cautions to the wind and take the side of desire against civilisation. Equally the Hegelian view that there is an ultimate harmony between desire, civilisation and knowledge is hard to sustain in the light of a succession of critiques running from Nietzsche through Freud and on into the present. Desire is not readily assimilable into any kind of unitary intellectual system. This statement applies very much to the figuration of desire in visual art. Yet even if the opening up of the depths of life in the flesh, such as we experience in relation to art, does not reveal any kind of perspicuous foundation for knowledge (enabling us, at most, 'almost' to 'locate a mystery', as Chesterton said) this does not mean that the desire which motivates such a process of opening up is to be regarded as negative or destructive in its impact on culture or on nature. Ruskin – and here we might acknowledge the significance of his essentially empirical temper – was able both to affirm the theoretic gratification of the eye and to establish a very positive conception of the relationship between art, nature and desire. In summarising his position I spoke of 'an aptitude for disinterested desire', desire, that is, which is fully connatural to the human subject, yet in which and through which the ego is liberated from its bondage to self-assertion and self-gratification. Or rather, in which its self-assertion and self-gratification opens it up for a full participation in the life of the 'given' world. We might link this also to Peter Fuller's use of the concept of biophilia, a biologically innate associative urge bonding all living creatures. In a quite different philosophical context we might recur to Merleau-Ponty's account of the blending of the 'seen' with our subjective 'motor projects' in the processes of vision. In such a blending our desire to enter ever more deeply into the never-objectifiable life of the flesh leads us ever closer to that God of depth which he identifies as the Christian God.[75]

At the start of this chapter I suggested that a contemporary theology of art should not be content to find a place for itself within the field of natural theology but should instead see itself in terms of a theology of redemption. We are now in a position to see why this should be so. For the implication of my argument is that there is an unsurpassable meaning and value to be found in the pursuit of those desires which draw us towards the world, and which enable or inspire us to affirm the goodness of that world in which we find ourselves. It should be clear by now that I regard art as having its unique place in the economy of human life precisely among such desires: arising from them, shaped by them and revealing them. It is in this context that we can recognise the force of Hans Küng's remark that art is an 'anticipation' of the 'still-awaiting humanizing of man'.[76] For art anticipates – perhaps in a fuller sense than that intended by Küng – the messianic kingdom itself, the return of the world to that created fulness in which we may declare, with God, that it is all 'very good'. In this way the activity of art, and of all good looking, proclaims that our desire towards the world is neither wasted nor futile. This desire rises from the eye of the flesh and sees in what it sees the presence of a good creation and the beginning of a more perfect consummation. Peter Fuller subtitled his study of Ruskin's ultimately sad vision 'art and the absence of grace'. Our argument has brought us to the point where we may, on the contrary, declare the presence of a 'structural grace in things',[77] a grace revealed to the rightly desiring heart and which we appropriate in our own acts of seeing and of shaping the visible things of this visible world.

Finally, we may ask where all this connects with that story of modern art with which we began? If my argument serves, as I hope, to support a theological engagement with art, what, if anything, might it have to offer art itself? Firstly, it suggests that artists would do well to resist a loss of faith in their own work. Art remains not only an important but, as I have suggested, an unsurpassable human activity. For Hegel, and many others since, art 'in its highest vocation' is a thing of the past. But on the view advanced here those processes from which art arises reach so deeply into the inalienable carnality of human existence that there can be no historical necessity placed on us to overthrow art – unless we are driven by some mad impulse to overthrow ourselves. The 'discovery' of the cave-painters of Lascaux is as irreversible as the 'discovery' of speech by some probably still more distant ancestor.

The theology of art does not require artists to become overtly religious in their work (though it does not exclude this). Rather it points them back into their own work, back to the figural space of desire and the play within it of its dance and travail with the world. It does not demand the surrender of artistic autonomy but declares the seriousness of art – though seriousness here does not, of course, mean ponderousness: there is a serious humour, a serious tenderness, a serious play and a serious joy as well as a serious doubt and a serious despair. Seriousness is not opposed to lightness but to triviality. In this respect the theology of art is open both to the dark vision of Rothko's final works and to the Neo-Romantic quest for a new unitary vision. All that is excluded is triviality, cynicism and the wanton or careless exercise of the creative gift. For these are not the principles of art but of kitsch.

9
The Theology of Art and the Meeting of Faiths

This book has been primarily concerned with developing a theology of art appropriate to the post-modern situation of contemporary western culture. But is that all? It could be argued that this situation is a highly localised phenomenon. Does the theology of art have any further function in the global perspectives within which modern theology increasingly operates? I should like to suggest that it does, and that a theology of art might make an important contribution to many areas of theological discussion. As an example let us take the ever more important dialogue between faiths. Clearly, different religions (and different movements within religions) have widely divergent attitudes towards the arts in general and the visual arts in particular and it is far too early (if it is desirable at all) to hope to construct any kind of universal theology of art. We must therefore proceed in terms of particulars and, as a particular example, I should like to take the specific case of Christianity and Far Eastern Buddhism, especially Zen. This should prove doubly interesting in that Zen is prominent among those religious traditions in which, as we shall see, artistic practices are accepted and acknowledged as part of the religious life. There are two issues which I shall seek chiefly to address: the capacity of art to reveal the fundamental values of a religious tradition, its 'world' (in a Heideggerian sense), and, secondly, the different understanding of art within different traditions as a further revelation of the 'style' of those traditions.

The first of these, the role of art in revealing the specific and unique character of a religious tradition is widely attested. An outstanding recent example of a Christian encounter with Buddhist art leading to a deeper engagement with the essential truth of Buddhism is recorded in the *Asian Journal* of Thomas Merton. Merton's account of his experience of Buddhist art provides an endorsement of the approach to art taken in this book in the way that it emphasises the actual bodily thereness (or *dasein* or 'thingliness') of the work of art as establishing a space within which further levels of meaning and interpretation can be opened up. In this way a point of reference is also provided in relation to which what is 'the same' and what is 'different' can be discussed, perhaps for the first time.

Merton received permission from his monastic superior to travel to the East in the latter part of 1968, with the official aim of attending an international monastic meeting in Bangkok at the beginning of December. He spent from mid-October travelling, reading and talking in an intense exploration of Indian and, especially, Buddhist culture and spirituality. He himself described the journey as a journey home[1] and, in fact, his interest in Eastern religion went back thirty or more years. His writing on Buddhism had received a striking accolade from D. T. Suzuki who, at a personal meeting in 1964, had told Merton, "Who is the western writer who understands best the Zen IT IS YOU they declare'.'[2] We cannot therefore pretend that he was a naive pilgrim but one who was already well-informed about Buddhist spirituality, one who had a definite pre-understanding and an equally definite question. The 'answer' to the question, however, was not to take the form of an intellectual breakthrough but was to occur in the context of a visit to the sacred Buddhist site of Polonnaruwa in Sri Lanka. The site is renowned for a number of huge statues of the Buddha, standing, sitting in meditation or reclining. This is how Merton described them.

> Then the silence of the extraordinary faces., The great smiles. Huge and yet subtle. Filled with every possibility, questioning nothing. Knowing everything, rejecting nothing. The peace not of emotional resignation but of Madhyamika, of Sunyata, that has seen through every question without trying to discredit anyone or anything – without refutation – without establishing some other argument.[3]

He describes his own reaction to them as total.

> I was knocked over with a rush of relief and thankfulness at the obvious clarity of the figures, the clarity and fluidity of shape and line, the design of the monumental bodies composed into the rock shapes and landscapes, figures, rocks and tree.

'Looking at these figures', he adds

> I was suddenly, almost forcibly, jerked clean out of the habitual, half-tied vision of things, and an inner clearness, clarity, as if exploding from the rocks themselves, became evident and obvious. The queer *evidence* of the reclining figure, the smile, the sad smile of Ananda standing with arms folded (much more 'imperative' than Da Vinci's Mona Lisa because completely simple and straightforward). The thing about all this is that there is no puzzle, no problem and really no 'mystery'. All problems are resolved and everything is clear. The rock, all matter, all life, is charged with dharmakaya . . . everything is emptiness and everything is compassion.

The account is interesting in several respects. It contains many features familiar to students of religious experience, and might, for instance, be compared with Tillich's 'Botticelli-experience' at the end of the First World War. We might note the sudden transformation of consciousness, the sense of a power or presence, 'not ourselves', a feeling of 'evidence' and obviousness, the conviction that what is revealed is beyond evidence and argument but has an immediate and incontrovertible veracity. At the same time the use of Buddhist terminology reminds us that Merton was well-prepared for this experience – perhaps, even, 'looking' for it. We cannot therefore pretend that in this encounter with works of visual art (whatever else they may also be) Merton learned the meaning of Buddhism for the first time. What we can say is that he learned to see it in a way he never had before. 'I don't know when in my life', he concludes, 'I have ever had such a sense of beauty and spiritual validity running together in one aesthetic illumination'.[4] In all this he lays particular emphasis on the *obviousness* of what is there to be seen at Polonnaruwa, its *openness* and *self-evidence*. What he saw there was simply what was there to be seen. There is nothing occult or hidden about these works. That is precisely the point. Their meaning is all out in the open. The seeing itself is what is both beautiful and holy and, as such, very much a part of the seeing of the rocks, trees, water and other features of the 'natural' landscape. The statues are 'there' as part of the landscape, things among things, not 'art-objects' set aside for purely 'aesthetic' contemplation.

Such an encounter, then, does not necessarily make us better informed about the content of another faith. What it does is to place us (literally) in the same space, the same presence, as that which another faith occupies. Whether or not one shares Merton's intellectual preparedness, the sheer physical actuality of the art-work creates the possibility of an experience in which we are – at least while it lasts – open to the reality of another spirituality (the art-work being such a reality). This need not be a step on the road to conversion, or the abandonment of one's own faith, but simply an extension of the double-perspective whereby one looks at other faiths and at one's own. What is at stake is not so much a matter of acquiring a fresh understanding of another faith (remember Gauguin's 'see without understanding') but of facilitating a response or a relationship which lies, in a sense, outside the line of understanding.

Though we in our time and from our perspective are, perhaps, more familiar with the concept of the journey to the East as a symbol of the getting of a new wisdom the situation can easily be reversed. During a visit of Japanese religious teachers to Europe an archery master was invited to hold an archery ceremony in a Church. Later he was told – apparently with an element of rebuke – that his ritual bow at the beginning and at the end of the ceremony had exceeded the customary forty-five degrees. "'He could only answer that he had not been aware of it but that, before the Crucifix, he felt an excess of reverence which *pulled his breast to the floor*"'.[5] The art-work creates its own response outside the line of intellectual comprehension.

Once more, however, it is necessary to re-iterate the conviction that although visual art is not to be treated as dependent on a realm of meaning or truth which is not in itself visual it may nonetheless fittingly be correlated with other levels or dimensions of communication, notably language. The image is open to the word, although in making the passage from one to the other we must stay close to the integrity of the visual image itself which may not be reduced to a mere cipher for verbal truth. With that proviso, the encounter with the art of another faith may not only yield the kind of wordless comprehension 'without understanding ' such as Merton describes or the archery master experienced: it may also lead on to an engagement with the doctrinal and conceptual dimensions of another religious community. Especially where such engagement, and the acts of interpretation which flow from it, are mutual, an enormously rich field of reflection and discussion is opened up.

A pioneering venture in this field has been made by Heinrich

Rombach, whose philosophy of images was discussed in the last chapter, and two Japanese respondents, Kōichi Tsujimura and Ryosuke Ohashi. The results of their exchanges are contained in the book *Being and Nothingness: Basic Images of Western and Eastern Thought*.[6] The title refers to what the authors regard as the two basic conceptions of the absolute in West and East respectively. They find these conceptions visually realised in two pictures, 'The Crowning of Mary' by Hans Baldung (called Grien), an early sixteenth century altarpiece, and 'Sakyamuni Descending the Mountain', a thirteenth century Chinese silk painting by L'iang K'ai. [Plates 12 and 13]

'The Crowning of Mary' is in the form of a triptych. The left and right-hand panels show contrasting groups of apostles, those on the viewer's left being headed by Paul, the apostle of the gentiles, those on the left by Peter, symbol of the Jewish Church. Their respective attributes, as interpreted by Rombach, are revealed in a wealth of pictorial detail, from the contrast between the open, forward-moving gesture of Paul to the defensive stance of Peter, and from the bright luminosity of the haloes of the gentile Church to the dimmer nimbuses around the heads of the Jewish Church. The one group, Rombach tells us, represents men of thought, the other men of action; the one stands for the Spirit, the other for the letter; the one is the new, the other the old dispensation. Together they represent a tension which runs right through the heart and the history of Christianity, a tension which is further heightened by the central panel of the work. This shows Mary being crowned Queen of Heaven by the persons of the divine Trinity. On the left (the same side as Paul and his group) is the Son, the inaugurator of the New Covenant, whilst on the right is the Father, in whom the symbolism of the Old Covenant is concentrated. Together they are holding a crown above Mary's head, Mary herself occupying the centre of the picture and shown kneeling, her hands joined in prayer in a downward-pointing 'v'. Above Mary, above the crown, is a sun-like halo, at the base of which hovers the white dove of the Holy Spirit. The various symbolic associations of the Father and the Son are revealed by many aspects of dress and posture. The Father, for instance, is fully robed, whilst the naked body of the Son, the Incarnate One, is partially revealed. The tension between the figures is such, Rombach claims, that they could easily find themselves locked into some mutually destructive conflict (witness some of the controversies touched on in Paul's letters) if there were not some third reconciling point. This is provided by the

central figure of Mary. The dynamic balance which she represents
is, Rombach shows, manifested in the geometrical structure of the
picture. The vertical line descending from the mid-point of the
dove to the apex of the 'v' made by her hands intersects with
the horizontal line joining the eyes of the Father and the Son to
make a symmetrical cross. Less abstractly, the love embodied in
Mary, subsumed under the symbol of the Spirit, provides the point
of unity of Father and Son. This cross, which Rombach refers to both
as the *Urkreuz* (primal cross) and the *Wesenskreuz* (essential cross), is
the dynamic structural principle which both unites and divides the
picture, assigning to each element and figure its place in a complex
whole. But there is still more to notice. By concentrating on the
central vertical axis of this cross he discerns what he calls a new
trinitarian principle implicit in the picture. The dove-spirit, Mary's
face and her praying hands constitute the three focii of this principle.
Its third element, the downward-pointing triangular shape made by
the hands, indicate (and, Rombach says, were explicitly understood
in this way in the artist's own time to indicate) the female principle
and, in particular, the womb. The movement of this 'new Trinity',
which Rombach sees as characteristic of the spirituality of the late
mediaeval/early Reformation period, is therefore revealed as being
fundamentally incarnational, a movement of Spirit descending into
and pervading the seamless density and complex finitude of the
flesh, its 'absolute thickness' (*Absolute Dichte*). The resolution of
what in the picture is portrayed as the 'horizontal' dialectic of Father
and Son, Old and New Covenants, points to this downward-moving
vertical axis, but in a spirituality which 'indeed hovers above everything, but realizes itself at the same time in the uttermost degree of
concretion . . . The spirituality of this Spirit has no need to fear the
flesh. Without a shadow this divinity finds itself in every reality.
Fulness'.[7] Moreover, this 'new theology' has moved beyond the
kind of dialectical contrast established along the horizontal axis and
in doing so, has also moved beyond the field of knowledge into the
density and actuality of incarnate life itself. In this way, Rombach
suggests, the picture reveals the transformation of the concept of
God as Being and Creator, the substantial principle of the unity
of all being, by extending the field of divine being to include all
that actually belongs to concrete existence. In such a perspective
theology will no longer be concerned with subordinating the finite
to the infinite but rather with grasping the infinite in the finite, that
is, it will not seek to determine God as the absolute ground which

unites and makes sense of all that is but to grasp the particular in its own irreplaceable actuality and uniqueness.

Kōichi Tsujimura responds to Rombach's analysis by means of his own 'counter-analysis' of L'iang K'ai's picture 'Sakyamuni Descending the Mountain'. This picture, chosen to highlight the relationship between finite and infinite as that is conceived and realised in Buddhism, is, at first glance, a much simpler work than the Freiburg altar-piece (itself a not insignificant point in the comparison between East and West). It contains only a single figure, Sakyamuni Buddha himself, descending a mountain path which slopes gradually down from left to right of the picture. Rising from the left side is an overhanging rock-face which virtually dissects the picture diagonally. Against it grows a bare, sparse tree. On the other side of the path (and of the picture) is the outline of another, less clearly-defined, rock wall. Sakyamuni himself is descending the path, barefoot, his hands concealed beneath the simple red robe he wears, though we can discern that they are joined in prayer (only here the 'v' is pointing upwards). In his way, taking up part of the path, is a rough thorn-bush. Tsujimura sets beside the picture a verse by the twentieth century poet and aesthetician Hisamatsu: Mu-Chu-Ari-Michi, literally translated in the German text as 'Nothing(ness) in the midst is a way' or 'In the midst of nothingness is a way'.

In his commentary Tsujimura draws attention to the barrenness of the scene, the bare rock, the wintry trees, the precipice on the left which rises up to hidden heights far beyond the realm of mortalkind. At the bottom right the few herbs growing by the path indicate (according to Buddhist iconology) the world of human desires. The path is thus seen to lead from the high mountain peaks down to the lower, human world, the abyss – as Tsujimura says, 'a very sharp contrast'.[8] But there is a way leading from one to the other, an open region, which he specifically identifies with the 'open region', the 'clearing' (*Lichtung*) spoken of by Heidegger as the region of the occurrence of truth. This open region is trodden by the figure, Sakyamuni himself. We are to note that this Buddha has no halo, although such a feature is as common in Eastern iconography as it is in the West. Why is this? Because the halo, the sign of a special, sacred 'other' dimension only appears when we define our own position over against it as 'worldly'. The halo is only there for those who see their own situation as profane. For God himself or for the Buddha himself the halo has no meaning or function. The absence of the halo is therefore taken to signify that this Buddha is not conceived of as standing over against us, but as journeying in the midst of 'the things that surround him in their deeper reality'.[9] If we look closer at him we will see that his eyes are not focussed on anything in particular. In this sense 'his eyes see *Nothing*'.[10] He himself, the seer, is *Nothing*; he sees nothing, says nothing, has no fixed standpoint, is no more than a simple, exposed human being. His praying hands (pointing upwards, we recall) have a further significance. According to Buddhist tradition the ten fingers stand for the ten regions of existence, from hell through humanity to Buddhahood. Their joining therefore signifies the unification of all these regions. They point upwards to indicate the Buddha's intention to work for the salvation of all beings. Yet they are concealed by the robe. Why? Because his work is a hidden work, an action prior to knowledge and revelation. His robes, caught by the wind, point downward to the world of men, the way he must go, whilst his firm posture shows his own firmness and security as he walks. Here too, Tsujimura concludes, we have a human figure in whom the dynamic union of worlds, finite and infinite, immanent and transcendent, is represented. It would seem, then, that whatever differences may be established between western and eastern spirituality are not determined by such characterisations as 'this-worldly' or 'other-worldly', 'world-affirming' or 'world-denying', since both manifest a knowledge of the ultimate union of the two. It is only now, Tsujimura finishes by saying, that 'a most difficult and fundamental problem emerges as between European and East Asian conceptions of the human world'.[11] This problem, however, can only be *seen* when we let go the structural analysis of the picture and look for ourselves into the void which Sakyamuni both sees and is.

This final, teasingly unexplained remark, is taken up in turn by Ryosuke Ohashi who summarises the previous discussing by saying that if the 'Crowning of Mary' can be taken as a representation of the absolute in the form of absolute Spirit, the 'Sakyamuni Descending the Mountain' represents the absolute as absolute Nothing(ness)'. Although both pictures show the unity of finite and infinite in the absolute they do so in distinct ways, which, he suggests, are manifest pictorially in the paintings themselves. To throw further light on this he turns to Hegel's understanding of the 'Spirit' and 'Nothing(ness)'. Nothingness, according to Hegel, is the ultimate principle of Buddhism and is 'pure abstraction . . . the absolute negative'. It is being in its most abstract form, featureless and without character. By way of contrast 'Spirit' means 'Return to Itself'. Spirit is not being in its raw immediacy: it is being which mediates itself through the myriad forms of its self-manifestation in nature and in history. Spirit is being which externalises itself in the forms and structures of the world and yet also *knows* itself in these forms. The problem of the relationship between the 'western' and 'eastern' motifs of being and nothingness therefore leads to the question of mediation.

This is, notoriously, a concept fraught with difficulties. According to Ohashi it is the movement of Spirit which in 'moving', that is, in transforming itself, nonetheless remains identical with itself. He cites Hegel's own definition of mediation as 'the movement of the "I" which is for-itself, the pure negativity or . . . simple becoming'.[12] He then draws attention to the role of the concept of the moment as an element in mediation. This is seen to be central to the whole structure of Hegel's thought, since mediation not only serves to link finite and infinite but also to establish time, and consequently history, as a field within which the absolute reveals itself. Time/history thus becomes for Hegel an eminent mode of the self-realisation of Spirit. If the principle of mediation is allowed then we have a theoretical basis for asserting that the Spirit can remain itself, remain absolute, even when it is immersed in the flux of time. The 'moment' is the precise point at which Spirit is both in and beyond time, a time-category – yet one which takes up no time. Referring back to Plato (and a Christian theologian might recall Book X of Augustine's *Confessions*) Ohashi observes that 'the moment, then, is not in time, has no place in it, thus it is ἄτοπον, that is, literally that without place'.[13]

He then directs his analysis back to Hegel's remarks about Buddhism. Whereas Hegel accuses Buddhism of denying mediation by the way in which it asserts the absoluteness of nothingness, his own concept of mediation can be shown to contain an element – the 'moment' – which, as place-less, is itself outside the process of mediation, ie., has no place in it. In this respect, he says, the concept of mediation is itself 'freed' and 'made fluid' and, most importantly, the Hegelian distinction between 'eastern' and 'western' thought rendered questionable.

We may seem to have digressed from the two pictures, 'The Crowning of Mary' and 'Sakyamuni Descending the Mountain', but Ohashi now returns to these in the light of his philosophical

investigations. In 'The Crowning of Mary' he notices a feature
which Rombach has overlooked. The picture itself is not a picture
of Mary *as* Queen of Heaven, it is a picture of the *moment* of her being
crowned. The crown is, as yet, suspended a small distance above her
head. In this small distance we can perceive the 'momentary' character of the scene. In it, in this small distance which is also a pause
in time, is reflected the tension between Father and Son, as the right
hand of the Father holds the crown from beneath, keeping it aloft in
'eternal elevation' and the left hand of the Son holds it from above,
pressing it downwards and earthwards. Mary herself remains still,
in her humility a point of rest at the centre of the tension around her
and, by virtue of this, able to receive and maintain in equilibrium
the opposing divine forces of which she is the focus. At the centre
of the picture, then, is a moment of dynamic stillness (*'bewegte
Stille'*) which is, as such, the abiding condition of the moment of
love-in-process-of-concretion (as analysed by Rombach). But it is
precisely this same moment which is thematically prominent in the
picture of 'Sakyamuni Descending the Mountain'. The difference
between the pictures, then, is not a crude difference between a
metaphysics of being and a metaphysics of nothingness. It is rather
a difference in the mode of representation of that moment, known
to both traditions, in which finite and infinite, earthly and heavenly,
time and eternity meet and engage in a process of mutual mediation.
Yet this moment, the point of unity of all zones of being, has in
itself no place, no time, no identity: it is nothing. In the Western
image this nothing is veiled by the solidity and thickness of the
action; in the eastern image it is this nothingness itself which is
made prominent. To re-iterate: neither tradition is immune from
the problematic concerning how finite and infinite, and similar
contraries, can be mediated and both are forced back onto the central
paradox of mediation. What remains distinctive is the standpoint
from which this paradox is approached; in the one case from the side
of stillness, in the other from the side of movement and dynamic
action. The unmediated reality which is in play in the eastern
image and the mediated reality ('Dichtheit') which characterises the
western image represent real differences – but they can no longer
be regarded as differences between two self-sufficient, mutually
exclusive 'world-views'.

In his postscript Rombach concludes that the perception of finite
and infinite as ultimately 'one and the same' is the theme of both
pictures, but approached from the standpoints of negation and

comprehensiveness respectively. He suggests that contemporary humanity may need to learn to tread both ways, 'the way of the crowning of humanity and the way of its negation and transparency'.[14] In this journey each will, perhaps, best learn its own truth by learning to recognise the truth of the other.

The participants in this conversation clearly bring to it a definite philosophical and religious apparatus which, to a considerable extent, determines what they see in the pictures. In such an exercise there can be no final safeguard against the pictures themselves being little more than the more or less accidental occasions for the elaboration of ready-made philosophical and religious arguments. But to the extent that the pictures themselves remain in view in the course of the conversation and, indeed, determine the course, acting as a kind of control on the discussion, then such a conversation exemplifies the theology of art at work in the dialogue of faiths. The image has been allowed to open a space within which discussion can orientate itself and the characteristic differences and similarities come into view. The scope for such discussions is immense, embracing the full range of western and eastern religious art, or, indeed, any art which (whether overtly religious or not) might be seen as typifying the approach of one or other religious tradition.

John D. Eusden has attempted a similar exercise in an article entitled 'Chartres and Ryōan-Ji: Aesthetic Connections between Gothic Cathedral and Zen Garden'. Recalling Tertullian's question, 'What has Jerusalem to do with Athens?', he comments that 'Today we can say that a Zen garden has much to do with a Gothic Cathedral'.[15] Like Rombach he not only affirms the timeliness of such encounters but also believes that what he calls the 'affective presence' of works of art provides unique access to the reality of other religious traditions, disclosing both differences and often quite unexpected points of meeting and contact. Much will depend in any particular case on the works chosen for comparison. They must be works which fall within a comparable field and yet which, by being highly characteristic of their respective traditions, stretch the possibilities of dialogue to the uttermost. In making such a selection we will, inevitably, be guided as much by our actual visual sensibility as by our considered theological intentions. In the context of a theology of art for which pictures are not merely 'illustrations' of ready-made theological positions, reflection must arise out of the processes of aesthetic making and responsiveness themselves. Such a venture therefore requires the willingness to take real risks by exposing that which we take (on essentially non-rational grounds) to be representative of our own religious orientation to rational reflection and cross-examination.

We may also conceive of a quite different area of discussion opened up by the theology of art, namely, the comparison of the different conceptions of art and of the place of art in the religious life which are found in the different religious traditions. I shall, therefore, conclude by examining the understanding of art to be found in Zen, bearing in mind the now familiar emphases of Western Christianity. A similar exercise could, of course, be conducted in relation to any one of a number of traditions. Zen just happens to be the one which, over many years, has most engaged my own attention, although it would not be hard to argue that it has had a unique impact on western culture and experience over the last forty or so years.

Zen is, as most of its interpreters agree, a spiritual way which gives a prominent role to the arts, understood in the broadest sense and embracing swordsmanship, flower-arranging and tea-making as well as poetry, pottery and painting. The difference between aesthetic and religious categories is narrowed to the point where *satori*, the enlightenment which is the goal of Zen disci-pline, can find a spontaneous expression in artistic activity or, con-versely, artistic activity can itself become a vehicle for the existential communication or transmission of *satori*. A poem or picture can show us the quality of – or be a test of the quality of – a Zennist's enlightenment. Writing about the seventeenth century Japanese poet Matsuo Bashō, Richard B. Pilgrim has described Bashō's stand-point as 'religio-aesthetic', a concept which he defines as 'that point where the aesthetic and the religious become synonymous and the distinction of religion and art is transcended'.[16] What, more precisely, is this point?

It is often described in terms of intuition. This, for instance, is how D. T. Suzuki defines *satori*: 'an intuitive looking into the nature of things in contradistinction to the analytical or logical understanding of it. Practically, it means the unfolding of a new world hitherto unperceived in the confusion of a dualistically-trained mind'.[17] Shades of theoria? Yet this quality of a direct and immediate intui-tion of the absolute truth of things characteristically marks Zen off from many aspects of the western philosophical and religious tradition, where the possibility of such a complete intuition in this life is either denied outright or hedged around with a multiplicity of cautions. Even when, as in Romantic philosophers such as Schelling, aesthetic intuition is given a certain primacy over the rational, discursive functions of the mind, knowledge remains a prime concern of western thought in a way which does not seem to apply to Zen.

Naturally there is a degree of mutual conditioning between art and religion in Zen. An art whose chief aim is to give an appropriate expression to the *satori*-experience will itself be shaped by that experience and the understanding of it. Zen does not merely provide art with a religious content: it also influences the forms and methods of art itself, in order to enable art to stand within the sphere of immediacy in which *satori* itself is experienced. Here is Suzuki again, describing the techniques of *sumi-e* painting:

> The artist must follow his inspiration as spontaneously and absolutely and instantly as it moves; he just lets his aim, his fingers, his brush be guided by it as if they were all mere instruments, together with his whole being, in the hands of somebody else who has temporarily taken possession of him. Or we may say that the brush by itself executes the work quite outside the artist, who just lets it move on without his conscious efforts. If any logic or reflection comes between brush and paper, the whole effect is spoiled.[18]

The requirement of such a high degree of spontaneity even governs the artist's materials, the soft, absorbent brush and the thin, fragile paper. Such materials exclude the possibility of working over a preliminary sketch and refining it into a final edition. The work can only be what emerges from the moment of inspiration. Suzuki acknowledges that this excludes certain artistic possibilities open, for example, to the western tradition of oil-painting, but it does enable *sumi-e* to be a direct expression of a living, moving spirit in a way which the more laboured discipline of oils cannot achieve. Its simplicity and (apparent) poverty of means is not in reality a lack. It is what it is and is, as such, final and absolute, perfectly suited to its aims. It does not claim to attain a high level of imitative truth but it is able to produce unique individual creations which appropriately represent the *satori*-spirit of the artist.

But, a sceptical and rationalistic westerner might want to ask, have we passed into a realm of wordless and formless wonderment where all differentiation has collapsed into a primal unity devoid of individual and concrete characteristics? Is *satori*, and the art which corresponds to it, that night in which all cows are black and 'cognition naively reduced to vacuity', as Hegel said of Schelling's doctrine of intellectual intuition?[19] Certainly a 'Romantic' reading of Zen is highly plausible. The numerous anecdotes about the extraordinary behaviour and sayings of the Zen masters; the *koan* exercise in which trainees are required to wrestle with such paradoxical and nonsensical sayings as 'the sound of one hand clapping'; the Zen dialogues in which all conventional logic is subverted – all these, together with numerous definitions and descriptions of *satori*, could seem to suggest that we have passed into a region where all rationality, all discipline, all structure has been discarded. With regard to art this would mean that any attempt to develop reliable criteria of meaning and value is flawed, if not misguided, from the very beginning. Religion and art have merged – but at the cost of our not being able to say anything coherent about either of them.

Such criticism is, however, superficial. Zen does have form, structure, coherence – but not necessarily of a kind we might expect. If it does subvert both religious and aesthetic norms and conventions (which can scarcely be denied) it does so in a rigorous manner.

We must for a start avoid confusing the kind of spontaneous self-expression exemplified in Suzuki's account of *sumi-e* with the cult of self-expression in post-romantic western art and culture. Whereas the western form of self-expression is usually found in connection with the assertion of artistic autonomy, the Zen doctrine is firmly rooted in a context of religious discipline and traditional skills and practices. The individualism and the avant-garde concepts associated with self-expression in the West are lacking in Zen. For the fundamental conjunction of religion and art means that (as in Neo-Thomist teaching) art is from the beginning conceived of as determined by religious experience and values. There are, of course, differences from the notion of religion-culture as found in the West. Because the focus of religious endeavour is experiential and, to a much lesser extent governed by doctrinally articulated truths, there is no *a priori* determination of content by religious concepts. What might be called secular themes in the West are treated as religiously significant: landscape, animal and bird life, still-life – not to mention non-representational arts such as calligraphy, archery and tea! Yet the religious requirement does impose a discipline and a direction on art. The aims and values of artistic practices are not free-floating. They serve a goal which even if it is entirely commensurable with aesthetic experience, perhaps even inseparable from it, is not exhausted by aesthetic enactment. Within art itself the methods of the Zen artist are not without discipline. The *sumi-e* painter, the haiku poet, the maker of the apparently random stone garden may aim to produce works which express something spontaneous – but they work within a clearly defined tradition in which the choice of tools, materials and forms is both circumscribed and nourished by accepted practice. Zen may not hold its rule-book open to the world – but we should not assume that there is no body of rules, no objectivity on which Zen draws, in religion and in art alike.

The structured quality of what might be called 'Zen experience' is apparent from another angle if we consider the variety of Zen moods. The emphasis on the intuitive quality of *satori* should not be interpreted as indicating that *satori* is a specific intuition, universally the same beneath all the variety of cultural and religious forms. In his treatment of Bashō's 'religio-aesthetic' Richard Pilgrim details a range of elements which go to make this up.[20] Firstly there is a complex of imagery connected with the wind; thus: *fūrabō*, 'a wind-blown hermit', *fūga*, 'wind eloquence', *fūryū*, 'wind style' and *fūsō*, 'wind-refined person'. Such imagery has many and varied connotations: wind and breath as life and as that which is the source of life; thereby also that which by pervading both man and nature is the living bond of unity between them; the bird who rides the wind, both as wanderer and pilgrim, courageously surmounting the colossal forces arrayed against it. Then, secondly, comes the concept of *hosomi*, literally 'slender' or 'narrow', which Pilgrim relates to the Zen doctrine of No-Mind, that is, the dissolution of the ego-consciousness in moments of great insight, and, on account of the sense of non-separation felt in such moments, appropriately mani-fested in images of that which is 'thin, sharp, narrow or delicate' since 'the mind of Tao . . . is so slender that it enters anything with plenty of room to spare'.[21] Thirdly, he discussed the concepts of *sabi* and *karumi*, 'loneliness' and 'lightness' respectively. *Sabi* has to do with 'detachment, quietness, slight melancholy, and tranquility'.[22] Suzuki, we may add, translates it as 'eternal loneliness', and, he says, it expresses 'the mysterious loneliness of human life, which is, however, not the feeling of forlornness, nor the depressive sense of solitariness, but a sort of appreciation of the mystery of the absolute'.[23] He relates this feeling to the extreme simplicity of many haiku poems and *sumi-e* paintings:

All things come out of an unknown abyss of mystery, and through every one of them we can have a peep into the abyss . . . Japanese artists more or less influenced by the way of Zen tend to use the fewest words or strokes of brush to express their feelings. When they are too fully expressed, no room for suggestion is possible, and suggestibility is the secret of the Japanese arts.[24]

If *sabi* thus points to depths of mystery and loneliness in Zen and in Zen art, *karumi* points to a 'down-to-earth, homely mundane' element which Pilgrim finds exemplified in the poem

> Under the trees
> A flurry of cherry-petals
> On soup and fish-salad.[25]

Pilgrim's analysis of Bashō's 'religio-aesthetic' is, of course, only an individual study and does not exhaust the full range of elements incorporated into the religio-aesthetic synthesis of Zen as a whole. What it does achieve, however, is (in the context of the present discussion) to show that the point of religio-aesthetic unity is, even in this individual case, complex and subtly differentiated. It may be that Zen does hinge on the possibility of some kind of undifferentiated intuition, but that intuition is embodied, articulated and expressed, religiously and aesthetically, in a coherent and structured way. In Zen art at least the experience of *satori* acquires cultural shape and communicability: the 'meaning' of such art is not to be looked for in some hidden depth of subjective consciousness but in the way in which it engages our bodily and visual attention.

'Nature' has been a recurrent theme in our survey of various Western theologies of art. It is also central to the Zen understanding of the relationship between religion and art, albeit in a quite distinctive way. Nature, in its beauty and in its sublimity, is not seen as a 'mere' veil of appearance from which we need to be emancipated. The appeal of nature is not construed as a temptation likely to divert the monk from pressing on single-mindedly to his goal of *nirvana*. It is instead itself a relation of the absolute in its suchness, giving itself to be apprehended in the manifold forms, materials, sounds, colours and textures of the natural world. Every aspect of nature participates in this absolute character, from the fragile cherry-blossom, beautiful in its transiency, to the sublime grandeur of a great mountain and the down-to-earthness of a frog jumping into a pond. Yet the Zen attitude to nature is not just an attitude of naive pastoralism. There is a well-known Zen saying which states that before Zen training begins the mountain is just a mountain, once training has begun it is no longer a mountain, and when training has finished it is, once more, just a mountain. This 'third' mountain is not, however, the same as the mountain which an undisciplined and unenlightened everyday mind sees. What happens in the process of Zen training is that we learn to see the mountain as it is for the first time. Our initial state is not a *tabula rasa* but a mass of confused and unexamined prejudices. It requires training precisely in order to undo the distortions of consciousness which characterise 'normal' looking. When this occurs we see the mountain in its being-there, rather than just taking it for granted. What we come to see is not the appearance of the mountain, what it looks 'like', but the sheer and astonishing facticity of its existence, very much in the sense of Etienne Gilson's comments on the power of still-life to evoke the simple *dasein*, the being-there, the thingly quality of being. It is this which is at stake in the religio-aesthetic response to nature.

The philosophical background to this view of nature lies in the Buddhist doctrine of suchness and the fundamental identity of the worlds of enlightenment and of change, *nirvana* and *samsara* respectively. The concept of suchness is conventionally traced back to the first century A.D. philosopher and writer Asvaghosha. At the simplest level suchness (or thusness at it is sometimes referred to) is defined as 'the oneness of the totality of things, the great all-including whole'.[26] In this respect it denotes the plenitude of being prior to verbalisation or conceptualisation. Alan Watts, one of the most successful popularisers of Zen in the West, summed it up in this way: '*Tathata* [suchness] therefore indicates the world just as it is, unscreened and undivided by the symbols and definitions of thought. It points to the concrete and actual as distinct from the abstract and conceptual'.[27] In a certain sense it is untrue even to speak of it as 'being' rather than as 'non-being' since it is prior to the dualistic standpoint which regards these as separate and opposed. It is the 'true or original nature' 'of all beings whatsoever'. Everything that is is ultimately included in suchness – including that which a dualistic philosophical viewpoint might want to discard as 'merely' phenomenal, mutable and transient.

The further implications of this were brought out a century later by the metaphysician Nāgārjuna. Nāgārjuna's teaching, which has

some affinities with Vedanta, denies the ultimate duality of enlightenment and non-enlightenment, *nirvana* and *samsara*. What does this
mean? Early Buddhism has regarded all earthly life as subject to
suffering, change and decay. It diagnosed the cause of this situation
to be the clinging desire which issues from the illusion of selfhood.
The world in which suffering holds sway is the world of *samsara*.
Over against it is the world of *nirvana*, often defined by analogy
with the blowing out of a flame. For in *nirvana* the desire which
causes us to be attached to the cycle of suffering is extinguished.
Nāgārjuna repudiated the dualism of this doctrine. In his view
nirvana was not to be understood so much in terms of the extinction
of a personal, individualised self but as the supreme insight into
the actual participation of all relative being in the absolute state
of suchness. Rather than marking a change of (ontological) state,
nirvana is interpreted more as a new perspective on existence, the
overcoming of ignorance. In its extreme form Nāgārjuna's teaching
is that 'this our worldly life is an activity of Nirvana itself, not the
slightest distinction exists between them'.[28] Nirvana, then, subjec-
tively, is the recognition that we are always ready 'in' the suchness
of absolute reality.

It is the further development of this doctrine which underpins
the Zen view of nature which, as we have seen, reveals in its
smallest details the absolute being which comprises all things, from
mountains to frogs.

This has important implications for the relationship between
religion and art, since it endorses the view that the manifest,
visible world can be regarded even in its material thingliness as
religiously significant. Moreover, the art-work itself, as an object
among objects, a thing among things, participating in the materiality
and visibility of phenomenal reality also by this token participates in
absolute reality. Its religious value is not just in the fact that it might
represent an important religious idea or scene (a Buddha descending
a mountain, perhaps) but in the way it can itself become a direct and
immediate presencing of being.

An important contribution to contemporary Zen aesthetics was
made by Yanagi Soētsu (1889–1961), a friend of the British potter
Bernard Leach, on whom Yanagi's aesthetic theories exerted considerable influence. Yanagi's essay 'The Dharma Gate of Beauty' (1948)
draws on many of the themes of Zen aesthetics and religion which
we have been examining. He also appeals to the Buddhist school
known as The Pure Land. This school is closely connected with Zen

but is distinctive in that it encourages votive prayers to Amidha Buddha to fully accomplish the salvation which he has wrought for humankind. Such prayer takes the form of invoking his name and, more than any other school of Buddhism, seems to involve ideas of what is called 'Other-power'. Yanagi's text starts from the Fourth Vow of Amidha Buddha as recorded in the *Sutra of Eternal Life*: 'When I come to obtain Buddhahood, unless all the beings throughout my land are of one form and colour, unless there is no beauty and ugliness among them, I will not attain highest enlightenment'.[29] This, Yanagi believes (perhaps surprisingly on a first reading), is to serve as the basis for a Buddhist aesthetic. Referring to the non-duality which characterises the condition of suchness and its transcendence of all forms of opposition, he suggests that this must, logically, include the duality beauty/ugliness. The Buddha-nature which is the source of all true beauty is thus beyond that level of aesthetic experience in which we might want to distinguish between beautiful and ugly art-works. Yanagi acknowledges that while we live in a world of change and multiplicity we will probably not be able to avoid using such dualistic concepts. Nonetheless since, as Buddhists believe, the Buddha has in fact accomplished his vow and attained enlightenment, there is a point at which the transcendence of the duality of beauty and ugliness has been achieved. Once more we are back with Nāgārjuna's paradox which Yanagi put like this: 'It is not that we are given salvation because we suffer. On the contrary, when we are suffering, we are suffering amid an accomplished salvation. There can be no suffering where there is no salvation'.[30] The same logic holds with regard to beauty and ugliness. Within the horizons of the relative world we are limited by their opposition, drawn to one and repelled by the other. But, Yanagi says, they are concepts of our making, they do not belong to reality as such; really there is no contradiction between beauty and ugliness. In response to the question, 'What then are we to do?' Yanagi gives what might be regarded as a classic Zen answer. 'Return to the original nature of "as-it-is-ness" or "thusness". Live in the plenty that heaven gave us. Be just as the Dharma makes you be, and all is well'.[31] Only in such a condition (or, should we say, absence of conditions) can we know the true beauty which is beyond the duality beauty/ugliness.

Now it might seem that in such a state we would neither be interested in involving ourselves in art nor capable of distinguishing between good and bad art, but this is not how Yanagi sees it. Instead he suggests that the conscious pursuit of beauty actually wrecks the cause of good art. It inevitably produces an element of contrivance, of conscious interference in the processes of creation and the being of natural reality, which prevents the making of a work of true beauty. The source of true beauty is Other-power, suchness – may we say 'grace'? – and, as such, is in no way dependent on the conscious intentions of the artist. As such true beauty can more easily co-exist with clumsiness and imperfection than with contrivance and 'art'. To show how beauty does not depend on conscious aesthetic culture Yanagi adduces the example of Korean Ido tea-bowls. Those who made them, he says, were 'poor artisans . . . workmen of the most ordinary kind. They were making low-priced articles. They were not giving any thought to making each piece beautiful. They threw them off simply and effortlessly'.[32] Yet the outcome is that they reveal precisely the quality and grace of a beauty which is beyond the duality of beauty and ugliness.

Nonetheless, though I have used the word 'grace', Yanagi does not pretend that such beauty comes about as if by magic, without human work, effort or skill. There is a combination of 'human' factors which facilitate the production of such works: 'The overall environment, the received traditions, the selfless work, the simple way of life, the natural materials and unsophisticated techniques, all combined in the flowering of these bowls'.[33] He also believes that such an achievement was typical of 'past ages of deep faith' when 'people were more innocent and humble and closer to the truth'.[34] Elsewhere he says that in East and West alike there was a time 'before the twelfth century or earlier' when 'it was almost impossible to find anything which was ugly'.[35] In the modern world, however, ugliness increasingly prevails – perhaps precisely because of the conscious but one-sided pursuit of aesthetic beauty, and because of the idolising of individual creativity at the expense of communal craft traditions.

The theological and philosophical background of Yanagi's ideas may seem strange, but these last remarks show a striking similarity to laments which we have heard elsewhere over the artistic deterioration of the modern world. They may, for instance, recall Maritain's eulogy of the mediaeval workman, and there are even stronger resonances with Eric Gill's advocacy of a renewal of craft traditions and his assertion of the value of a 'hieratic canon' as a counterweight to individualism in art. Yanagi's canon, rooted as it is in Zen ideas is less overt than that of the complex theological edifice of which the

Gothic cathedral is (or is said to be) the architectural realisation. Its religious and aesthetic ambience is quite distinct from that of any canon with which the West is familiar, but Yanagi's lament over a lost tradition endorses our view that Zen, for all its emphasis on immediacy and spontaneity, is a quite different beast from western aesthetic individualism. Zen too draws on subtle but nonetheless real structures, traditions and disciplines in its religious and artistic practices alike. And, like so much of Western Christianity, it experiences the conscious autonomy and individualism of the modern world as a profound threat to its religo-aesthetic synthesis. Yet in responding to this crisis Zen may, arguably, find itself at an advantage compared with Christianity. This advantage lies quite simply in the fact that its tradition takes a more benevolent view both of nature and of art than Western Christianity. Although it requires the artist to live within the framework of a religious orientation it finds in his work and in the realm of material objects in which, with which, and among which he works a proper focus for religious concern. At the theoretical level this was, as we saw, made possible by the identification of the worlds of *nirvana* and *samsara*.

In Chapter 8 I argued for the relocation of the theology of art within the field of the theology of redemption. Perhaps we may now go further and suggest that so long as theology operates with a sharp dualism of nature and grace (or nature and redemption) it will help to perpetuate the carelessness which has so characterised the Western theological attitude towards art. Such a reorientation, however, may require a revolution no less dramatic and no less paradoxical than Nāgārjuna's teaching of the identity of *nirvana* and *samsara*. It will involve developing a kind of Christian worldliness which sees redemption in terms of a total transformation of our relation to nature, to the visible, material world and to our carnal, bodily involvement in the world – rather than in terms of deliverance from that world. To put it another way: it is precisely the knowledge of God the redeemer which enables us to recognise the goodness and the beauty and the sublimity of nature, and it is in such a recognition and in no other way that we show our knowledge of God as redeemer.

There have, as any student of modern theology knows, been many, many calls with varying emphases for just such a folding back of the sphere of redemption into the sphere of natural existence. The limits and consequences of such a rethinking remain controversial, however. The more interest theologians take in art – and this may be read as an invitation or as a warning – the more tempting a firm commitment to such Christian worldliness is likely to appear. The very fact of such an interest indicates that theologians are already falling under the spell of that lust of the eye which is of the essence of a fully carnal spirituality.

That is a provocative way of putting it. Here is another. In his essay 'The Pure Land of Beauty' Yanagi spoke of the consolation which art brought him during a long and, in fact, terminal illness. 'As I lie in bed', he wrote, 'I have had pots and pictures brought into my room for me to look at. I have got into the habit during long sleepless nights of allowing my thoughts to ponder over the strange miracle of the quiet beauty of each object'.[36] Remembering that Yanagi's conception of beauty points us beyond narrowly conceived conventions of beauty and ugliness, I should like to suggest that both theologians in their thinking and artists in their making may also ponder over 'the strange miracle of the quiet beauty' of visual art, and spend time in the space which this 'strange miracle' opens up.

10

Seeing is Believing

If this book is read as the quest for a Christian theology of art, it seems to have arrived at an impasse. This impasse is generated by a knot of issues around which the last two chapters have circled without being able to find a satisfactory resolution. The deepest knot of all is both very simple and very complex, being concerned with the relationship between image and meaning in art and how this relationship gets worked out in the context of religious art. The issue is easily stated, but the preceding pages have provided considerable evidence to suggest that answers are less easily come by. The problem is given a further twist by the specific historical timing of the question, since we live in an age that is both extraordinarily uncertain and extraordinarily pluralistic. There is no agreed agenda in either art or religion, nor even a clearly defined or defining tradition of authority against which to mark out our own position. If we call this situation 'post-modern', that simply under-lines the point: that we are having to take our bearings from an ideology and a culture (modernity) that is itself pervaded by the spirit of critique, irony and social transformation.

If the condition of postmodernity in this way problematizes the discussion of religion and art in general, it raises particularly sharp issues for a Christian theology of art. I have argued that art has to be justified out of its own resources, and its own unique way of being present in the world. If art works, it works because of the way it works through the specific media of visual experience. If we are not moved by art in its own terms, we will not be moved to attend to it as part of a larger theorization of Christian self-understanding. However, Christian theology seems to be singularly ill-placed to allow art an appropriate autonomy, since it is congenitally reluctant to concede its privilege of judging art in terms of its relation to a (verbally determined) dogmatic meaning or narrative. This is true even of theology's attempts to interpret important works of secular art: it is especially true of theology's approach to art in and for

Churches. Even apart from the vexed issue of getting a new work accepted by a particular congregation, a work of Church art must be able to survive a theological interrogation that can easily distort or destroy its artistic integrity, as the values of art are subordinated to the demands of doctrinal formulations or narrative reference. The results are well-known: that much of the Church art of the nineteenth and twentieth centuries is mediocre or kitsch. Confronted by the new, the Churches have habitually opted for the familiar and safe – a strategy that may have placated the faithful in the short term, but that has further attenuated the already weakened links between the communities of art and Church. Buddhism, on the other hand (at least in its Zen form), seems to permit an aesthetic that allows art to be itself, thereby facilitating a theology of art that is both contemporary and spiritual.

Is this a situation we simply have to accept, or can things be otherwise?

Having stated repeatedly that the primary source of any theology of art has to be art itself, the only appropriate way of addressing this question is by looking at particular art works that promise a positive response. I have therefore chosen four examples of contemporary works of art in British Churches that, in my judgement, are both true to the exigencies of contemporary artistic production and that also 'work' in their Church context. These works are 'Pietà' by Glynn Williams (in Worcester Cathedral), 'Sound II' by Antony Gormley (in Winchester Cathedral), 'The Messenger' by Bill Viola (a temporary installation in Durham Cathedral in 1996) and 'Crucifixion 1994' by Craigie Aichison (in King's College Chapel).

Although the principles argued for in this book allow no other way forward than that of engagement with particular works in particular situations, this procedure does have two major drawbacks. The first is that it depends upon judgements that are individual and contestable, the second that it falls into the trap of localism. Before proceeding to the works themselves, then, I shall briefly address these problems.

The belief that individual taste is subjective and non-negotiable is one of the most widespread assumptions about art in comtemporary culture. It is an assumption that continually threatens to block off all discussion of art at source. Ultimately it means that all one can ever do is give voice to gut-level reactions and express personal preferences more or less extensively. Now it is true that persuading someone to like a picture they don't like is notoriously difficult and perhaps impossible. However, it should none the less be possible to *explain* and not merely to report on one's own likes and dislikes, to say what it is about a work that elicits admiration, and where and how that admiration is marred or limited, and also how it relates to the larger contexts within which, as you see it, the work works. If we cannot hope to persuade others to share our tastes, we can at least hope to persuade them to understand them. That, however, only mitigates the problem; it does not solve it. But perhaps it is a mistake to want to solve it. Perhaps we must accept that there *is* an irreducible subjective element in our response to art and that, this being the case, the point is not to try (vainly) to get rid of it but to take responsibility for the judgements we make, and not to shrink from the contestation of opinions that makes up the realm of art criticism. If there is no objectively 'right' view, this is not a reason for shrinking from the expression of our own opinions but rather underlines the need for us to speak up for the judgements we make. Judgements *are* always particular, always personal and always contestable and, since anything worth saying about art always involves particular judgements about particular works, that is simply the situation under which any philosophy or theology of art is going to operate. There is no theoretical high ground above and beyond the cut and thrust of opinion. It is probable that it was precisely his insight into this situation that made Plato uncomfortable with the world of art.

In choosing these works, then, I am not holding them up as universal examples of how Church art might or should reconstruct itself for a post-modern age, for neither the works themselves nor my response to them can be exempted from the larger process of production and reception that might lead to the dismissal of works and response to the dustbins of art-history. Equally, however, a sense for the provisionality of our own judgements does not exempt us, here and now, from saying 'This is what works for me, and it does so in this way and for these reasons.'

If the following discussion is therefore necessarily coloured by a certain subjectivity, it is also, for similar reasons, necesssarily local. In focusing on works in four British Churches I am accepting the limitations of place as well as of personality that constrain the world of art, but this should not at all be taken as implying that these are the best or the only examples available. There are many other situations and works that could also be mentioned, and there are other artists whose work is congruent with the argument I have been advancing, but who have not yet been represented in any significant Church commissions.[1]

With these provisos in place, then: to the works themselves.

Glynn Williams' early work has been negatively characterized by Peter Fuller in the following terms: 'His work became drained of imagery; and he pursued collage, mixed media and construction rather than carving. Mere placement of material, often without discernible aesthetic or symbolic intent, became a substitute for imaginative and physical working.'[2] In the 1970s, however, Williams returned to carving, producing a range of figures in complex and dynamic positions. 'Squatting, Holding and Looking' (1982) featured a mother and child doing just that, whilst 'Walking' (1984) depicted a mother bending down and guiding her toddler's first steps. 'Stone Rise East' showed a nude male figure doing a shoulder stand. The kinetic quality of these works expressed Williams' ambition to give stone an illusory lightness of being, an anti-gravitational 'lift' that defied its own solidity. These works have an impact quite different from that of the massive monumentality of Henry Moore or, to look further back, Rodin. This almost counter-intuitive effect is exaggerated in some works where Williams has cut up and rearranged the stone, as in carvings of a vase of flowers or a piece commissioned for the Purcell tercentenary. The material itself is redefined in the virtual explosion of its raw materiality. 'Pietà' is related to these latter works in that it too is, in its final form, the result of having been, literally, carved up. But it also has other sources in Williams' work.

At the height of the civil war in the Lebanon, Williams was deeply affected by the images of civilian suffering appearing daily on the television and in the newspapers. His own 'Shout' (1982) is a response to that, although (as is so often the case for artists) it is also the resolution of a technical challenge. This challenge was how to combine two planes, horizontal and vertical, in a single work. The image shows the figure of a kneeling mother, holding the body of her dead child across her lap, while her head is thrown back, her mouth torn open like a gaping wound, in a silent 'shout' of anger and grief. As a representation of the power of raw emotion it is almost unequalled in modern British sculpture.

'Pietà' also takes up the theme of a mother and a dead child. In this case, however (and in contrast to both 'Shout' and the traditional iconography of the Pietà theme), the mother is standing, her left arm curving over and round the sprawling body of the child and her right arm holding it up from underneath. The child is, perhaps, adolescent, but of no determinate gender; its legs, arms and head hang limply down. After the first showing of this work Williams took his saw to it, carving off the mother's head and lower legs, with the result – seen in the work as it now exists – of heightening both the universality and the violence of the work. The emphasis is not, as in 'Shout', on her grief, but on the objective tragedy of the cruel and untimely death.

Neither the position of the figure nor the age of the child accord with accepted representations of the dead Christ in his mother's arms, nor was the Pietà originally intended for a Church. In 1991 Worcester Cathedral arranged a fund-raising sale of works by fifty leading artists, with a percentage of the sale price going to the Cathedral Appeal. Williams' piece in fact failed to sell at the auction, but the then Dean, Robert Jeffrey, quickly raised funds to purchase it for the Cathedral, where it is now sited in the Norman crypt. Although it is no traditional Pietà, it none the less works as such, precisely because Williams has returned the imagery to the context of primary human emotion and the bare statement of suffering's terror and pity. In the Church context it becomes a reminder that the violence of the cross belongs in a continuing sequence of appalling violent acts, and that that is the precondition for any dogmatic or doctrinal interpretation that might be added to it. Abstracting from any particular political or historical context it simply depicts a grief without a cause, beyond all causes: Rachel weeping for her children and knowing no consolation. As such it states directly what violence always signifies before and beyond any interpretation.

Thus far 'Pietà' belongs in a modern tradition of works that tear away the veil cast by doctrine and sentiment over the primal obscenity of the crucifixion. But it is not brutal or confrontational. The very fact that our response is not determined or directed by the expression of the mother's face means that the work allows us and, indeed, requires us to stand back and think for ourselves upon the significance of what it means. The thoughtfulness induced by the work corresponds well to the prayerfulness of its ancient site. In contrast to media images of violence that cut us to the quick for an hour or day only to be buried beneath new and yet more disturbing images, the 'Pietà', because its object is grief as such and not this grief or that, reaches out into the universality of the human condition and thereby calls for a more patient and a more sustained effort of appropriation and interpretation. Its religious value is therefore not simply that it reminds us of the actual historical violence of the passion (although it does do that), but the way in which it constitutes a question concerning ourselves, concerning what, for good or ill, we are capable of.

Antony Gormley's 'Sound II' is a figure of a very different kind. Insofar as it contains an allusion to the suffering inherent in the human condition, it is an allusion that is by no means immediately apparent in a figure that creates around itself an atmosphere of serenity and concentrated peace.

Gormley is perhaps best-known for his innovative body-casts, lead figures made from plaster casts built round his own bandaged body in a variety of postures, subsequently sited in unusual and counter-intuitive positions, like the group of figures in 'Learning to Think' (1991), whose heads disappear into the ceiling from which they are suspended. 'Sound II' was itself conceived as part of an ambitiously large project involving thirty-six figures, but never completed. The body-cast is of an upright figure, whose head is bowed and whose hands are cupped at the level of his heart. A hole is inserted in the sternum which allows water falling into the hands to flow into the cavity of the body, or, conversely, water accumulating in the body to overflow into the hands. This is important in terms of its siting in the crypt of Winchester Cathedral, for, unlike the crypt at Worcester, this is not ordered as a Chapel, since it is liable to seasonal flooding, during which the rising and falling water levels interact dynamically with the figure of 'Sound II'.

The fact that the crypt is a space devoid of specifically Christian imagery and has a character determined by the ebb and flow of the waters is important to Gormley in interpreting its spiritual significance. Like many of his contemporaries, Gormley is intensely preoccupied by the issue of humanity's relation to the elemental life and rhythms of the planet. Instead of seeing humanity as a separate creation, Gormley seeks to revision human being as an integral part of planetary life. He has, for example, written that 'Nature is within us. We are sick when we do not feel it. The sickness of feeling separate from the world is what is killing it. We are earth above ground, clothed by space, seen by light.'[3] Our own bodies provide the most obvious and immediate means by which to re-establish our link to the world. In fact the body *is* our way of being in the world as a part of the world. If, under the influence of Neo-Platonism, the body has long been conceived of as 'dark' in comparison with the 'light' of reason, we must now learn that this 'darkness' is the darkness of an earth rich with possibilities for renewal. If the body is also that which makes us mortal, that very mortality and the encounter with death is seen by Gormley as 'a doorway' to understanding the mystery of life itself. It is not surprising that Gormley has had important spiritual encounters with Buddhist spirituality, and the ecological orientation of some contemporary Buddhist spirituality resonates with aspects of his own artistic programme.

In the unique space of the crypt of Winchester Cathedral, 'Sound II' evokes, in Gormley's own words, 'languages before language, moving elemental dynamics that happen before symbolism ... that don't need to be limited by iconographical or biblical or textual ... readings',[4] he also sees a fittingness in the siting of the work in this elemental space, without doctrinal symbols or liturgical functions, beneath the more formal Christian space of the Cathedral above. 'Sound II' thus sites itself in the pre-history of the Cathedral, establishing a link between the dark, sustaining life of the planet and the conscious 'world' of history and public religion. The resonances with Heidegger's vision of art belonging to the ceaseless struggle between 'earth' and 'world' are congenial to Gormley, though not specifically intended in his work.[5] It is also relevant to allude back to my own previous comments[6] regarding the way in which Heidegger privileges language. For language is only one dimension of a process that must always root itself in the unconscious, pre-linguistic, but still formed and expressive life of the body in its primordial continuity with earth.

Christian readings of the work are obviously not intended by the artist. However, its siting (which Gormley himself regards as 'felicitous') suggests that it is congruent with the conscious life of the Cathedral Church. The posture of the figure can be read as alluding to the iconography of the baptism of Christ, its bowed head suggests prayer, the water flowing periodically from its heart recalls biblical imagery of Christ as the source of living waters and there are also fainter echoes of sacred heart imagery and of the passion. Gormley does not reject such readings, although he does not want to see them as in any way exclusive. The work is open to but does not require such interpretation. Rooted in the elements that encompass the human condition, the work is open to interpretation at various levels of meaning and intention, according to the interpreter him- or herself.

Yet it would be foolish to deny the very clear tension between Gormley's vision and much Christian theology. He is outspokenly critical of the role of the crucifixion in Christian iconography, seeing in it a manifestation of the Christian view that, in his words, 'the only good body is a body that is nailed down to prescription, and it's in some senses the mortification of the flesh that will allow the release of the spirit, rather than the body [being] the instrument by which the spirit finds a prayer or form of celebration'.[7] However, it is open to question how far this hostility towards the body is integral to Christianity, and how far it is the result of the particular historical circumstances of Late Antiquity, the period when Christianity established itself as the dominant cultural force of the Western world. This question has been extensively revisited in much recent theology, particularly in feminist and green theology, and the argument of this book has involved appealing to art as one way of overturning the Neo-Platonic prejudice against thorough-going incarnationalism.

Despite these theoretical tensions, the installation of 'Sound II' has proved almost entirely uncontroversial. Modern art and controversy are, however, old friends, who cannot stay apart for long, and the next work to be considered, Bill Viola's video installation in Durham Cathedral entitled 'The Messenger' provoked instant controversy. Much of this was, inevitably, uninformed, but the fact itself is a reminder that we are journeying in a region where there are no universally accepted prescriptions and no guaranteed successes. Every new work is a venture into the unknown, encountering an infinitely variable and unpredictably volatile press and public. John McEwen, writing in the *Sunday Telegraph*, damned the installation as merely a 'trendy art show', asserting that the centrality of the body in the work exemplified a 'concentration on the physical [that is] the reverse of spirituality'. Apropos the nudity of the figure featured in 'The Messenger' he commented that 'there does indeed seem very good reason for an outraged member of the public to take [the Dean and Chapter] to court'.[8]

What was the object of this attack? 'The Messenger' is a twelve foot high video image of a man, seen from above and facing the viewer, who repeatedly sinks down into water, his body dissolving into shimmering patterns of watery light as he goes down into the depths, and gradually re-assuming recognizable human form as he re-ascends back to the surface, after an excruciatingly long interval. Although not permanently sited in Durham Cathedral, 'The

Messenger' (unlike the previous works I have been considering) was originally site-specific, commissioned by the Dean and Chapter and realized by the artist as the fruit of a long period of absorption in and reflection on the distinctive atmosphere and history of the Cathedral. Like 'Sound II' its primary impact is connected with its bodily and elemental immediacy. Looking at it over the half-hour period of each cycle, we are bodies facing a body, responding to it by virtue of our own experiences of immersion, experiences re-evoked in us by sound and image. Animal anxieties about drowning mingle with no less primal desires to regress to the aquatic life-before-life of the womb, and the whole experience is refracted through the dazzling fluctuations of shape and colour in the ceaselessly changing surface of the water. Like 'Sound II' also in this, 'The Messenger' was not made with any specific doctrinal intent or iconographical reference. However, its positioning near the nave font of the Cathedral opened rich seams of doctrinal symbolism around the themes of baptism, death and resurrection. Though the work is not doctrinal, Viola was happy for it to dialogue with its Christian environment, since, as he saw it, its subject-matter was concerned with 'that which gave rise to the ritual of baptism itself in the beginning'.[9] It represents an 'elemental' experience familiar throughout history and pre-history, bringing us into contact with fundamental realities such as birth and death. Viola conceives of the relation between the work and those who read it religiously by analogy with the experience of parenting: what is conceived in the realm of pre-rational instinct and feeling acquires a life of its own on coming out into the world, and becomes independent of its maker. The artist has no copyright on the meaning of the work. Although Viola himself is informed more by Buddhist than by Christian spirituality, the work projects itself almost effortlessly towards Christian appropriation precisely because of its use of a language before language that is the primary matrix of symbolic formation and that is shared by Christian and non-Christian art alike. If it is successful, it is so precisely because it does not impose a theological narrative, doctrine or interpretation on the viewer, but, engaging the unconscious mind before appealing to conscious reflection, it offers the possibility for religious symbol-making, while leaving open a space for the viewer's own interpretative effort.

In introducing 'The Messenger' I referred to the brief scandal surrounding the opening of the work, but it is important to note that it had its defenders as well as its detractors. For Waldemar Januszcak it is 'one of the finest pieces of twentieth-century church art I have seen – perhaps the finest'.[10]

Finally, I come to a work that is explicitly Christian in content, if unorthodox in treatment: Craigie Aichison's 'Crucifixion (1994)', awarded the Jerwood prize in that year and subsequently loaned to King's College, Cambridge, where it is hung as an altarpiece in one of the side-chapels, a space used for quiet, intimate early morning services and for private prayer.

This is one of many 'Crucifixions' painted by the artist, and, like many of his other works on this theme, it has a number of unusual features. Virtually all of his Crucifixions share a number of striking characteristics: large, geometrically ordered areas of single colour are composed into the landscape background of the cross, a landscape that is empty of other human figures; the figure on the cross is reduced and rendered without detail, while a beam of light or a star signals the salvific significance of the scene. In many of these paintings (though not 'Crucifixion [1994]') a number of animals or birds are present. The landscapes in which these Crucifixions are set recur in Aichison's other landscape works, which also sometimes include a distant cross without a figure, as in 'Landscape and Trees (1981)' or 'Goatfell, Isle of Arran (1993)'. There are also important links between the Crucifixions and a number of works responding to the deaths of the artist's Bedlington terriers, and, indeed, these dogs appear in some of the Crucifixion paintings. If this seems fanciful, we should note that, as Andrew Gibbon Williams has commented, as well as being a vehicle for personal feeling, these dogs have a symbolic quality, and their similarity in appearance to lambs admits of allusions to paschal lamb imagery.[11] The presence of birds is also not unprecedented in the tradition, being a feature characteristic of the kind of early Renaissance crucifixions that provide the most immediate art-historical analogy to Aichison's own treatment of the theme. Their stillness and simplicity, their iconic lack of overt or forced sentiment or emotional expressiveness, point back to a pre-modern and pre-Romantic period of art. At the same time, the freedom, quasi-abstraction and studied naiveté with which Aichison goes to work are distinctively modern. His is an art that incorporates the iconoclastic current of modernity, stripping away Romantic indulgence and excess to arrive at a tender, delicate minimalism.

'Crucifixion (1994)' is perhaps one of his strongest and potentially most tragic treatments of the theme. Much of the force of the painting comes from the two great blocks of colour that dominate its composition: the green earth, occupying the bottom third of the picture, and the deep blue sky, weighing down upon it from above. The cross, situated to the right of centre, spans the division between them, breaking through the smudgy red horizon. The Christ figure itself is unusual, in that the arms are not spread out and nailed to the cross by the hands, but are draped over the horizontal beam of the cross, heightening the effect of limpness and defeat conveyed by the pale body. The bloody spear-shaped wound in Christ's side is reflected in the red of the horizon and in subliminal blotches of red scattered throughout the green earth. Is this a visual suggestion that the link between heaven and earth is forged by the blood of the cross? That the cross ascends from an earth spattered with an ancient history of blood and sacrifice into the profound serenity of the sky, still and receptive as a deep evening twilight?

The head of Christ lacks distinctive features, and hangs down, as if in death or at the very point of death. Its halo emits three beams of light that radiate out towards a small star, itself cross-shaped, hanging just above the cross and within the angle of the beam and upright. This reciprocity of cross and star reinforces the message of the relationship between earth and heaven: that the heavenly light itself cannot exist for us other than as refracted through the outline of the cross. In this respect 'Crucifixion (1994)' is more tragic than those of Aichison's 'Crucifixions' in which a continuous light-beam comes down from beyond the picture frame to touch the figure of the Crucified One with heavenly light.

If this 'reading' of the picture seems to be returning us to the sort of allegorizing reading invited by paintings such as Watts's 'Hope', we need to remember that here, as there, such readings work only to the extent that they are integral to the painting *qua* painting. However, Aichison does not appear to have a deliberate allegorical programme, and if his painting gives itself to theological explication it does so first and foremost because it works as a painting and as a distinctively modern painting, rather than as the bearer of doctrinal or narrative references. Its media are the intensity and tonality of colour, the relationship between colour and spatial organization, and the primordial language of the body itself, not conventional iconographical signs.

The very ambiguity of the work, as focused in the chiasmic

relationship between cross and star, means that it stops short of being an unqualifiedly 'Christian' work. The relationship between earth and heaven remains broodingly mysterious, marked by enigmatic blood and open to multiple interpretations. However, if this might make some hesitant with regard to its suitability as a focal work in a place of Christian worship, it should be said that its particular siting is, as has been said, in a side Chapel used for quiet early morning services or for private meditation. Precisely because the work invites reflection, rather than imposing a predetermined meaning onto the viewer, it 'fits' its space. Here, to one side of the extroversion of public worship, is an opportunity to become open to the quiet miracle of art that, for us, is only accessible through the individual's solitary, exploratory, pondering gaze.

In the last decade there has been an enormous growth of interest in 'art-and-religion', an interest reflected both in the installation of new works in Churches and in an expanding theological and critical literature. All this is not without its dangers. Doubtless many works will be installed in Churches to critical and congregational acclaim, only to be embarrassedly withdrawn to the obscurity of dusty store rooms as the wheel of taste turns. Artists will be heralded as harbingers of a new renaissance of Church art, only to vanish from sight within a generation. But the history of Church art has always been a history of trial and error. On the whole we probably have a better opinion of the achievements of the past simply because much of the ephemera and dross has vanished. Conversely, we may expect that works will emerge from out of the experiments and errors of our time that will outlast us and communicate important truths we have not yet deciphered to those who come after. Whether the works discussed in this Chapter will be amongst them is impossible to say. What they illustrate, each in its distinctive way, is my argument that the elemental materials and forms of art, and the 'language before language' of the body, are the primary sources on which any significant Church art of the future must be based. If the trauma of modernism has achieved anything permanent it is – hopefully – to wean us once and for all from giving inappropriate eminence to an art that is merely illustrative and that functions as language rather than as painting or sculpture (or video). In this way, modern art, through focusing its gaze on the all-pervasive reality of embodiment, offers the religion of the incarnation the possibility of being re-awakened to the redemptive meaning of carnality itself.

However, this is also a profound challenge to Christianity as it exists institutionally today. It is a challenge sharpened by the habit of modern theological thought to preoccupy itself with the attempt to define or to articulate what is distinctively and decisively Christian. This attempt is understandable in a situation in which, on the one hand, Christianity has in so many areas become simply identified with 'Western culture' and, on the other, finds itself fighting for its identity in the global super-market of faiths and ideologies. None the less, it obscures what is infinitely more important: what Christianity shares, across and beyond all boundaries of doctrine and Church order, with all planetary life. Art is only one clue amongst others to another way. Perhaps a theology of art can never claim the urgency of feminist, green or liberation theologies. Its task is, one the less, to journey with them towards a more open theology in which the Church does not imagine itself as the sole purveyor or channel of grace, but as responding, with all sentient beings, to the structural grace of life itself.

Notes

1   ART, MODERNITY AND FAITH

1. Quoted in U. Apollonio (ed.), *Futurist Manifestos* (London: Thames and Hudson, 1973) p. 25.
2. Ibid., p. 21.
3. W. Kandinsky, *Concerning the Spiritual in Art* (New York: Dover, 1977) p. 2.
4. Ibid., p. 12.
5. R. Hughes, *The Shock of the New* (London: BBC, 1980) p. 323.
6. S. Gablik, *Has Modernism Failed?* (London and New York: Thames and Hudson, 1984) p. 71.
7. J.-F. Lyotard, *The Postmodern Condition: A Report on Knowledge* (Manchester University Press, 1984) p. 79.
8. Cf. the extensive discussion of Augustine's relevance to the contemporary cultural situation in A. Kroker and D. Cook, *The Postmodern Scene* (London: Macmillan, 1988)
9. M. Roskill (ed.), *The Letters of Vincent Van Gogh* (New York: Atheneum, 1963) p. 122.
10. D. Cupitt, *Radicals and the Future of the Church* (London: SCM, 1989) p. 26.
11. Jane Dillenberger, *Style and Content in Christian Art* (London: SCM, 1986) p. 214.
12. John Dillenberger, *A Theology of Artistic Sensibilities* (London: SCM, 1987) p. 193.
13. This point was brought home to me in a recent interview with Dame Elisabeth Frink. Cf. G. Pattison, 'Elisabeth Frink Talks about Art and the Church' in *Modern Painters* vol. 2, no. 3 (Autumn 1989) pp. 53ff.
14. *Stanley Spencer RA* (London: Royal Academy of Arts in association with Weidenfeld and Nicolson, 1980) p. 92.
15. I have chosen Spencer as an example precisely because of the explicit references in his work to Christianity. I also believe that he *was* capable of producing great religious art, an eminent example of which is his work in the Sandham Memorial Chapel, expecially the painting on the East Wall which shows newly-resurrected soldiers handing in their crosses to Christ. Here the 'otherness' of the resurrected world is clearly and movingly alluded to. But if theological caution is needed in the case of a painter like Spencer it is going to be *a fortiori* necessary in the case of those far more numerous modern artists whose relation to

191

traditional sources of iconography is far more tenuous. As the argument of the book develops, however, it will become clear that such explicit references are not the only, nor even the main, means of giving art a religious significance and value.

16. P. Fuller, *Images of God* (London: Chatto and Windus, 1985) p. 188.
17. S. Gablik, *op. cit.*, p. 90.
18. Ibid., p. 97.
19. H. R. Rookmaaker, *Modern Art and the Death of a Culture* (London: Inter-Varsity Press, 1970) p. 222.
20. Ibid., p. 156.
21. Ibid., p. 228.
22. P. Fuller, *op. cit.*, p. 91.
23. Ibid., p. 92.

2 THE BREAKING OF IMAGES: CHRISTIAN ICONOCLASM

1. M. Aston, *England's Iconoclasts* (Oxford: Clarendon Press, 1988) p. 45.
2. Cf. John Dillenberger, *op. cit.*, pp. 15f.
3. Ibid., p. 3.
4. Plato, *The Republic* (London and New York: Everyman edn., 1935) pp. 296ff. (Book X).
5. Ibid., p. 207 (Book VII).
6. Cf. John Dillenberger, *op. cit.*, pp. 3ff.
7. Cf. Kroker and Cook, *op. cit.* For an extensive discussion of Augustine's view of asceticism and bodily life cf. Margaret R. Miles, *Augustine on the Body* (Missoula: Scholars Press, 1979)
8. Saint Augustine, *City of God* (Harmondsworth: Penguin, 1972) p. 462.
9. *Idem.*, *Confessions* (Harmondsworth: Penguin, 1961) p. 241. Cf. also pp. 239ff.
10. Ibid., p. 231.
11. Ibid., p. 328.
12. R. J. O'Connell, *Art and the Christian Intelligence in St. Augustine* (Oxford: Basil Blackwell, 1978) pp. 37–8.
13. J. Calvin, *Institutes of the Christian Religion* (London: SCM Library of Christian Classics, 1961) p. 43.
14. Ibid., pp. 52–3.
15. Ibid., p. 100.
16. Ibid., p. 105.
17. Ibid., p. 107.
18. Ibid., pp. 113–14.

19. Ibid., p. 112.
20. Ibid., pp. 106–7.
21. Quotations are from an Oxford edition of 1683. As there is no readily accessible standard edition I have not given page references.
22. M. Aston, *op. cit.*, p. 97.
23. Ibid., p. 83.
24. K. Barth, 'The architectural problem of Protestant places of worship' in A. Bieler (ed.), *Architecture and Worship* (Edinburgh and London: Oliver and Boyd, 1965) pp. 92–3.
25. Cf. Chapter 5, below.
26. W. H. Wackenroder, *Werke und Briefe* (Heidelberg: Lambert Schneider, 1967) p. 33 (Author's Translation).
27. Cf. G. Pattison, *Kierkegaard's Theory and Critique of Art: Its Theological Significance* (Durham: Ph.D. thesis, 1983).
28. S. Kierkegaard (ed. Hong and Hong), *Sören Kierkegaard's Journals and Papers*, 6 vols (Bloomington: Indiana University Press, 1967–78) Entry no. 1455, (entries are numbered consecutively through the six volumes).
29. From a contemporary review of Kierkegaard's *Either/Or* in Faedrelandet 4. 1227/8 (May 1843), (Author's translation).
30. Ibid.
31. S. Kierkegaard, *Journals and Papers*, Entry No. 1019.
32. *Idem., Samlede Vaerker* (Copenhagen: Gyldendal 1962) vol. 8, p. 255 (Author's translation).
33. A. Schopenhauer, *The World as Will and Representation*, vol. 1 (New York: Dover, 1969) p. 185.
34. H. Steffens, *Inledning til Philosophiske Forlaesninger* (Copenhagen: Gylendal, 1905) pp. 21–2.
35. From the poem 'Die Götter Griechenlands.'
36. From the poem 'De Levendes Land'.
37. Kierkegaard, *Samlede Vaerker* vol. 4, p. 83.
38. Cf. Chapter 6, below.
39. L. Bloy (ed. Maritain), *Pilgrim of the Absolute* (London: Eyre and Spottiswoode, 1947) p. 112.
40. Ibid., p. 103.
41. Ibid., p. 104.
42. Ibid.
43. Ibid., p. 105.
44. Ibid., p. 108.
45. Ibid., p. 110.
46. Ibid., p. 109.
47. Ibid., p. 111.
48. Ibid.
49. Ibid., p. 114.
50. Ibid.

51. J. H. Newman, *On the Scope and Nature of University Education* (London: Everyman edn., 1915) p. 61.
52. Ibid., pp. 62–3.

3   THE DREAM OF A CHRISTIAN CULTURE

1. H. Heine, *Die Romantische Schule* (Munchen: Wilhelm Goldmann, 1964) p. 11 (Author's translation).
2. W. Anderson, *The Rise of the Gothic* (London: Hutchinson, 1985) p. 22.
3. Ibid.
4. Ibid.
5. E. I. Watkin, *Catholic Art and Culture* (London: Burns and Oates, 1942), contents page.
6. Ibid., pp. 47–8.
7. Ibid., pp. 46ff.
8. Ibid., p. 47.
9. Ibid., p. 51.
10. Ibid., pp. 68–9.
11. E. Panofsky, *Gothic Architecture and Scholasticism* (London: Thames and Hudson, 1957).
12. J. Maritain, *Art and Scholasticism* (London: Sheed and Ward, 1933) p. 22. Further references are given in the text after the abbreviation *AS*.
13. E. Gill, *Beauty Looks After Herself* (London: Sheed and Ward, 1933) pp. 208–9.
14. *Idem.*, *The Necessity of Belief* (London: Faber and Faber, 1936) p. 337.
15. *Idem.*, *Beauty Looks After Herself*, p. 244.
16. *Idem.*, *The Necessity of Belief*, p. 351.
17. *Idem.*, *Beauty Looks After Herself*, p. 28.
18. Ibid., p. 17.
19. Cf. also the essays 'Sacred Art and the Spiritual Life' and 'Absurdity in Sacred Decoration' in T. Merton, *Disputed Questions* (London: Hollis and Carter, 1961).
20. Gill, *Beauty Looks After Herself*, p. 36.
21. Ibid., p. 38.
22. U. Eco, *The Aesthetics of Thomas Aquinas* (UK: Radius, 1988) p. 193.
23. Ibid.
24. Ibid., p. 200.
25. Ibid., p. 201.
26. Cf. *idem.*, *The Name of the Rose* (London: Picador, 1984) p. 492.

27. E. H. Gilson, *Painting and Reality* (Princeton: Princeton University Press, 1969) p. 9. Further references are given in the text after the abbreviation *PR*.

4   CHRISTIAN THEORIA

1. J. Ruskin, *Modern Painters* (London and New York: Everyman edn, 1906) vol. II, p. 156. Further references are given in the text after the abbreviation *MP* and the Volume number.
2. P. Fuller, *Theoria: Art and the Absence of Grace* (London: Chatto and Windus, 1988) pp. 28ff.
3. Cf., for example, the section 'Of Truth of Clouds'.
4. J. Ruskin, *The Seven Lamps of Architecture* (London: Cassell and Co., 1909) pp. 179f. ('The Lamp of Beauty', sections 25–29).
5. Cf. Chapter VIII, below.
6. Fuller, *Theoria*, p. 113.
7. Ibid.
8. Ibid., p. 116.
9. Ibid., p. 114.
10. Ibid., p. 168.
11. P. Fuller, 'Exhibition Notes' for Michael Williams, 'Recent Land-scapes' at Austin/Desmond Fine Art 1988.
12. Fuller, *Images of God.*, p. 189.
13. *Idem., Theoria.* p. 230.
14. Ibid., p. 232.
15. Ibid., p. 233.
16. Cf. Chapter VIII, below.

5   PESSIMISM AND PROGRESS

1. P. T. Forsyth, *Religion in Recent Art* (London: Hodder and Stoughton, 1905) p. 220. Further references are given in the text after the abbreviation *RRA*.
2. *Idem., Christ on Parnassus* (London: Hodder and Stoughton, 1911) p. viii. Further references are given in the text after the abbreviation *CP*.
3. G. W. F. Hegel, *Aesthetics* (London: Oxford University Press, 1975) vol. 2, p. 625. Not, of course, according to Gilson!
4. Ibid., p. 824.
5. Fuller, *Theoria*, p. 146.
6. W. Blunt, *'England's Michelangelo'* (London: Hamish Hamilton, 1970).
7. G. K. Chesterton, *G. F. Watts* (London: Duckworth, 1909) p. 23.

8. Ibid., p. 169.
9. Rookmaaker, *op cit.*, p. 75.
10. Fuller, *Theoria*. p. 146.
11. Hegel, *op. cit.*, p. 2.
12. Ibid., pp. 30–1.
13. Ibid., p. 11.
14. Ibid.

6 INTO THE ABYSS

1. P. Tillich (ed. J. and J. Dillenberger), *On Art and Architecture* (New York: Crossroad, 1987) p. xxvi. Further references are given in the text after the abbreviation *AA*.
2. P. Tillich, 'The Kingdom of God and History' in *The Kingdom of God and History: Papers for the Oxford Conference 1937* (London: Allen and Unwin) p. 123.
3. *Idem.*, 'Mensch und Staat' in *Gesammelte Werke* (Stuttgart: Evangelisches Verlagswerk) vol. 13, p. 173.
4. *Idem.*, *Theology of Culture* (New York: Oxford University Press, 1959) p. 114.
5. *Idem.*, *Systematic Theology* (Welwyn: James Nisbet, 1968) vol. 2, p. 206.
6. Ibid., p. 14.
7. Ibid., p. 15.
8. Ibid., pp. 14–15.
9. Ibid., p. 15.
10. Ibid.
11. Ibid., p. 10.
12. Ibid., vol. 3, p. 128.
13. Ibid., p. 132.
14. Ibid., vol. 2, p. 133.
15. Ibid.
16. Ibid., vol. 3, p. 132.
17. Ibid., vol. 2, p. 132.
18. *Idem.*, *The Shaking of the Foundations* (Harmondsworth: Penguin, 1962) pp. 82–92.
19. W. Kaufmann, *Existentialism, Religion and Death* (New York: New American Library, 1976) p. 115.
20. John Dillenberger, *op. cit.*, p 159.
21. M. Rothko in *Mark Rothko* (London: The Tate Gallery, 1987) p. 80.
22. Ibid., p. 81.
23. Ibid., p. 87.
24. Ibid., p. 78.
25. Ibid., p. 16.
26. Stanley Cavell 'Kierkegaard on Authority and Revelation' in

J. Thompson (ed.), *Kierkegaard: A Collection of Critical Essays* (Garden City: Anchor, 1972) p. 383.
27. Rothko, *op. cit.*, p. 194.
28. Hughes, *op. cit.*, p. 323.

7 ICONS OF GLORY

1. A. Nichols, *The Art of God Incarnate* (London: Darton, Longman and Todd, 1980) p. 55.
2. Ibid., p. 81.
3. V. L. Lazarev, *Novgorodian Icon-Painting* (Moscow: Iskusstvo, 1976) p. 5.
4. L. Ouspensky and V. Lossky, *The Meaning of Icons* (Crestwood, New York: St. Vladimir's Seminary Press, 1983) p. 47.
5. C. Scouteris, 'Never as Gods: Icons and their Veneration' in *Sobornost* 6. 1 (1984), pp. 10ff.
6. V. Lossky in Ouspensky and Lossky, *op. cit.*, p. 15.
7. Ibid., p. 22.
8. Ibid.
9. Ibid., p. 30.
10. Nichols, *op. cit.*, p. 86.
11. Ouspensky and Lossky, *op. cit.*, p. 165.
12. Nichols, *op. cit.*, p. 86.
13. Ouspensky and Lossky, *op. cit.*, p. 32.
14. V. Lossky, *The Mystical Theology of the Eastern Church* (Cambridge and London: James Clarke, 1957) p. 126.
15. Ouspensky and Lossky, *op. cit.*, p. 35.
16. Ibid.
17. V. Lossky, *In the Image and Likeness of God* (New York: St. Vladimir's Seminary Press, 1974) p. 68.
18. Ouspensky and Lossky, *op. cit.*, p. 36.
19. Ibid., p. 38.
20. J. Zizioulas, *Being as Communion* (London: Darton, Longman and Todd, 1985) p. 100.
21. Ibid.
22. Nichols, *op. cit.*, p. 93.
23. Ibid., p. 95.
24. J. Baggley, *Doors of Perception* (London and Oxford: Mowbray, 1987), pp. 82f.
25. V. N. Lazarev, *Moscow School of Icon-Painting* (Moscow: Iskusstvo, 1971) p. 26.
26. Ibid., p. 34.
27. Ouspensky and Lossky, *op. cit.*, p. 41.
28. Baggley, *op. cit.*, p. 69.
29. Ibid., p. 66.

30. John Dillenberger, *op. cit.*, p. 244.
31. Cf. W. Kandinsky, *op. cit.*, Also cf. Fuller, *Theoria.* p. 155.

8   RESTORING THE IMAGE

1. N. Wolterstorff, *Art in Action* (Grand Rapids: Eerdman, 1988) p. 89.
2. Ibid., p. 92.
3. Ibid., p. 72.
4. Ibid., pp. 70–1.
5. Cf. Gilson, *op. cit.*, pp. 55ff., 107ff. Also, Chapter III, above.
6. John Dillenberger, *op. cit.*, p. 231.
7. Ibid., p. 240.
8. Ibid., p. 243.
9. Ibid.
10. Ibid., p. 244.
11. Hegel, *Aesthetics,* p. 101.
12. J. Derrida, *The Truth in Painting* (Chicago: University of Chicago Press, 1987) p. 257.
13. Nichols, *op. cit*, p. 90
14. Ibid., p. 93.
15. M. Heidegger (ed. Krell), *Basic Writings* (London: Routledge and Kegan Paul, 1978) p. 157.
16. Ibid., pp. 151ff.
17. Ibid., p. 153.
18. Ibid., p. 156.
19. Ibid., p. 157.
20. Ibid., p. 158.
21. Ibid.
22. Ibid.
23. Ibid., p. 159.
24. Ibid., pp. 162 ff. Cf. Derrida's partial defence of Heidegger who has been much criticised for misappropriating Van Gogh's boots in the cause of what some would claim reeks of a Nazistic peasant ideology. Derrida, *op. cit.*, pp. 257ff.
25. Heidegger, *op. cit.*, p. 164.
26. Ibid., p. 170.
27. Ibid., p. 165.
28. Ibid., p. 168.
29. Ibid., p. 169.
30. Ibid., p. 170.
31. Ibid., p. 171.
32. Ibid.
33. Ibid., p. 185.
34. Ibid., p. 186.

35. H. Rombach, *Leben des Geistes* (Freiburg im Breisgau: Herder, 1977) p. 7. This and other extracts are my own translation.
36. Ibid., p. 8.
37. Ibid.
38. Ibid.
39. Ibid.
40. Ibid., pp. 301ff.
41. M. Merleau-Ponty, *The Prose of the World* (Evanston: Northwestern University Press, 1973) p. 61.
42. *Idem.*, 'Eye and Mind' in J. O'Neill (ed.), *Phenomenology, Language and Sociology* (London: Heinemann, 1974) p. 286.
43. Ibid., p. 285.
44. Ibid., p. 304.
45. Ibid., p. 305.
46. Ibid.
47. *Idem.*, *The Prose of the World*, pp. 59–60.
48. *Idem.*, 'Eye and Mind', p. 284.
49. Ibid., p. 283.
50. *Idem.*, *The Phenomenology of Perception* (London: Routledge and Kegan Paul, 1962) p. 377.
51. *Idem.*, 'Eye and Mind', p. 287.
52. Ibid.
53. Ibid., p. 295.
54. Ibid., p. 297.
55. Ibid., p. 300.
56. Ibid., p. 301.
57. Ibid., p. 298.
58. Ibid.
59. *Idem.*, *The Prose of the World.*, p. 83.
60. Ibid., p. 84.
61. Ibid., p. 110.
62. Ibid., p. 88.
63. *Idem.*, *The Visible and the Invisible* (Evanston: Northwestern University Press, 1968) p. 153.
64. Ibid., p. 155.
65. P. Dews, *Logics of Disintegration* (London and New York: Verso, 1987) p. 112. Cf. J-F. Lyotard, *Discours, Figure* (Paris: Klincksieck, 1971) pp. 9ff ('Le Parti Pris du Figural'). Dews's book contains a useful summary of Lyotard's position in *Discours, Figure* and its place in contemporary French thought.
66. Lyotard, *Discours, Figure*, p. 18.
67. Ibid., p. 9.
68. Cf. John Lane's commentary on Bonnard's painting 'Almond Tree in Flower', which is in some respects similar to the treatment of Monet offered here. There are also, of course, significant differences, as when Lane alludes to what he calls 'the two

lights', i.e. the light of the external, visible world and 'the other light perceived by his (Bonnard's) imagination.' My position tends towards the conflation of these 'two lights' into one. J. Lane, *The Living Tree: Art and the Sacred* (Bideford: Green Books, 1988) pp. 109ff.

69. Fuller, *Theoria*, pp. 1ff, and elsewhere.
70. Chesterton, *op. cit.*, p. 102.
71. Ibid., p. 98.
72. Ibid., p. 102. For a slightly different view cf. Blunt, *'England's Michelangelo'*, pp. 58ff. The point is not exactly whether Watts is or isn't to be called a 'literary' painter; it is rather whether in accommodating itself to a literary interpretation the work allows its visual integrity to be diminished.
73. Lyotard, *Discours, Figure*, pp. 271ff.
74. As well as Lyotard, philosophies which take the part of desire include those of Georges Bataille, Gilles Deleuze and, in a different context, Herbert Marcuse, who also sees art as a kind of 'ark' for instinctive forces in the hostile climate of 'late capitalism'. Cf. H. Marcuse, *Die Permanenz der Kunst* (München: Karl Hanser, 1977). For a summary of some of the issues involved cf. P. Dews. *op. cit.*, and, from a theological perspective, Don Cupitt, *The Long-Legged Fly* (London: SCM, 1987)
75. A similar proposal is to be found in Heidegger's interpretation of Kant's definition of aesthetic delight as 'disinterested', an interpretation at variance with that given by Schopenhauer. Cf. M. Heidegger, *Nietzsche, Volume I: The Will to Power as Art* (London: Routledge and Kegan Paul, 1981) pp. 107ff.
76. H. Küng, *Art and the Question of Meaning* (London: SCM, 1981) p. 50.
77. U. Eco, *Art and Beauty in the Middle Ages* (Newhaven and London: Yale University Press, 1986) p. 76.

9   THE THEOLOGY OF ART AND THE MEETING OF FAITHS

1. T. Merton, *The Asian Journal of Thomas Merton* (London: Sheldon Press, 1974) p. 5.
2. M. Furlong, *Merton: A Biography* (London: Collins, 1980) p. 249.
3. Merton, *Asian Journal*, p. 233. The following quotations are all from pp. 233ff.
4. Ibid., p. 235.
5. The incident is cited by John D. Eusden in his article 'Chartres and Ryoan-Ji: Aesthetic Connection between Gothic Cathedral and Zen Garden' in *The Eastern Buddhist* vol. XVIII, Part 2, 1985, p. 17.
6. K. Tsujimura, R. Ohashi, H. Rombach, *Sein und Nichts: Grundbilder westlichen und östlichen Denkens* (Basel: Herder, 1981). All

translations from this book are my own.

7. Ibid., p. 24.
8. Ibid., p. 36.
9. Ibid., p. 40.
10. Ibid.
11. Ibid., p. 44.
12. Ibid., p. 54.
13. Ibid., p. 56.
14. Ibid., p. 69.
15. Eusden, *op. cit.*, p. 9.
16. R. Pilgrim, 'The Religio-Aesthetic of Matsuo Basho' in *The Eastern Buddhist* vol. X, May 1977, p. 35.
17. D. T. Suzuki, *Essays in Zen Buddhism, First Series* (London: Rider & Co., 1949) p. 230.
18. *Idem.*, *Essays in Zen Buddhism, Third Series* (London: Rider and Co., 1953) p. 324.
19. Hegel, *Phenomenology of Spirit* (Oxford: Oxford University Press, 1979) p. 9.
20. Pilgrim, *op. cit.*, pp. 35ff.
21. Ibid., p. 48.
22. Ibid., p. 51.
23. Suzuki *Essays, Third Series*, p. 330.
24. Ibid., p. 331.
25. Pilgrim, *op. cit.*, p. 52.
26. L. Stryk, *World of the Buddha* (New York: Anchor, 1969) p. 248.
27. A. Watts, *The Way of Zen* (Harmondsworth: Penguin, 1962) pp. 87–8.
28. Stryk, *op. cit.*, p. 283.
29. Yanagi Soētsu, 'The Dharma Gate of Beauty' in *The Eastern Buddhist* vol. XII Part 2, October 1979, p. 5.
30. Ibid., p. 7.
31. Ibid., p. 9.
32. Ibid., p. 15.
33. Ibid., pp. 15–16.
34. Ibid., p. 16.
35. *Idem.*, 'The Pure Land of Beauty' in *The Eastern Buddhist* vol. IX, Part 1, May 1976, p. 26.
36. Ibid., p. 18.

10   SEEING IS BELIEVING

1. See, e.g., Doug Adams, *Transcendence With the Human Body in Art: Segal, De Staebler, Johns and Christo* (New York: Crossroad, 1991); Joseph Beuys, *In memoriam Joseph Beuys: Obituaries,*

Essays, Speeches (Bonn, 1986); Mark Cazalet, 'The Dialectic Between Art and Faith' in *Modern Believing*, Vol. XXXVII, 1996, no. 4, pp. 8–18; G. Pattison, 'Letters from America: Robert Natkin and Friends' in *Arts: The Arts in Religious and Theological Studies*, 6:2, Spring 1994–5, pp. 22–5.

2. P. Fuller, Catalogue notes to 'Glynn Williams. Piccadilly Festival 1985'. See also, idem., 'Glynn Williams: Carving a Niche for Sculpture' in *Images of God*.

3. In E. H. Gombrich, John Hutchinson and Lela B. Njatin, *Antony Gormley* (London: Phaidon, 1995), p. 124.

4. From a taped interview with the author.

5. Commented on by him in the unpublished paper 'Still Moving' delivered at the 'Art and Spirituality' conference at Durham Cathedral, 2.10.1996.

6. See Chapter Eight, above.

7. See note 4 above.

8. J. McEwen, 'The not-so grand organs of Durham Cathedral' in *The Sunday Telegraph*, 15.9.1996.

9. See note 4 above.

10. W. Januszcak, 'Closer to Godliness' in *The Sunday Times*, 15.9.1996.

11. See A. G. Williams, *Craigie: The Art of Craigie Aichison* (Edinburgh: Canongate, 1996).

Select Bibliography

Apostolos-Cappadona, D. (ed.) *Art, Creativity and the Sacred* (New York: Crossroad, 1984).

Aston, Margaret, *England's Iconoclasts* (Oxford: Clarendon Press, 1988).

Baggley, J., *Doors of Perception – Icons and their Spiritual Significance* (London and Oxford: Mowbray, 1987).

Barth, K., 'The architectural problem of Protestant places of worship' in A. Bieler (ed.) *Architecture in Worship* (Edinburgh and London: Oliver and Boyd, 1965).

Bloy, L., *Pilgrim of the Absolute* (London: Eyre and Spottiswoode, 1947).

Dillenberger, Jane, *Style and Content in Christian Art* (London: SCM, 1986).

Dillenberger, John, *A Theology of Artistic Sensibilities* (London: SCM, 1987).

Eco, U., *The Aesthetics of Thomas Aquinas* (UK: Radius, 1988). *Art and Beauty in the Middle Ages* (Newhaven: Yale University Press, 1986).

Eusden, J. D., 'Chartres and Ryōan-ji: Aesthetic Connections between Gothic Cathedral and Zen Garden' in *The Eastern Buddhist* Vol. XVIII Part 2, 1985, pp.9–18.

Forsyth, P. T., *Christ on Parnassus* (London: Hodder and Stoughton, 1911). *Religion in Recent Art* (London: Hodder and Stoughton, 1900).

Fuller, P., *Images of God* (London: Chatto and Windus, 1985). *Theoria: Art and the Absence of Grace* (London: Chatto and Windus, 1988).

Gablik, S., *Has Modernism Failed?* (London: Thames and Hudson, 1984).

Gill, E., *Art-Nonsense and other essays* (London: Cassell and Francis Walterston, 1929). *Beauty Looks After Herself* (London: Sheed and Ward, 1933).

Gill, E., *The Necessity of Belief* (London: Faber and Faber, 1936).

Gilson, E. H., *Painting and Reality* (Princeton: Princeton University Press, 1960).

Heidegger, M., 'The Origin of the Work of Art' in Heidegger, M., (ed. Krell) *Basic Writings* (London: Routledge and Kegan Paul, 1978).

Lyotard, J. -F., *Discours, Figure* (Paris: Klincksieck, 1971). *The Postmodern Condition: A Report on Knowledge* (Manchester: Manchester University Press, 1984).

Maritain, J., *Art and Scholasticism* (London: Sheed and Ward, 1933).

Merleau-Ponty, M., 'Eye and Mind' in J. O'Neill (ed.), *Phenomenology, Language and Sociology* (London: Heinemann, 1974). *The Prose of the World* (Evanston: Northwestern University Press, 1973). *The Visible and the Invisible* (Evanston: Northwestern University Press, 1968).

Merton, T., *The Asian Journal of Thomas Merton* (London: Sheldon Press, 1974). *Disputed Questions* (London: Hollis and Carter, 1961).

Nichols, A., *The Art of God Incarnate* (London: Darton, Longman and Todd, 1980).

O'Connell, R. J., *Art and the Christian Intelligence in St. Augustine* (Oxford: Basil Blackwell, 1978).

Ouspensky, L., and Lossky, V., *The Meaning of Icons* (Crestwood, New York: St. Vladimir's Seminary Press, 1983).

Panofsky, E., *Gothic Architecture and Scholasticism* (London: Thames and Hudson, 1957).

Pattison, G. L. *Kierkegaard's Theory and Critique of Art: Its Theological Significance* (University of Durham, Ph. D. thesis, 1983).

Rombach, H., *Leben des Geistes* (Freiburg im Breisgau: Herder, 1977).

Rookmaaker, H. R. *Modern Art and the Death of a Culture* (London: Inter-Varsity Press, 1970).

Ruskin. J., *Modern Painters* (Everyman edn., London and New York: Dent-Dutton 1906).

Tillich, P., *On Art and Architecture* (New York: Crossroads, 1987).

Tsujimura, K., Ohashi, R. and Rombach, H., *Sein und Nichts* (Basel: Herder, 1981).

Suzuki, D. T. *Essays in Zen Buddhism, 3 Series* (London: Rider, 1949, 1953 and 1953). *Zen and Japanese Culture* (New York: Pantheon, 1959).

Watkin, E. I., *Catholic Art and Culture* (London: Burns and Oates, 1940).

Wolterstorff, N., *Art in Action: Towards a Christian Aesthetic* (Grand Rapids: Eerdmans, 1980).

Yanagi, S., 'The Dharma Gate of Beauty' in *The Eastern Buddhist* Vol. XII Part 2, October 1979, pp. 1–21. 'The Pure Land of Beauty' in *The Eastern Buddhist* Vol. IX, Part 1, May 1976, pp. 18–41.

Index

Abgar, King of Edessa 119
abstract art 2, 51, 115–17, 132–3
abstract expressionism 2, 115–17
Aichison, Craigie 178, 186
Albertus Magnus 38
Anderson, William 31
Angelico, Fra 41
Aquinas, Thomas, *see under* Thomas Aquinas, St.
Arras, Synod of 43
Aston, Margaret 10, 20
Asvaghosha 171
Augustine, St. 3, 13–16, 17, 163

Bach, Johann Sebastian 21, 92
Baggley, John 129, 131
Baldung, Hans 159–61, 163–4
Barth, Karl 21, 55, 56, 72, 74, 99, 111
Bashō 166, 169–70
Baudelaire, Charles 40
beauty 14–16, 37–41, 46–7, 56, 60–8, 73–4, 116, 172–4, 176
Bible, the 11, 16, 18, 19, 21, 48, 69, 71, 93, 113
biology, (and art) 50, 73–4, 75, 153
Bloy, Léon 26–8, 34, 52
Bonnard, Pierre 4, 185–6
Botticelli, Sandro 100, 112, 157
Braque, Georges 4
Breughels, the 102
Browning, Robert 93
Buddhism 155–76, 178, 183
    Pure Land School 172–6
    Zen 155, 156, 166–76, 178
Bultmann, Rudolf 113
Burne-Jones, Sir Edward 78, 87, 89, 90, 91

Calvin, Jean 16–17, 19, 27, 134
Cavell, Stanley 116
Cézanne, Paul 108
Chagall, Marc 4
Chesterton, G. K. 90, 150–1, 152

Christ *see under* Jesus Christ
Cimabue 86
Claude Gelée 59
Collins, Charles 149
Constantine, the Emperor 120
Cook, D. *see under* Kroker, A.
Correggio, Antonio 69, 86
Couturier, Jean Marie–Alain 4, 45
cubism 39–40, 41
Cupitt, Don 4, 7, 117, 186
Cuyp, Aelbert 59

Dante 33, 93
de Hooch, Pieter 7
Derrida, Jacques 138
Descartes, René 146
Dillenberger, Jane 4
Dillenberger, John 4, 11–12, 13, 115, 135–6, 138, 152
Dowsing, William 20

Eco, Umberto 45–7, 50
Enlightenment, the European 1, 30, 74, 105
Enlightenment, Buddhist 166–8, 169, 170, 171–2, 173, 175
Epiphanius of Salamis 120
Eusden, John D. 165
existentialism 108–9, 110, 114–15
expressionism 101–4, 105, 106, 108, 109, 151
expressive style 106–8

Feuerbach, Ludwig 22, 75
formal element in art 35, 36, 38, 46
form/matter distinction 36–7, 39–40, 48–50, 138–41
Forsyth, Peter Taylor 77, 78–100, 114, 150, 151
Francia, Francesco 70
Freud, Sigmund 75, 152
Frink, Dame Elisabeth 177
Fuller, Peter x, xii, 6, 8, 55–6, 71–7,

88, 93, 94, 114, 117, 138, 145, 149, 153, 180

Gablik, Suzi 3–4, 6
Gauguin, Paul 50, 158
Gill, Eric 43–5, 122, 174
Gilson, Étienne 47–53, 136, 151, 152, 171
Giotto 1, 86, 93
Goethe, J. W. von 23
Gorky, Arshile 115
Gormley, Antony, 178, 182, 183, 184
Gottlieb, Adolph 115–16
Goya, Francisco 1, 108
Greece *see under* Hellenism
Gregory Palamas 126
Grünewald, Mathias 108
Gruntvig, N. F. S. 25

Hals, Frans 87
Hegel, G. W. F. 79–80, 81, 83, 84, 86, 95–8, 108, 137–8, 152, 154, 162–3, 168
Heidegger, Martin 76, 138–41, 142, 143, 147, 161, 183
Hellenism 10, 12–13, 41, 66, 68, 80, 82, 84
Hinduism 44, 80–1
Homilies, Book of 17–20, 21, 27, 119, 120, 121
Hughes, Robert 117
Hume, David 55
Hunt, William Holman 78, 87, 89, 92–5
Husserl, Edmund 76
Hussey, Canon 4
iconoclasm 10–29, 120–1
  in the Early Church 11–12, 13, 19, 27
  in Islam 120
  in Judaism 10–11, 82
  in modern art 26, 115–17
  in the Reformation 87, 97
Iconoclastic Controversy, the, 120–1
icons 118–33, 134, 151
  see also Moscow school of icon-painting; Novgorod school of icon-painting; and Rublev, Andrei

Irene, the Empress 19, 121
Islam 19, 120

Jeffrey, Robert 181
Jesus Christ 6, 8, 19, 21, 27, 34, 41, 67, 68, 69–70, 71, 78, 83, 86, 92–3, 94, 95, 96, 97, 98, 99, 102, 103, 112–13, 119–20, 123, 124–7, 159, 160, 164
Judaism 10–11, 80, 82–3

Kandinsky, Wassily 2, 132–3
Kaufmann, Walter 114–15
Kiefer, Anselm xii, 5
Kierkegaard, Sören 22–6, 27, 28, 79, 98, 99, 108, 115, 116
Klee, Paul 143, 147
Kroker, A. and Cook, D. 13
Küng, Hans 153

Lane,John 185–6
Language/word 9, 42–3, 97, 112–13,123, 141, 147–8, 150–1
Lazarev, V. N. 122, 129–30, 131
Leach, Bernard 172
Léger, Fernand 4
Leo II, the Emperor 121
Leonardo da Vinci 86, 157
L'iang K'ai 159, 161–5
Lipchitz, Jacques 4
Lossky, Vladimir 123
Lurçat, Jean 4
Luther, Martin 109
Lyotard, Jean–François 3, 147–8, 150, 152

Malraux, André 34, 144
Mandelbrot, Benoit B. 73
Mandylion, the 119–20
Manet, Eduard 1
Mann, Thomas 104
Marcuse, Herbert 186
Maritain, Jacques 34–43, 44, 45, 46, 47, 48, 50, 52, 74, 119, 151
Marinetti, Filippo 1–2
Matisse, Henri 4, 143, 147
McEwen, John 184
Merleau–Ponty, Maurice 76, 143–7, 150, 151, 153

Merton, Thomas 155–7, 180
Michael Angelo 86
Middle Ages, the 16, 27, 30–4, 43,
    44–5, 47, 85–6, 87, 102, 151, 174
Mondrian, Piet 51
Monet, Claude 149, 152
Moore, Henry 143, 180
Moscow school of icon–painting
    121, 122–3
Motherwell, Robert 116
Munch, Eduard 102, 114

Nāgārjuna 171–2, 175
natural theology 34–5, 53, 54–6,
    74–5, 111, 118, 134, 153
nature 12, 15, 16, 34–40, 50–1,
    56–60, 63–8, 71–4, 80–1, 92–6,
    113–14, 131–2, 135–6,148–9, 153–
    4, 170–1, 175–6
Newman, John Henry 28
Nichols, Aidan 128, 138
Nicephorus, St. 124
Nietzsche, Friedrich 75, 152
Nolde, Emil 110
Novgorod school of icon–painting
    121, 122

O'Connell, R. J. 15–16
Ohashi, Ryosuke 159, 162–4
orthodoxy 118–33, 134, 138, 151
    see also icons, iconoclastic
    controversy
Ouspensky, Leonid 123, 124, 126,
    127, 129, 130

Paley, William 55
Panofsky, Erwin 33, 47
Perugino 70
phenomenology 76–7, 138–48
Philaret, Bishop 126
Picasso, Pablo 7, 109–10, 149–50
Pilgrim, Richard B. 66, 169–70
Plato/Platonism 12–13, 14, 16, 51,
    138, 163, 179, 182, 184
Polonarruwa 156–7
postmodernism 2–3, 147–8, 152
Poussin, Nicholas 40, 59
Pre–Raphaelites 71, 78, 87–95

Protestantism 8, 10, 16–21, 55, 70–1,
    86–7, 92–3, 109–10, 113, 119

Racine, Jean 40
Raphael 22, 70, 85–6
Reformation *see under* iconoclasm in
    Reformation; Protestantism
Renaissance 1, 28, 32, 36, 70, 85–6,
    102–3, 106, 107, 121
Renan, Ernest 93
Richier, Germaine 4
Rodin, Auguste, 180
Roman Catholicism 4, 10, 27–8,
    31–53, 70, 105, 112, 127
romanticism 1, 2, 8, 21–5, 30–1, 83,
    136–7, 168
Rombach, Heinrich 141–3, 152,
    158–65
Rookmaaker, H. R. 141–3, 152,
    158–65
Rossetti, Dante Gabriel 78, 79, 87,
    88–9, 91
Rothko, Mark 2, 4, 115–17, 154
Rouaul, Georges 4, 40, 110
Rubens, Sir Peter Paul 103
Rublev, Andrei 122, 128–31, 151
Ruskin, John 54–77, 78, 80, 85, 86,
    93, 95, 96, 114, 126, 138, 149, 151,
    152–3

Salvator 69
Sartre, Jean–Paul 108, 145
Schelling, F. J. W. 21, 167, 168
Schiller, F. 25
Schlegel, Friedrich 21
Schnabel, Julius 6
Schopenhauer, Arthur 78, 79
Scouteris, Constantine 123
Servaes, M. 41
Shakespeare, William 40, 72
Spencer, Stanley 5–6, 177–8
Steffens, Henrik 24
Strauss, David Friedrich 22, 93
Sutherland, Graham 110
Suzuki, Daisetz T. 156, 166, 167,
    168, 169–70

Tarkovsky, Andrei 123
Theodore of Studios 125

Theophanes the Greek 122
Thomas Aquinas, St. 34–47, 48, 55,
   74
Tillich, Paul 99, 100–17, 119, 151,
   157
Timanthes 81–2
Tintoretto, Jacopo 69–70
Titian 86
Tsujimura, Kōichi 159, 161–2
Turner, J. M. W 1, 54, 56, 60, 85, 151

Uhde, Fritz von 108

Van Eyck, Jan 51
Van Gogh, Vincent 3, 5, 102, 108,
   140, 184
Vermeer, Jan 87
Viola, Bill 178, 184, 185

Virgil 40

Wackenroder, Wilhelm H. 21–2
Watkin, E. I. 31–3
Wagner, Richard 78–9
Watts, Alan 171
Watts, George Frederick 78, 79, 87,
   89–92, 150–1, 187
Wells, H. C. 32
Williams, Andrew Gibbon, 186
Williams, Glynn, 178, 180
Williams, Michael 73
Wilson, E. O. 73
Wolterstorff, Nicholas 135, 138, 151–2
Yanagi, Sōetsu 172–5, 176

Zen Buddhism *see under* Buddhism,
   Zen
Zizioulas, John 127